Islamic Futures and Policy Studies

Series editor   *Ziauddin Sardar*

EXPLORATIONS
in Islamic Science

Ziauddin Sardar

MANSELL

LONDON AND NEW YORK

First published 1989 by Mansell Publishing Limited
A Cassell imprint
Artillery House, Artillery Row, London SW1P 1RT, England
125 East 23rd Street, Suite 300, New York 10010, U.S.A.

British Library Cataloguing in Publication Data

Sardar, Ziauddin
    Explorations in Islamic science.
    1. Science—Islamic viewpoints
    I. Title   II. Series
    297'.1975

    ISBN 0-7201-2004-7

Library of Congress Cataloging-in-Publication Data

Sardar, Ziauddin.
    Explorations in Islamic science / by Ziauddin Sardar.
        p.   cm.—(Islamic futures and policy studies)
    Bibliography: p.
    Includes index.
    ISBN 0-7201-2004-7
    1. Science—Middle East.   2. Islam and science.   I. Title.
II. Series.
Q127.M628S27   1989   88-30368
509'.17'671—dc19   CIP

This book has been printed and bound in Great Britain: typeset in Singapore by Colset Private Limited, printed on Redwood Book Wove paper by Redwood Burn Ltd, and bound by WBC Bookbinders.

In the name of Allah, the Beneficent, the Merciful

And they say:
Had we but listened or used reason,
We would not be among the dwellers in the flames
The Quran, Surah Al-Mulk 67:10

for Zaid

Contents

Acknowledgements

These explorations would not have been possible without the support of certain key people, although none of them is to blame for the results. Major support for my work has come from Abdullah Naseef, General Secretary of the Muslim World League, Makkah al-Mukkaramah, who not only motivated my quest for a contemporary Islamic science, but also funded a great deal of research. Thanks are also due to one of my best and longstanding friends, Jerry Ravetz, who has been my guide to history and philosophy of science and who was always there when I needed to iron out some tricky philosophical or intellectual problem. Some of his ideas, not to mention his words, appear in these essays. I have been fortunate enough to have two editors who believed in me when I needed that belief most. Robert Walgate, former European editor of *Nature*, was among the first to understand what I was talking about. Colin Tudge, former features editor of *New Scientist*, gave me unparalleled advice and support during the formative phase of the thoughts expressed in this book. Both to Robert and Colin, I will be eternally grateful. I must also record my obligation to Sam Nilsson, former Director of the International Federation of Institutes of Advanced Studies (IFIAS), for his appreciation of my work and support for the 'Science and Technology in Islam and the West' study that helped me crystallize so many ideas on the contemporization of Islamic science. I have been able to try out many of the ideas expressed in this anthology at certain lectures that I was honoured to be asked to give. In particular, I am grateful to Zaki Kirmani for asking me to deliver the keynote address at the Centre for Science Studies, Aligarh, seminar on 'Quest for New Science'; and to Anwar Ibrahim, Minister of Education of Malaysia, who asked me to expose many of my half-baked ideas at a number of 'Intellectual Discourses' held in Kuala Lumpur. I am grateful to all those who were present at these occasions for comments and criticisms.

Introduction

The first steps towards the explorations collected in this book were taken over a decade ago. During research for a book on the role of science and technology in the development of the Muslim World, I visited science institutions and universities in many Muslim countries and was struck by the extent of the discussion on Islam and science. I was unprepared for this debate, for me, at least up to then, there was no contradiction between science and Islam. Why, then, were so many scientists and university professors insisting on finding Islamic justifications for their scientific activities?

I discovered that despite the lip service many working scientists paid to the empathy between Islam and science, many felt that there were some problems between their religious ethics and their professional work as scientists. No one actually articulated the problem in any clear way—it was slipped in during complaints about how science is ignored, lack of funding, absence of adequate research facilities and so on.[1] When posed a direct question, most scientists avoided talking about ethics in science or the notion of Islamic science. The explanation offered by a Turkish scientist placed this reluctance in perspective: 'Obviously', he said, 'I have my own opinion on the relationship between science and Islam, but I would not discuss the subject in my office or indeed at any scientific or public gathering. This would be the fastest way to lose the respect of one's colleagues, become isolated and labeled as a fanatic. In fact, such a discussion would mean the end of my scientific career.'

In less than five years the whole situation had changed. When I surveyed the scene again on behalf of *Nature*,[2] crossing the entire global middle belt from the shores of Senegal and Morocco to the Pacific Ocean and the islands of Indonesia, Muslim scientists were more assertive about their religious and ethical concerns. It had now become respectable to talk about Islamic science.

It was quite evident that there were certain problems between the world view of Islam and science. These problems had absolutely nothing to do with Islam and the pursuit of knowledge, for Islam encourages the quest for knowledge, making it a sacred duty for both men and women. The problems had to do with the actual practice of science, perceived in different ways by different scientists. Even those who declared that 'science has no home, no religion, no particular bias' accepted that something needed to be done to give science indigenous roots in Muslim societies. Perhaps 'Arabization' could make 'the link between our past and present'? 'Only through Arabic', a noted Egyptian scientist told me, 'can we encourage cultivation of sciences in the Arab and Islamic countries, encourage science to become a genuine component of Arab and Islamic thought, and assimilate the love of science in the mentality and minds of our citizens'. So, the vehicle for the communication of scientific ideas presented one problem.

A broad spectrum of scientists in the Muslim world talked about Islamic and secular approaches to science. While science itself is neutral, it is the attitude by which we approach science that makes it secular or Islamic. The Islamic approach recognizes the limitations of the human mind and reason and acknowledges that all knowledge is the property of God. Also, 'science is Islamized by the way we practice it and utilize it'. One noted expert on solar energy, who eventually became the first director of the Islamic Foundation for Science and Technology for Development, declared, 'Science is intricately linked with ideology in its emphasis, scale of priorities, control and direction of research, to such an extent that scientists have now become ideologues. Their craft is not neutral but promotes certain patterns of growth and development and a certain ideology.' The problem for Muslim scientists is that it links them scientifically and emotionally with western establishments. 'So we are working for a society that is elsewhere, in the West. Most of our work ultimately benefits the developed countries.'

There was also a small group of scientists who spoke of Islamic science as a science based on entirely different assumptions from those of modern science about man and man, man and nature, universe, time and space. 'Under Islam, science is subservient to the goals of society. The goals of an Islamic society are to increase brotherhood, reduce consumption and increase spiritual awareness. A science with these goals has to be different in nature and style from science as it is practised today. Furthermore, these goals cannot be pursued by any means. They can only be pursued by those goals which are permitted by Islam.'

I decided to explore the last viewpoint in more detail. By the time the first tentative essay on the subject appeared in *New Scientist*,[3] the notion of a contemporary Islamic science had acquired a small, committed and growing following. Apart from Muslim scientists and thinkers, certain Western institutions also began to take an interest in the whole question of science in the Islamic civilization. One such institution, the International Federation of Institutes of Advanced Studies (IFIAS), then based in Stockholm, commissioned a comparative study on 'Science and Technology in Islam and the West'. I was thus able to organize a number of seminars to discuss the basic issues involved in the Islamic and Western approaches to science and explore the topic of Islamic science more thoroughly. The outcome was a second, more forthcoming essay in *New Scientist*[4] and *The Touch of Midas: Science, Values and Environment in Islam and the West*. The first essay in this book, 'The Return of Islamic Science' is based on my two contributions to *New Scientist* and serves as a curtain raiser to the entire discussion.

Both the *New Scientist* articles and *The Touch of Midas* generated considerable discussion and a few fireworks, but, to my surprise, the discourse on Islamic science began to move in a strangely irrational direction, being squeezed by two strangleholds. The first arose from our difficulty in defining what we actually mean by Islamic science: different groups give their own interpretations and take the discussion in their own eclectic directions. The second results from the conventional discussion on 'Islam and science' being woolly, confused and not infrequently intellectually shambolic. This legacy, dating back to the early 1950s, has introduced uninformed, emotional and rather irrational elements into the discourse. Much of the discussion on 'Islam and science' reveals an acute inferiority complex. Perhaps this is natural. In its thriving, dynamic form, Muslim civilization existed in a distant past and Muslim intellectuals have been out of touch with the operational form of their civilization for over six centuries. During this time Muslim civilization degenerated to its nadir, was colonized, and has only recently re-emerged in the form of autonomous nation states to face what are probably the most fundamental material changes human life has ever experienced. It appears that many Muslim intellectuals cannot free themselves from their colonial pasts and conditioning. As a result we now have, on the one hand, a growing body of apologetic literature attempting to prove the divine origins of the Quran by reading science into it, and, on the other hand, a growing movement of intellectuals retreating into mysticism and equating Islamic science with gnosis. 'Anatomy of a Confusion' dissects this segment of the discussion and is based on my contribution to *Inquiry* where the term 'Bucaillism'—the tendency to find every scientific fact and theory in the Quran—was first introduced, causing a great deal of controversy.

With the emergence of two research groups, one in Pakistan and the other in India, the discourse on Islamic science entered a new phase. The establishment of a 'Research Unit for Science in Islamic Polity' at the National Science Council of Pakistan, which publishes the quarterly journal *Science and Technology in the Islamic World* and organized the 'International Conference on Science in Islamic Polity' in Islamabad, in November 1983, further focused attention on the idea that there is an Islamic solution to the problem of ethics and values in science.[5] The basic thesis of 'science in Islamic polity' is that while science itself is neutral, value-free and universal, it has a specific role in an Islamic polity that gives it a unique flavour. Islamic polity somehow 'Islamizes' science by changing its character and style. However, it seems to me that science is such a powerful agent of change, and the historical forces behind it are so strong, that it is not science that changes in an Islamic polity, but Islamic polity that changes to adopt science. This is particularly so when the contemporary concept of Islamic polity is so ill defined. 'Islamic Science or Science in Islamic Polity?', which first appeared in *Pakistan Studies*[6] and was later republished in the *MAAS Journal of Islamic Science*[7] argues why the notion of science in Islamic polity is untenable.

Following on the heels of the 'International Conference on Science in Islamic Polity', was the April 1984 seminar on 'Quest for New Science', organized by the newly-established Centre for Science Studies in Aligarh, India. The seminar set out to produce cogent arguments to justify the notion of Islamic science. The Centre, established by the Muslim Association for the Advancement of Science (MAAS), introduced a much needed research component into the debate. When MAAS began publication of the bi-annual *Journal of Islamic Science* in 1985, Islamic science had arrived. 'Arguments for

Islamic Science' was my key-note address to the seminar; it appeared in the proceedings of the seminar and has also been published as a booklet by the Centre for Science Studies.[8] The essay's four arguments for the justification of a contemporary notion of Islamic science are: (1) different civilizations have produced distinctively different sciences; (2) Islamic science in history had a distinctive identity expressed in its unique nature and characteristic style; (3) Western science is inherently destructive and is a threat to the well-being of mankind; and (4) Western science cannot meet the physical, cultural and spiritual needs and requirements of Muslim societies. The essay also compares the norms between Western and Islamic science.

Finally, 'Where's Where? Shaping the Future of Islamic Science' takes a closer look at the major actors in the debate and puts my own position in perspective. It examines the ideas of four schools of thought that have been published in *MAAS Journal of Islamic Science*. The first, 'Islamic science is gnosis', is associated with the works of Seyyed Hossein Nasr and his followers. Although Nasr has made a major contribution to the discussions on Islamic science, he is also responsible for creating a great deal of confusion—hence, his appearance in 'Anatomy of a Confusion'. In 'Where's Where?', I look at his *oeuvre* in an attempt to discover where he is taking the debate. The second, and dominant view among Muslim scientists, is the 'business as usual' school of thought. The view that science is neutral, value-free and universal, and what Muslim countries need is more science rather than a futile discussion of ethics and values in science, has been repeatedly expressed by, for example, the Nobel Laureate Abdus Salam. I present evidence from the philosophy and sociology of science to show why this view is increasingly becoming obsolete. The third school of thought has emerged around the Centre for Science Studies in Aligarh; while most of the work of this group is focused on criticism, it has produced a number of original ideas. I explore their work and counter some of their criticisms of my own efforts. The last school of thought, in which I include myself, is the Ijmalis, who seek synthesis through conceptual analysis with the style of aesthetics, and include such scholars as Munawar Ahmad Anees and S. Parvez Manzoor. I present the Ijmali position, including an attempt to formulate a definition of Islamic science, and delineate where Ijmali thought on Islamic science differs from other schools and from such Western trends as positivism, relativism, radical science and the new paradigm and epistemological schools associated with the work of

Fritjof Capra and Francis Verala. The last section of this essay also presents a programme for constructing a contemporary Islamic science.

Underlying these explorations are a number of assumptions that ought to be noted at the outset. Perhaps my main assumption is that the 'purpose' of science is not to discover some great objective truth; indeed, reality, whatever it may be and however one perceives it, is too complex, too interwoven, too multidimensional to be discovered as a single objective truth. The purpose of science, apart from advancing knowledge within ethical bounds, is to solve problems and relieve misery and hardship and improve the physical, material, cultural and spiritual lot of mankind. The altruistic pursuit of pure knowledge for the sake of 'truth' is a con-trick. An associated assumption is that modern science is distinctively Western. All over the globe all significant science is Western in style and method, whatever the pigmentation or language of the scientist.

My next assumption follows from this: Western science is only a science of nature and not *the* science. It is a science making certain assumptions about reality, man, the man-nature relationship, the universe, time, space and so on. It is an embodiment of Western ethos and has its foundation in Western intellectual culture. Different constellations of axioms and assumptions may lead the sciences of two different societies to highly divergent interpretations of reality and the universe, interpretations which may either be spiritual or materialistic according to the predisposition of the society.

The basic assumptions of Western science have led it to a purely materialistic interpretation of reality and the universe where values serve no purpose. The intellectual climate produced by this science favours the rise and dominance of, what Skolimowski has called, the 'Bazarovs'. Yevgeny Bazarov (from Turgenev's novel *Fathers and Sons*) is an embodiment of materialism, scientism and positivism— a technocrat and an arch believer in cold facts, clinical objectivity and scientific reason. In his world, scientific facts and positive knowledge are supreme values. The Muslim world is full of bearded Bazarovs whose ritual observance of Islam bears no relationship to their work as scientists and technocrats. There is an ethical missing link, for it does not occur to them that ethics and values have a role to play in what they do in laboratories. They accurately reflect the spirit of the age—*Espiritu del tiempo*—which has inhibited them from considering values as one of the central concerns of human thought and human life. One of the great misfortunes of Western thought of the last centuries was to link intrinsic values with institutionalized religion. The bankruptcy of one form of institutionalized religion was tantamount, in the eyes of many, to the bankruptcy of religion as such, and of intrinsic values woven into this religion. This identification was based on a faulty logic. Religion, and especially values, are not the tools of the clergy to keep the masses in control (though occasionally they are used to such purposes) but are the forms and structures, worked out over the millennia of human experience, through which the individual can transcend himself and thereby make the most of himself or herself as a human being, through which man's spirituality and humanity can acquire its shape and maintain its vitality, through which we define ourselves as self-transcending beings. As such . . . intrinsic values outline and define the scope of our humanity[9]

The assumption, then, that science is not above intrinsic values, that such values play an integral part in shaping science, that man's spiritual needs are as great, if not greater, than his outer requirements is central to the ideas expressed in these essays.

Western science and technology are producing a homogenized, acultural world. My assumption is that the world should evolve towards a plurality of civilizations rather than a universal, Western civilization. The two predominant systems of economic organization—capitalism and socialism—are apparently mutually opposed. But in reality they are the two faces of the same coin: in one, economic growth is controlled by the corporations, while in the other the control lies with the state. Both systems follow similar models of development and growth; which is why, in the post-glasnost era, the two systems are coming progressively close to each other. However, the developing nations of the globe, two-thirds of mankind today, and four-fifths in the year 2,000, which includes the Muslim world, are totally excluded from the economic benefits of this technological civilization. Moreover, the developing nations are realizing, particularly after four decades of development, that the way to prosperity lies not in the footsteps of Western civilization, which is the way to annihilation of their intrinsic cultural values. Their survival depends on their being true to themselves; on choosing their own destinies; on rediscovering their own ways of being, doing and knowing; on constructing their own science and technologies; and on undertaking their own civilizational projects.

The current efforts to rediscover a contemporary style of science that can legitimately be called Islamic should be seen as one strand—notable among other strands are the 'Islamization of knowledge' movement and the theoretical and practical work undertaken towards the realization of Islamic economics—in the civilizational project to recompose the divided Muslim self and restore the sanity of Muslim people by integrating their intrinsic values with their culture and environment, science and technology, politics and law. The despotism and dependency, and the accompanying emotional, volatile and unstable politics in vogue in the Muslim world today, is the prime product of this divided self. The debate on Islamic science is one outcome of the realization that the state of our knowledge is an important characteristic of the state of our being.

References

1. I discuss these problems in the book that was the outcome of this research, *Science, Technology and Development in the Muslim World*.
2. All the quotations from Muslim scientists are from 'A revival for science, a boost for science?'.
3. 'Can science come back to Islam?', *New Scientist* **88**, 212–16 (1980).
4. 'Why Islam needs Islamic science', *New Scientist* **94**, 25–8 (1982).
5. International Conference on Science in Islamic Polity, *Science and Technology Potential and its Development in the Muslim World* (2 volumes) and *Islamic Scientific Thought and Muslim Achievements in Science* (2 volumes), Ministry of Science and Technology, Islamabad, 1983.
6. *Pakistan Studies* **2** (3), 3–16 (Winter 1983–84).
7. *MAAS Journal of Islamic Science* **1** (1), 31–44 (1985).
8. Ahmad and Ahmad, *Quest for New Science*.
9. Henryk Skolimowski, *Ecology* **5** (1), 8 (January 1975).

One

The Return of Islamic Science

The current interest in Islamic science is undoubtedly due to the re-emergence of the Muslim people in the twentieth century, the arrival of Islam as a force in international relations and as a political factor in Muslim societies themselves. Islamic science is receiving increasing attention, both in its historic and contemporary aspects, because of the growing consciousness in Muslim societies of their traditional heritage and distinct cultural identity. With the granting of independence to most of the Muslim countries by their imperial masters in the 1940s and 1950s, these newly autonomous states began a progression through various conditions. They passed through a phase of self-conscious emulation of the former metropolitan powers into one of equally self-conscious apologetics for their cultural difference from their erstwhile rulers, and thereafter into a state of trying to marry together their cultural and religious distinctiveness with those institutions and practices inherited from the West which were perceived as being beneficial. By and large, they now seem to have entered a phase of increasing emphasis on the Islamic side of this marriage, so that without much change of the outward form of the inherited practices and institutions, there is identifiable progressive Islamization of the social and political culture.[1]

This may be a phenomenon of new, urban middle classes, but this is not the whole story. The post-independence pattern of change in the Muslim countries is also the story of changes in outlook of the occidentalized élite that was the inheritor of the colonial powers. In many cases, the individuals who fought for and gained independence are the same individuals who are participating in the growing movement for Islamization. Perhaps the need to adapt culturally to the practices of the imperial powers had a decreasing relevance and impulsion after independence. When the new rulers became deeply involved in the minutiae of governing a country and giving reality to its ambitions and aspirations, their inherent Muslimness became progressively more assertive. Without realising the transformation, even the occidentalized élites became the vehicle for cultural change and a return to the values and ethos of Islam. Islamization or Islamic revivalism is not the exclusive province of the so-called Islamic fundamentalists. (If this term had any meaning at all, it would simply tell us that all Muslims—no matter how bad or lapsed—are fundamentalist since they all believe that the Quran is verbatim the revealed word of God, freely participated in by all political, intellectual and professional groups of Muslims each in their own way.)

Muslim scientists have played a major role in the intellectual revival of Islam, as evidenced by the debate on the nature and characteristics of a contemporary Islamic science.[2] Apart from political and cultural impetus, this debate has also received an impulse from the recent discoveries in the history of Islamic science. The new historical research debunks the 'conveyor belt' theory—which sees Islamic science as only a conveyor belt that preserved the Greek heritage and then passed it on to its rightful descendant, the post-Renaissance European civilization—and would lead to an eventual rewriting of world and European intellectual history. For example, the work of the Turkish science historian, Fuat Sezgin, and the scholars at the University of Aleppo's Institute for the History of Arab Science,[3] has shown that a rewriting of the history of science has now become a matter of Western intellectual integrity.

Sezgin's *Geschichte des Arabischen Schrifttums*—eight out of the planned twenty volumes of which have now been published—provides ample evidence that the medieval Western world diligently imitated, copied and plagiarized the works of Muslim scientists.[4] Sezgin, who teaches history at Frankfurt University and won the first King Faisal Foundation prize for Islamic scholarship in 1979, shows that this piracy was so common that as early as the twelfth century a decree was issued in Seville, forbidding the sale of scientific writings to Christians because the latter translated the writings and published them under another name. Sezgin's research has taken almost forty years and includes a survey of 1.5 million Arabic manuscripts that he has located throughout the world. He stops in the middle of the twelfth century and shows how even for those first five centuries of Islam, the depth and the scope of Islamic scientific scholarship is truly staggering.

While the works of Muslim scientists and technologists and their tremendous influence on Western science are relatively unknown, their achievements in astronomy, physics, biology, medicine, chemistry and mathematics are still attributed to Western scientists; for example, the discovery of planetary motion to Kepler and Copernicus, of the circulation of blood to Harvey, and of gravity and various discoveries in optics to Newton. Western historians of science have systematically and consistently played down the contribution of Muslim scientists to civilization. Pick up any introduction to the history of science and it will jump from the Greeks to the Renaissance as though the centuries in between were intellectually sterile. In his four-volume, 1,325 page *Science in History*, J.D. Bernal devotes ten pages to 'Islamic science'![5] Clearly, all areas of the history of science must be seriously rectified; for whether they discovered the lesser pulmonary circulation or undertook complicated eye operations 600 years earlier than in Europe, invented spherical trigonometry in the late tenth century, solved equations of third and fourth degree or further developed differential and integral mathematics, measured the circumference of the earth and values for specific gravities correct to three decimal places almost a thousand years ago, used the camera obscura three hundred years before Europe, or anticipated relativistic motion, there is scarcely a field where Muslim scientists did not think out, investigate or invent something exemplary.[6]

If Muslim scientists were capable of such achievements, it is legitimate to ask what caused the demise of Islamic science and the consequent colonization of the Muslim world? Was it something inherent in Islam? Or was it purely a result of certain historical coincidences?

The rise of the Muslims to the zenith of civilization in a period of less than one hundred years and the evolution of Islamic science were based on Islam's insistence, indeed over-insistence, on learning. The Quran and the traditions of the Prophet Muhammad are saturated with references to learning, education, observation, and the use of reason. The very essence of Islam is summed up in the first verse of the Quran revealed to the Prophet Muhammad on the fateful night of 27th Ramadan, 611:

Read: In the Name of thy Lord who created,
Created Man of a blood-clot.
Read: And thy Lord is the Most Generous
Who taught by the Pen
Taught Man, that he knew not. (96: 1–5)

'The Pen' has the most exalted place in Islam. 'And they shall say, had
we but listened or used reason, we would not be among the inmates of
the burning fire'. (67: 10) 'Are those who have knowledge and those
who have no knowledge alike? Only the men of understanding are
mindful'. (39: 9) 'He causes crops to grow for you, and the olives and
the date palm and grapes and all kinds of fruits. Lo! Herein is indeed a
portent for people who reflect. And He has constrained the night and
the day and the sun and the moon to be of service to you, and the stars
are made subservient by His command. Lo! herein indeed are portents
for people who have sense.' (16: 11–12)

The Prophetic traditions supplement these teachings of the Quran.
'The ink of the scholar', Prophet Muhammad is reported to have said,
'is more sacred than the blood of the martyr.' He also said, 'Seek
knowledge from the cradle to the grave'; 'An hour's study of nature is
better than a year's adoration'; 'To listen to the words of the learned
and to instil unto others the lessons of science is better than religious
exercises'; and 'Acquire knowledge:–it enables its possessor to distinguish right from the wrong; it lights the way to Heaven; it is our friend
in the desert, our society in solitude, our companion when friendless;
it guides us to happiness; it sustains us in misery; it is an ornament
among friends and an armour against enemies.' These teachings drove
many Muslim scientists to their accomplishments: al-Khwarizmi
(d. 850) whose *Kitab al-jabr wal muqbala* laid the foundations of modern
algebra; al-Battani (d. 928) who measured the solar year as being only
24 seconds longer than the currently accepted value; al-Khazini
(d. 971) whose *The Books of the Balance of Wisdom* first introduces the
concept of centre of gravity; ibn Sina (d. 1037) whose *Canons of Medicine*
was the standard medical text in Europe for some 800 years; and twelfth
century Muslim technologist, al-Jazari, who produced a number of
original inventions described in his *A Compendium of the Theory and
Practice of the Mechanical Arts*. For them, science was integral to Islam
and equivalent to piety. Some of the best and most eloquent praises of
science ever written come from the pens of Muslim scientists who considered their work to be acts of worship; such as the great Andalusian
scholar Abu Umar Yusuf al-Qurtubi (d. 1071) whose book, *The
Comprehensive Account of the Enlightenment and Virtue of Science and of the
Pre-requisites of Telling Its Truths and of Carrying Its Mission* has no contemporary parallel.[7] The same motives led to the establishment of
al-Azhar (c. 800), the first university in the world,[8] the Shammasiyah
observatory (c. 828), the first in the world,[9] and the celebrated House

of Wisdom (c. 815) of Baghdad.[10] Clearly there is nothing in the teachings of Islam that militates against learning, against science and against technology.

The Decline of Islamic Science

Although Islam exalts the use of reason, it also places reason under the control of revelation. In other words, in Islam, the use of reason is not divorced from the ethics and morality of the exercise. It is significant that the twelfth century technologist, al-Khazini, entitled his treatise on mechanics, hydrostatics and physics, *The Book of the Balance of Wisdom*. That he associated and equated his work with the acquisition of wisdom is not incidental.[11] Al-Biruni, most exact of scientists, insisted that his experimental work was subject to the moral principles of Islam; for him revelation was the supreme authority. The ethics and morality of Islam are all pervasive; both theoretical and experimental science must be guided by them.[12]

Yet it was the perversion of reason which lead to the fall of Islamic science. Revelation in Islam is above reasoning, but not above reason. Neither is reason above revelation. This rather subtle relationship was destroyed when Greek thought became dominant in Muslim societies. The introduction of Greek classics, through translations mainly by Christian Arabs, introduced two alien elements on the Muslim intellectual scene: Greek philosophy and gnosis; both were to lead to suffocation of indigenous thought and the eventual downfall of Islamic science.

Rationalism, as a philosophical movement, made an appearance in Islamic history almost immediately after the death of the Prophet Muhammad. Citizens of the newly established state and expanding empire, would question and argue with the officials about their unreasonable and cruel behaviour. Often Muslim scholars would be approached with complaints about the behaviour of the official. For example, the noted Muslim scholar Hasan Basri (b. 621), known as Abu Said ibn Jafar, was approached by a group of citizens who said: 'O Abu Said, these rulers shed blood of the Muslims and do grievous things and say that their works are the decree of Allah.' Hasan replied: 'The enemies of God, they are liars!' and set about producing rational arguments to show the falsehood of the position of the rulers.[13]

It was a pupil of Hasan Basri who actually established the dominant school of rational thought in Islamic history. The story goes that during a lecture by Hasan Basri, one of his students, Wasil ibn Ata

(b. 699), seriously disagreed with him. During the lecture a member of the audience said: 'There are two views with regard to man's deeds. One holds that there is no benefit from good deeds or pardon from bad deeds for those who refrain from evil yet are unbelievers. Conversely, a true believer has his sins pardoned at death. The second view advances that a sinner is nothing but a total unbeliever. What stand are we to adopt on the matter?'. But before Hasan Basri could answer, Wasil replied, 'Any sinner is neither believer nor unbeliever. There lies another distinction between belief and unbelief.' After his answer, Wasil turned to Hasan Basri and announced, 'I am separating from you'. He then left Hasan Basri's lecture, went to the other end of the hall and continued to elaborate his point: 'The state of believer or faithful is a rewarding state. The sinner, the one who believes and does not perform what he ought to, is not deserving of reward because he is not a true believer. Yet the sinner, however heavy his sins may be, when publicly expounding his faith, and abiding by religious rulings, cannot be branded as unfaithful. However, when shifting to the other world, his place will always be among the damned. On the Judgement Day men will be parted into two separate groups: the blessed and the damned, while there is no third group. But, as the sinner's state is higher than the unbeliever's, his suffering will be less'.[14] The followers of Wasil became known as the Mutazilites (Separatists), and came to describe themselves as 'the Followers of Justice and Monotheism'.[15]

Rationalism in Islam, thus, began both as a weapon against injustice and a method for elaborating religious beliefs. During the first two hundred years of Islam, philosophy stemmed from the Quran and Sunnah and was used to provide rational grounds for the beliefs that the world and matter are created and not eternal and was used to demonstrate the existence of a creative God, unique and incorporeal. Intellectual discourse and debates were a common occurrence of this period; and there was not much difference in the positions of those who described themselves as theologians and those who labelled themselves Mutazilites. Indeed, the theologians themselves produced a rational philosophy, Kalam. Kalam means speech or conversation and was based on the idea that truth can be found through a process of interrogation involving questions and answers. Someone proposes a thesis, and someone else questions it. This form of argumentation is apparent in the grammatical structure of the works of Kalam themselves. Within all shades of opinion, this period produced a rational philosophy which was intrinsically Islamic.

However, the appearance of Greek philosophy on the Muslim intellectual scene changed all this. When the rationalist thinkers acquired
the knowledge of Greek philosophy and armed themselves with new
weapons for speculation and polemics their attitudes changed: they
came to believe in the absolute validity of Aristotelian logic. The
common Muslim myth has it that when Muslims came into contact
with Greek thought, they were able to synthesize it totally—indeed,
this alleged synthesis is presented as a major achievement of Islamic
science.[16] Historical reality was somewhat different; Greek philosophy
and gnostic tradition tried to co-opt Islam, and indeed succeeded to
some extent; Muslim theologians fought back and managed to retain
certain territory that was free from Greek influence.

The Mutazilites were totally overwhelmed by Greek philosophy.
While the Mutazilites were highly critical of Islamic sources, they
uncritically accepted all the basic assumptions of Greek philosophy,
even where they were clearly contradictory to the basic teachings of
Islam. Al-Farabi (870–950), for example, accepted Plato *in toto*.
Mutazilites now came to believe that by the use of reason alone one
could know God's existence, essence and characteristics; the possibilities of prophecy and revelation, what it is to act morally and
immorally, and the structure of the physical world and its relation to
its maker. The ethics of the Quran and Sunnah were replaced by the
ethics of reason. Islamic philosophy was thus transformed into *falsifa*
(by which is meant *Greek* philosophy) and Muslim philosophy became
a deformed commentary on the systems of Aristotle and the neo-
Platonists. Every time the Muslim philosophers noticed that Aristotle
had left certain points obscure or incomplete they increased their efforts
to clarify them and fill in the gaps, in the process producing philosophical doctrines which were alien to Islam. Because the philosophers
slavishly and zealously followed Aristotle on the topic, the *falsifa*
deliberately set out to produce a model which tended to undermine the
religious notions of *ex nihilo* creation. A casual remark of Aristotle that
the intellect is 'part of the soul' lead al-Farabi to produce a whole
doctrine of the active intellect. Ibn Sina took Plotinus's ideas to develop
a connection with the doctrines of necessity and the model of creation
of the world.

Mutazilite thought was now throughly based on Greek philosophy.
Its postulates were based on five main points: (1) rejection of all
attributes in matter of exposition and critical consideration of the
Oneness of God; (2) God is not responsible for human acts which

result in evil, and, consequently, conviction that man has free will conferred on him to do as he wills; (3) nobody is in a position to see God, neither will anybody ever see Him; (4) ability of the human mind to perceive the truth without God sending Messengers; and (5) conviction that the Quran was revealed under the impact of circumstances and spontaneously.

Muslim rulers, many of whom saw themselves as Plato's philosopher kings, were quick to realise that Greek philosophy provided certain legitimacy for their authoritarianism and perpetuation of their dynasties—positions which could not be justified within Islam. The Abbasids, for example, were very impressed with Greek philosophy. Caliph al-Mamun, who funded the translation of a vast corpus of Greek thought into Arabic, made Mutazilism the official doctrine of the state between 833 and 848. Mutazilites now not only believed in the absolute supremacy of reason, but were also in a position, with the help of the state, to ensure that everyone shared their interpretation of Islam. Thus rationalism, which originally emerged as a tool to fight injustice, changed sides and was allied with the state.

The majority of Muslim scholars, however, rejected the *falsifa*. Why? Simply because it was clearly an alien way of thinking: *falsifa* demonstratively bore the hallmarks of its Greek creators. But there were other reasons too. The place Greek philosophy sought to occupy was already filled by theology, theory of language and a well-developed jurisprudence. And the conclusions that Greek philosophy offered as the only demonstratively respectable conclusions often ran against the principles of Islamic theology, not to mention the Quran itself. But in rejecting Greek philosophy, the Muslim scholars did not reject reason; indeed, they were aware of and rather enthusiastic concerning the importance of reason in arguments in general, and exposition of religious arguments in particular. What they were objecting to was the dogmatic belief that reason alone can lead to absolute truth and that reason can become the basis of an ethic. Indeed, from the point of view of some scholars, there was nothing new about the methodology of Greek philosophy. Al-Ghazzali went so far as to demonstrate that logic and Aristotelian syllogisms were already used and recommended in the Quran, and even illustrated Aristotelian logic with examples from Islamic law![17]

The reaction against *falsifa* produced the Asharite school of thought, which is traced backed to the teachings of Abu al-Hasan Ali ibn Ismail al-Ashari (d. 945). The Asharites, however, were not the only school to oppose the Mutazilites. Major Muslim centres produced schools of thought with the sole function of demolishing the *falsifa*: the Zahirites in Spain, al-Tahawi school in Egypt and Maturidi school in Samarkand. But Asharites became the dominant *anti-falsifa* school because they boasted such brilliant thinkers among their ranks as al-Razi (d. 924), al-Ghazzali (d. 1111) and ibn Khaldun (d. 1406). The Asharite philosophy centred on five points: (1) the uniqueness of the characteristics of God which are inapplicable to human beings; (2) the eternity and the uncreatedness of the Quran; (3) the possibility of seeing God; (4) God's seating Himself upon the throne; and (5) the notion that while man has free will, he has no power to create anything.

The battle between the Asharites and Mutazilites reached its apex with al-Ghazzali and ibn Rushd (1126–98). While the Asharites drew their positions directly from the Quran, the exponents of *falsifa* sought to append their philosophical views to the Quran. This is why, in *Incoherence of the Philosophers*,[18] al-Ghazzali accuses the philosophers of using the verses of the Quran to camouflage their real views, pretending that their doctrine is in accordance with Islam. He asks what difference the introduction of God makes to a philosophical theory? If it makes no difference at all, then surely it is just an attempt to mislead readers when religious vocabulary and Quranic passages are used as though they fitted into philosophical arguments when plainly they do not.[19] Al-Ghazzali's sustained, systematic and formidably argued demolition of *falsifa* utterly destroyed the Mutazilites and the philosophical system built by al-Farabi, the 'Brethren of Purity' who sought to purify their souls by philosophy, and ibn Sina (980–1037). Al-Ghazzali has so much confidence in his analysis that he not only presents the philosopher's arguments well, shows their weaknesses and why they don't work, but even provides the philosophers with counter-arguments which they could use to justify their original positions. Indeed, over one hundred years later, ibn Rushd uses arguments not too dissimilar to those suggested by al-Ghazzali.[20] However, despite its power and eloquence, ibn Rushd's defence of *falsifa* is not a match for al-Ghazzali and his efforts to reconcile Islam with Aristotelian metaphysics fail.

The Asharite victory led to the emergence of three divergent trends in Islamic history, all based on reduction and sharing two basic characteristics: blind imitation and authoritarianism. The theologians reduced Islam first to Sunnah and then to hadith, demanded its uncritical acceptance and often relegated those who did not comply to a position outside the boundaries of Islam. The philosophers reduced religious beliefs to rational categories, demanded logical proofs of religious premises and ridiculed everyone who did not surrender to the power of reason. The gnostics reduced everything to mysticism, and demanded absolute surrender of their followers to the Master. The theologians wanted *taqlid* (unquestioning following) of the opinions and judgements of the classical jurists; the philosophers argued for the *taqlid* of the Greek masters; and the gnostics asked for *taqlid* of Greek mystery religions and occult sciences. Thus the dominant paradigm of Muslim civilization became the tyrannical attitude of passive acceptance.

To consolidate their victory, the theologians went a step further. The opposite of *taqlid* is *ijtihad*, to exert the utmost effort, to struggle, to do one's best to know something. *Ijtihad*, after the Quran and Prophetic traditions, is the third source of Islamic law. The theologians, fearing misuse of *ijtihad* by the followers of *falsifa* and the gnostics, and consequent deviation from the true teachings of Islam, closed the gates of *ijtihad*. This was not achieved by a conference or a meeting, but by the theologians reaching consensus over a period of several decades that it should not be allowed for anyone to exercise independent reasoning in matters of religion. As Islam does not separate the sacred from the profane, it was only natural for such an injunction to be generalized. With *taqlid* accepted as the dominant paradigm by all schools of thought and the gates of *ijtihad* firmly closed, Islamic science truly became a matter of history.

Islamic Science Today

And this is largely where matters stand today—with one difference. Many Muslim scholars, scientists and intellectuals are now arguing for the rediscovery of Islamic science. The concerns for contemporization of Islamic science are a product of the intellectual awakening of the Muslim people and an outcome of the present crisis in science.

It has long been claimed in the name of science that we can gain important and true knowledge of nature, that can be used to ameliorate human conditions, and that the method of science can beneficially be extended to cover all worthwhile human affairs. However, disillusion has set in: philosophers despair of ever getting certain scientific knowledge, students turn away in boredom, science is blamed for suicidal assaults on humanity and the natural environment, and the scientific method is denounced as being generally dehumanizing. This disillusion with Western science has fueled the debate on evolving a contemporary Islamic science.

But the rediscovery of Islamic science is not an easy task, particularly when we do not know exactly what we mean by 'Islamic science' and certain historical forces are poised to appropriate Islamic science. The problems in the conception of a contemporary Islamic science arise from a missing link in the practice and traditions of the discipline. When *taqlid* came to be perceived as the dominant paradigm of Muslim civilization around the fifteenth century, the *practice* of Islamic science all but disappeared. There is thus a five-hundred-year gap between the traditions of Islamic science as they existed and the contemporary attempts to rediscover these traditions. Had there been a continuous link in the tradition of Islamic science, there would have been no need to rediscover the discipline; it would have just existed. But because there is a missing link in the chain of tradition, it is difficult for contemporary Muslim scientists to conceive how the discipline can be practised today.

The history of Islamic science itself presents certain difficulties. Which tradition—the Mutazilites, the Asharites or the Gnostics—do we take as the genuine exponent of Islamic science? In the contemporary debate, the gnostics seem to have appropriated Islamic science to themselves. Part of the crisis of science in the West is the realization that the abandonment of the claim to truth by science—without the substitution of an adequate alternative epistemology—could contribute to a collapse of standards and an immediate flight from reason. The contemporary debate on Islamic science and its domination by the gnostics, who equate science with mysticism and gnosis with method of science and are concerned largely with occult, alchemy and astrology, provide a good example of this realization.

Then there are problems with the historiography of Islamic science. Despite the new found impetus in research on its history, there is a conspicuous absence of analysis in the existing histories of Islamic science. On the whole they tend to be catalogues of the achievements of individual scientists, translations of individual works, biographies of noted figures, learned comments on this or that manuscript, and sweeping accounts of the rise and fall of Islamic scientific culture. There is an acute need for analytical works on the methodologies of great Muslim scientists, their philosophies of science and, most of all, their rationale and ability for integrating their work with their worldview. We need models and theories for the historical practice of Islamic science that can either be adopted *per se* or used as guides for contemporary practice. Without these models modern Muslim scientists have nothing tangible to which to relate. Given this situation, the contemporary rediscovery of Islamic science becomes an intellectually formidable task, requiring research on a number of different fronts and a sustained effort over several generations.

However, even at this preliminary stage, we can suggest in a positive way that the study of Islamic science must be undertaken within the living, dynamic, thriving civilization of Islam. Essentially, the rediscovery of Islamic science is the rediscovery of the moral and ethical principles of Islam. As such, it is irrevocably linked to the cultural and religious awakening of the Muslim people.

There are two prerequisites that must be met before the process of rediscovering the methods and principles of Islamic science can begin. The first is obvious: the institution of *ijtihad* must be invoked, for only then can the Muslim people develop the kind of Islamic perception that can relate the teachings of Islam to the problems of today and meet the challenges of tomorrow. To some extent, the rebirth of *ijtihad* is already taking place. In particular, in the new science-based universities that have mushroomed over the past twenty years in the Muslim world, there is hardly a graduate who does not wish the hold of *taqlid* to break away and disappear. It is unlikely that the domination of *taqlid* will continue in Muslim societies in the future.

The second is the integration of science policy in the Muslim world with the values and culture of Islam. The value and normative perspective of Islam does not allow any form of knowledge to be cultivated independently, without social responsibility, outside the value structure of society. This is not to say that the freedom of inquiry is limited, but that the parameters of inquiry are integrated in a single world view. Muslim countries must ensure that their science policies— including research priorities, science education structures, technological choices—reflect values and the rich cultural heritage of Islam and the aspirations of indigenous people. Without a certain correspondence between science policies and Islamic values, hopes of rediscovering Islamic science would appear unrealistic.

We are also in a position to delineate the differences between Islamic science and Western science, that is science as it is practised today. Two scientists from different cultures may not disagree in their observation of the same physical phenomenon. Significant differences are

philosophical and sociological—they lie in the epistemological framework in which science is done; the reasons why it is done (whether for
the benefit of the people, private profit, technological expansion or
military gains); the people who do it (is it an élitist activity or can a
mass of people be trained to be scientists?) and the problems that are
tackled.

The philosophical and sociological differences between Western
and Islamic approaches to science are quite distinct. For example, in
the European and American civilizations, science and religion exist in
two water-tight compartments; indeed, the conflict between institutionalized Christianity and scientific rationality during the
Enlightenment has come to be known as the war between science and
religion. However, in Islam there is no division between the sacred
and the profane, the secular and the religious. All intellectual traditions,
the Mutazilites, the Asharites and even the Gnostics, used systematic
rationality to argue their positions. Thus, while it is possible for science in the West to develop outside the framework of religion and
values and still have meaning for Western peoples and society, for
Muslim societies a science that develops outside the worldview of
Islam carries no real meaning and cannot be psychologically and
sociologically internalized. In other words, it cannot become part and
parcel of Muslim society and the amalgam of people who constitute
that society. Classical Muslim scholars who tried to impose Greek
philosophy on the Muslim civilization were well aware of this. Hence,
in his *The Concordance Between Religion and Philosophy*, ibn Rushd goes to
great lengths to define Greek philosophy in Islamic terms; only by
setting it within the Islamic conceptual matrix could ibn Rushd hope
that Greek philosophy could be totally accepted by the Muslim
community.

Moreover, while the Western philosophy of science considers the
scientific method as the only valid way of understanding the universe,
Islamic tradition considers the scientific method to be only *one way of
knowing*. Even though Muslim scientists made many discoveries, scientific method never came to dominate Islamic civilization—it remained
one among many methods of gaining knowledge and appreciating the
signs of the Creator. Exact science was done not just by the Mutazilites,
as one would expect, but also extensively by Asharites such as al-Razi
and the Sufis such as Sadr al-Din Shirazi (Mulla Sadra). Thus, a method
of knowing that excludes all other equally valid ways of knowing, and
downgrades what Muslims see as higher forms of knowledge, namely

intuition and revelation, can never be fully accepted by the Muslim psyche. While Muslim scientists may give lip service to this method, they may acquire an evolutionist garb when inside a laboratory and become creationists once outside its confines, they may ape its techniques of experiments, but they can never accept its all-pervasive domination. It is the dichotomy between how Western science sees its method and the place that this method has in Islamic culture that is the basic reason why science as it is practised today has not been embraced wholeheartedly by Muslim societies. Muslims, even though they may express secularist views, are incapable of seeing anything outside their value systems; they can never accept a method that places itself emotionally and psychologically above their value system.

Classical Muslim scientists always considered scientific method to be subservient to the values and cultural imperatives of the worldview of Islam. For example, ibn al-Haitham (965–1039) studied the camera obscura, demonstrating experimentally that light travels in straight lines. He set up a laboratory on optics where he discovered and demonstrated a number of optical laws, but he did all this work within the matrix of the Islamic philosophical and sociological universe. While performing experiments with light, he never failed to remind himself and the readers of his textbooks that 'God is the light of the heavens and the Earth'. Al-Biruni measured the circumference of the Earth, latitudes and longitudes, and the specific density of several metals and precious stones with remarkable accuracy; but he consciously rejected the tyranny of method. He argued that the methodology of particular inquiry depends on the nature of the questions, the area we decide to study, and the way the questions are formed. Al-Biruni himself used a number of methods that conformed with the nature of his subject of study. Where he felt it necessary he used deduction, observation and experimentation, induction, or had recourse to intellectual intuition. But always he returned to revelation as the supreme authority. For al-Biruni no scientific answer obtained through reason and experience, experimentation and dissertation, was considered to be absolute. He was the most exact of scientists operating within a well-defined philosophical framework, yet he never lost sight of the spiritual empyrean, the knowledge of which he found not illogical or irrational but merely unattainable through logic and reason alone.

These philosophical and sociological differences also mean that the priorities and emphases of Islamic science are different from those of

Western science. For example, cultural and value considerations have a much higher priority than purely scientific ones. Classical Muslim scientists strongly rejected the notion of science for science's sake. As they operated within a defined value framework, there was an organic balance in their approach to science. Al-Biruni, for example, argued on one hand that the purpose in studying a subject was its importance to the community; on the other, he rejected the notion of purely utilitarian science. In their survey of *Islamic Technology*, Ahmad Y. al-Hassan and Donald R. Hill show how pure research and community interests were integrated in the works of Muslim scientists.[21] There is no question of technology creating needs, but needs being fulfilled by technology.

For the scientists of early Islam, science was a vehicle of understanding and the mandate for the pursuit of this understanding was to be found in the Quran where man is commanded to contemplate the heavens and the earth and all that is enclosed within. These scientists did not see the natural world as something hostile or evil to be controlled and dominated, but something that needed to be understood so that life could be lived in harmony with it. In fact, it was something sacred whose spirituality needed to be preserved; as such the sanctity of nature had a higher priority for classical Muslim scientists than the pure pursuit of science. Moreover, for classical Muslim scientists both the means and ends for doing science had to be based on Islamic ideals.[22] A pragmatic problem that was being tackled for the benefit of the community, or a pure problem that was being pursued, in al-Biruni's words, 'for the perfection of man', could not be solved by unethical means. Thus scientists such as al-Razi (d. 925) whose observations of smallpox are considered to be classic, and ibn Sina (d. 1037)—the arch defender of pure reason—whose *Canons of Medicine* was a standard text for over 600 years, could never have considered, to give a contemporary example, the use of dogs as experimental animals in studies of cancer. They would have acknowledged the pragmatic benefits of the research in reducing human suffering, but would have insisted on finding an alternative mode of research. Moreover, they were conscious of the end product: it could be put only to an Islamically acceptable use. Thus the physician Hunain ibn Ishaq (d. 877) refused to make poisons when asked by the ruler of the state, and declared: 'I have skill in what is beneficial and have studied nothing else'. He was prevented from making poisons, he claimed, by two things: 'my religion and my profession. My religion commands us to do good, even to our enemies, so much more to our friends, and my profession forbids us to do harm to our kindred, as it is instituted for the benefit and welfare of the human race, and God imposed on physicians the oath not to compose mortiferous remedies.'

These then are the philosophical and sociological considerations and some of the priorities which make Islamic science an entirely different enterprise from science as it is practised today. These considerations, values and emphases shaped scientific activity from the eighth to the fourteenth centuries in the civilization of Islam. It can be seen that the motivational and governing forces of this science were religious and cultural. They gave it a direction that was different from the direction of contemporary Western science. And they produced an entity which in finer detail and spiritual make-up was radically different from Western science.

The biggest hurdle in incorporating this philosophical and sociological system with the practice of science in the Muslim world comes from the Muslim scientists themselves, who are too deeply entrenched in Western scientific practice to be able easily to break away from it. However, the irony is that despite four decades of 'science development', Western science is refusing to take *social* root in Muslim societies. Muslims may, and indeed have, produced great individual scientists, just as history produced great Muslim exponents of Greek philosophy, but as with Greek philosophy, Western science has not flourished in the Muslim world. This is partly because of the colonial legacy, partly because of global structures that induce dependency, but largely because it is an embodiment of values, priorities and emphases that, to some extent, undermine cherished Islamic values and go against the deep historical consciousness of the Muslim community. Indeed, because Muslim scientists and engineers operate in the Western system of science, they tend to propagate two different sets of values: one that is evident in their professional output and another that they cherish in their personal lives.

One explanation given for this dualistic behaviour is that Muslim scientists have two types of knowledge, operational and non-operational knowledge.[23] Their operational or working knowledge is that of the Western system of science, based on a practical model they have learned either in Western or Western-type institutions. The model works something like this: there are scientists who discover facts which they pass on to technologists who apply these facts for the creation of new devices and processes. The products of technologists are then manufactured and tested and selected by the market, which expresses consumer choice. Finally, individual people have their lives enriched by the steady stream of such science-based technology.

This scheme is attractive for several reasons. First, we do have scientists, technologists, a market and, up to quite recently, an increasing welfare. Islam, after all, makes it a duty for everyone to seek knowledge and discover facts, and increase the welfare of mankind. Could scientists discover anything other than facts? Could technologists market things that didn't work, or were designed to wear out? Could consumers be wrong about their needs? At every stage, the various people acting autonomously, but in the proper sequences, ensure that all will be well. It seems that the vast majority of Muslim scientists still believe this folklore: they have complete faith in their colonial masters and occidental or occidentalized teachers. It is this supreme inferiority complex that ensures that no one thinks that reality may be considerably different.

The non-operational knowledge that Muslim scientists have concerns Islamic values. While the scientists give verbal support to these values, they cannot incorporate them into their work. Yet, as committed Muslims, they seek to assert their identities and personalities, by expressing personal piety, announcing the love of God and meticulously observing everyday Islamic rituals. Because they are part of the Western system of science and the philosophical and sociological world view that it produces, it is difficult for them to comprehend an alternative model of science that integrates Islamic values with science and technology. In the absence of a working model of Islamic science, they are led to think that their personal piety makes their professional output relevent both to Islam and to their society.

Indeed, this folklore is believed so strongly by the majority of Muslim scientists that they shun any discussion of science, technology and values because they see this as an attempt to get them away from the path of 'true science', deny them modern technology and ultimately deprive them of the fruits of science and technology from which Western civilization has so conspicuously benefited. Some see the very mention of Islamic science as a threat to their professional integrity. After all, if they are good scientists they are good at solving puzzles within the dominant paradigms using the methodology in which they have been trained. How they will perform in different paradigms, on different problems, is an open question. Yet, if Muslim scientists continue to operate within the system of Western science, they risk separating their societies from the very values they cherish, wasting their potential and resources by working on problems that are foreign to their societies, alienating themselves from their societies and their individual spiritual being. The entrapment of Muslim scientists in this framework has meant that they no longer hear the fundamental question facing the Muslim *ummah*: how can we get science and technology to solve the compelling and monumental problems of Muslim society without dislocating the essential values and cultures that make these societies Muslim.

This question has been wholly ignored, despite the fact that imposition of alien science and technology in Muslim societies has produced a revolution in Iran, has led to the emergence of Islamic activists in Egypt, Algeria, Tunisia, Pakistan and the Sudan, destroyed the sacred environment of the Hajj—the holy cities of Makkah and Madinah and their environs—and has stimulated the world-wide Islamic revival. The reasons lie in the fact that the majority of Muslim scientists still believe science to be a value-free, neutral, pursuit of objective truth and, hence, subscribe to the norms, values, priorities and emphases of the international culture of science.

Most Muslim scientists, therefore, suffer from an acute schizophrenia, the seeds of which are planted at the beginning of their education. A student's journal aptly describes the process that produces the split mind.

> The committed Muslim student is presented with a problem; his education will be rooted in an intellectual tradition which is different and hostile to his basic religious beliefs. As he approaches graduation he will learn to cope with this by assigning the secular and religious knowledge he acquires into two separate mental compartments: of matter and spirit, of physics and meta-physics, of nature and supernature, of scientific method and mysticism, of science and religion. Sooner or later he will forget the early tensions in his mind which first forced reality to be divided in this way. The boundaries will become firmly established as natural rather than arbitrary demarcations. This is the trap to be avoided, for the start of the process of 'de-Islamization' is when one's single, integrated worldview becomes compromised.[24]

That, basically, is the challenge before the contemporary proponents of Islamic science. How do we practise science without compromising the wholistic, integrated worldview of Islam? The process of reintegration could perhaps begin by adopting those elements of Islamic science that can be readily identified as among its basic characteristics.

One of these elements is humility. Al-Haitham concludes his monumental work, *Optics*, the foundation stone on which Newton built his theories, with the words that while all he knows about the subject is in his book, his knowledge is limited and there may even be errors in his work. 'Only Allah knows best.' Ibn Rushd (Latin name, Averroes), after one of the most powerful defences of rationalism ever written, ends his *Incoherence of the Incoherence*, the last chapter of which deals with the natural sciences, with an apology for taking the reader's time and asks for forgiveness both from the reader and God for his errors, excuses and stumblings. These are not isolated cases; humility was the norm in all Muslim intellectual traditions—no matter how hard they fought with each other—and it is a basic tenet of Islamic science.

Another element of Islamic science is the recognition of the limitations of scientific method. Al-Biruni, who produced some 180 works on such diverse subjects as geometry, geography, light and astrolabe, time and seasons, comets, religion, astrology and sociology, repeatedly reminds his readers of the limitations of his method. In fact, in al-Biruni there is no method, but *methods* in conformity with the nature of the subject under study. No scientific answer obtained through reason and experience, experimentation and dissertation was considered by al-Biruni to be absolute, contrasting sharply with Bacon's notion that the job of science is to do all things possible!

A third element of Islamic science is respect for the subject under study, whether it is nature, as in al-Haitham's study of optics, or people, as in al-Biruni's study of India. Muslim scientists sought to understand, not to dominate the object of their study, their respect for which was almost reverential. Bacon's dictum that 'nature yields her secrets under torture' would have sent shudders down al-Biruni's spine! Humility, recognition of the limitations of scientific method, respect for the object of study: these primary lessons can be adopted at the very start of the journey to rediscover the heritage and contemporary meaning of Islamic science. And this, in essence, is also the message of Islamic science to the world. The scientific tradition of Islam is based on the profound intuition of the interdependence and interrelation of all things in the universe, let alone our planetary environment. The rediscovery of this tradition will, among other things, remind man of the necessity of humility and respect in preserving the harmony and equilibrium of nature, if his science is not to lead to the destruction of its own object of study.

References

1. In this respect, see my *Islamic Futures: The Shapes of Ideas to Come*, Mansell, London, 1985; Mohammad Ayoob (ed.), *The Politics of Islamic Reassertion*, Croom Helm, London, 1981; A. E. H. Dessouki (ed.), *Islamic Resurgence in the Arab World*, Praeger, New York, 1982; and Y. Y. Haddad, *Contemporary Islam and the Challange of History*, State University of New York Press, Albany, 1981.
2. For a discussion of the role of Muslim scientists in the Islamic revival and a survey of their views, see Sardar, 'A revival for Islam, a boost for science?'.
3. The institute's *Journal for the History of Arabic Science*, its numerous publications and conference proceedings have contributed considerably to the new appreciation of the history of Islamic science.
4. Brill, Leiden, 1967- .
5. Watts and Company, London, 1954; Pelican, London, 1969.
6. See Sarton, *Introduction to the History of Science*; Nasr, *Science and Civilization in Islam*; al-Hassan and Hill, *Islamic Technology: An Illustrated Study*; and numerous entries in the *Dictionary of Scientific Biography*, Charles Scribner, New York, 1974.
7. Cairo, Matbaat al Mawsuat, 1320/1902.
8. For background to al-Azhar, see Bayard Dodge, *Al-Azhar: A Millennium of Muslim Learning*, The Middle East Institute, Washington, D.C., 1961.
9. For background to Muslim observatories, see M. Dizer (ed.), *International Symposium on the Observatories in Islam, 19–23 September 1977*, Istanbul, 1980.
10. See Sardar, *Information and the Muslim World*, chapter 2.
11. For the contents of al-Khazini's *Book of the Balance of Wisdom*, see Donald R. Hill, *Arabic Water-Clocks*, Institute of History of Arabic Science, Aleppo, 1981, chapter 4.
12. See Hourani, *Reason and Tradition in Islamic Ethics*.
13. Sheikh, *Studies in Muslim Philosophy*, p. 4.
14. Sheikh Saleh Firuz, 'The Mutazilah and the beginnings of rationalism in Islam', *Islamic Review* **49** (7–8), 19–23, 25–8 (1961).
15. For a background to Mutazilism, see Mir Valiuddin's article in Sharif, *A History of Muslim Philosophy*, volume 1, pp. 199–219.
16. Seyyed Hossein Nasr, in particular, propagates this myth. See his *Islamic Science: An Illustrated Study*, chapter 1.
17. Leaman, *An Introduction to Mediaeval Islamic Philosophy*, p. 19.
18. Al-Ghazzali, *Incoherence of the Philosophers*.
19. For a detailed account of the arguments between al-Ghazzali and ibn Rushd, see Leaman, *op cit.*, part one: 'Ghazzali's attack on philosophy', chapters 1, 2, and 3.
20. In Averroes's *Tahafut Al-Tahafut* (*Incoherence of the Incoherence*).
21. CUP, 1986.
22. See Ali Kettani, 'Science and technology in Islam: the underlying value system' in Sardar, *The Touch of Midas*.
23. For an analysis of the impact of the operational and non-operational types of knowledge on Muslim societies, see Ziauddin Sardar, *The Future of Muslim Civilization*, Mansell, London, 1987, chapter 3.
24. *The Muslim*, 'Science and Values' **15** (5), 99 (1979).

Two

Anatomy of a Confusion

The basic characteristics of Islamic science—humility, the recognition of the limits of human reason, and respect for the subject under study—can all be derived from the study of the Quran. Indeed, the Quran provides the basic guidelines for the pursuit of knowledge. However, Muslim scientists and intellectuals have not used the Quran for distilling the values which should shape their scientific activity; rather, they have either treated the Quran as a textbook of science or have used it to justify the activities and excesses of science as it is practised today. Over the last three decades a fashion for reading science into the Quran has emerged in Muslim learned circles.

The headline on the April 1985 issue of *Bulletin of the Islamic Medical Association of South Africa* provides a good example of this vogue. It announced a staggering discovery: 'Canadian scholar confirms Quran and Ahadith on Human Embrylogy'. The story tells us that Dr Keith Moore, chairman of the anatomy department of the University of Toronto's school of medicine, has discovered the 'happy marriage' between the Islamic revelation and contemporary human developmental anatomy. 'I am amazed at the scientific accuracy of these statements which were made in the seventh century. . . . It is quite reasonable for Muslims to believe that these verses are revelations from God', Moore is reported to have said.[1]

What has Keith Moore discovered that has so excited the Muslim doctors, scientists and scholars? His article, first presented at the seventh Saudi Medical Meeting, has been reprinted in a number of places.[2] It simply reads modern biology into certain Quranic verses, describing the development of a foetus and illustrating them with clinical drawings and textbook descriptions. For example, the Quranic verse, 'Verily, we fashioned man from a small quantity of mingled liquids' (76: 2), is explained by Moore as referring to the mixture of a small quantity of sperm with the oocyte and its associated follicular fluid, or the male and female sexual secretion. The resulting mixed drop, made up of the ovum and penetrating sperm, becomes the zygote, the precursor of the embryo. Similarly, many other verses of the Quran are given scientific legitimacy. Consider, for example, the following verses: 'Verily, we created man from a product of wet earth; then placed him as a drop (of seed) in a safe lodging; then fashioned We the drop a clot, then fashioned We the clot a little lump, then fashioned We the little lump bones, then clothed the bones with flesh, and then produced it as another creation. So blessed be Allah, the best of Creator!' (23: 12–14). Looking into these verses, Moore shaped some plasticine like the embryo at 28 days and put his own teeth marks on it. The chewed plasticine was a carbon copy of the embryo, with the embryo's somites similar to the teeth marks. Further examination showed that in an embryo of six weeks, bones begin to form and muscles attach to them. By the seventh week the bones give a human shape to the embryo. The ears and eyes begin to form in the fourth week and are visible by the sixth, or forty-two days after the zygote has been formed. All these developments are in conformity with the Quranic description, Moore tells us.

So what does all this prove? Does it confirm the divine origins of the Quran? Or does it merely tell us that the Quran is a treasure chest of scientific 'facts'? What is the function of the exercise?

Benign Bucaillism

On the surface, such attempts to legitimize modern science by equating it with the Quran, or to prove the divine origins of the Quran by showing that it contains scientifically valid facts, appear to be harmless, indeed, even commendable exercises. However, when pursued on a naive basis, as is often done by Muslim scholars, such methods can be dangerous; and when undertaken deliberately, albeit sincerely, often by non-Muslim scholars, they can have mischievous consequences. The inference drawn by comparing the Quran and science is two-fold: if the facts and theories mentioned in the Quran, which was revealed fourteen hundred years ago, are supported by modern science, the divine nature of the Quran is confirmed (if confirmation is what we are looking for); and conversely, if modern scientific facts and theories find a reflection in the Quran, then modern science must also have the same universal and eternal validity as the Quran. My counter argument is simple: the Quran does not need confirmation from any other source because, for Muslims, it is *a priori* valid and eternal. Any attempt at reading science into the Quran makes the eternal scripture subservient to science; and it elevates science to the level where it becomes the arbitrator of what is and what is not truth. It further enforces the mythical notion that scientific theories are neutral, universal and eternally valid. Moreover, trying to read science in the allegorical, metaphorical and symbolic verses of the Quran often stretches analogical reasoning beyond its limits and leads to absurd conclusions and, in some authors, to ones quite contradictory to those intended by the Quran. It is apologia of the worst type.

Apologetic Muslim authors, trying to prove that the Quran is scientific and modern, often start by stating that the Quran places great emphasis (and indeed it does) on the pursuit of knowledge and use of reason. Some 750 verses, almost one-eighth of the Quran, in contrast to only 250 legislative verses, exhort the believer to study nature, reflect, make the best use of reason, and make 'scientific' enterprise an integral part of the community life. It is further pointed out that the Quran mentions several scientific facts and theories, all of which are supported by the most recent discoveries and advances.

This type of apologetic literature, trying to give scientific legitimation to the Quran, goes back to the early 1960s. In fact, one of the earliest pamphlets came out of Cairo: *On Cosmic Verses in the Quran* by Muhammad Jamaluddin El-Fandy.[3] El-Fandy tries to prove that every recent (that is in the 1950s) astronomical discovery and scientific theory has already been mentioned in the Quran. He considers the Quran as 'the best example of scientific expression' (an unsustainable claim since the ideal form of scientific expression is a mathematical equation; and there are certainly no equations in the Quran). Thus, from almost any Quranic verse referring to any astronomical phenomenon, El-Fandy can draw modern astronomical parallels and comparisons. For example, from the verses, 'Allah is He who raised the heavens without any pillars that you can see', and 'neither can the night outstrip the day, and each revolve in an orbit', El-Fandy draws the following inference:

'If we consider the sky a name given to anything which is over our heads, then it will surely mean the entire universe which surrounds us and which begins with the space around the earth followed by the planets, the sun and other stars found in the depth of the space, in our galaxy or in the other galaxies. All these heavenly bodies move in their orbits. This is the sky. It is created by Allah and each body in the space is similar to the brick in its lofty structure. All these heavenly bodies split one after the other and are held in their relative position by centrifugal force and universal gravity. The gravity and this centrifugal force, produced by rotation in semi-circular orbits or ellipses, could be treated as actually built pillars. Although we may not detect such forces with our eyes yet that does not mean that they are not there in any case, since we can measure and give their specifications correctly. If anyone of us is granted a suitable sense in addition to the normal ones we have, he will be able to feel these (tubes of forces) exactly as we can feel any material body with our normal senses.'[4]

El-Fandy does not stop here. He goes on to argue that the atmosphere can be regarded as a pillar and that light itself is like a pillar, with the colours of the spectrum being minor pillars! In the other verses of the Quran, El-Fandy finds evidence for the creation of red giants, white dwarfs, existence of ether (sic), the evolution of the planets and the big bang theory. And there is more: science supports the Quran's claim, writes El-Fandy, that life exists on other planets. After quoting numerous verses, including, 'And thy Lord best knows those who are in the heavens and the earth' and 'To Him submit whosoever is in the heavens and the earth', he ventures to describe what aliens may look like (here it is not clear whether he is drawing inferences from the Quran or science):

> If we try to define the shape or form which developed races living outside our planet will have, we should, in this case, and without inviting compli-cations, act on the assumption that nature has made no dissimilarity whatsoever in its method. Accordingly such creatures, in their attempt to make good show, share with us the following:
> 1. The body's reliance on an inner osteology made of hard material.
> 2. The existence of a main centre for nerves (the brain) and a net which communicates with the various parts of the body directives (the nerves).
> 3. The best shelter for the brain which exists inside a safe movable organ either in the fore or the top part of the body . . .
> 4. The creature's dependence upon legs used in motion.
> 5. The existence of a mouth for speaking and feeding . . . [5]

All this is not just bad science; it makes a mockery of the Quran. But compared to some others, El-Fandy is quite sane. Azizul Hasan Abbasi, a Pakistani neuropsychiatrist, in his pamphlet, *The Quran and Mental Hygiene*, [6] manages to find in the Quran modern cures for diabetes, tuberculosis, stomach ulcers, rheumatism, arthritis, high blood pressure, asthma, dysentery and paralysis.

In recent years, this rather banal comparative approach to science and Islam has been legitimized by the French surgeon, Maurice Bucaille. His *The Bible, the Quran and Science* is essential reading for Muslims with a larger-than-life inferiority complex and has been translated into almost every Muslim language, from Arabic, Persian, Turkish, Urdu to Indonesian.

Bucaille sets out thoroughly to analyse the 'holy scriptures in the light of modern knowledge'. He focuses on four topics: astronomy, the earth, animal and vegetable kingdom, and human reproduction. The methodology followed is the well-established one of quoting Quranic verses and then giving a scientific commentary on them. Bucaille tries to be more objective and takes pains to point out that the Quran contains scientific information that was not available at the time of revelation and, in fact, some of the information contained in it is contrary to what people believed at the time of the Prophet. After going through the standard motions of examining verses about the orbit of the moon and the sun, the water cycle, the reproductive procedure, he concludes:

> The Quran most definitely did not contain a single proposition at variance with the most firmly established modern knowledge, nor did it contain any of the ideas current at the time on the subjects it describes. Furthermore, however, a large number of facts are mentioned in the Quran which were not discovered until modern times. So many in fact, that on November 9, 1976, the present author was able to read before the French Academy of Medicine a paper on the 'Physiological and Embryological data in the Quran'. The data, like many others on differing subjects, constituted a veritable challenge to human explanation—in view of what we know about the history of the various sciences through the ages. Modern man's findings concerning the absence of scientific error are therefore in complete agreement with the Muslim exegetes' conception of the *Quran as a Book of Revelation*. It is a consideration which implies that God could not express an erroneous idea.[7]

The Bible, of course, did not meet the stringent criteria of modern knowledge and the 'clear-cut' conclusion of Bucaille is that 'it is impossible not to admit the existence of scientific errors in the Bible'. However, all this simply states the obvious with a sense of real discovery: the Muslim belief that the Quran as the Word of Allah cannot contain any errors and that the Bible, as it exists today, is not true divine revelation.

Bucaille's assertions are not wild; he is quite objective about his undertaking and remains more or less within the boundaries of common sense. However, where Bucaille stops, Bucaillism takes over. A number of recent studies have tried to look for almost every scientific fact and theory in the Quran. Thus, Shamsul Haq, for example, manages to find the 'seeds of the theory of relativity and quantum mechanics in the Quran' and produces Quranic evidence to support the Big Bang theory.[8] M. Manzoor-i-Khuda manages to find Quranic evidence for the theory of the development of the biosphere, the water cycle of life on earth and even a justification for the geological development of earth![9] Moore notwithstanding, the entire field of embryology has been discovered several times in the Quran!

The extent to which this activity has caught the imagination of Muslim scholars and scientists can be judged by the contributions to the first international conference on scientific miracles of the Quran and Sunnah, which range from 'the origin of terrestrial iron' to various aspects of meteorology, cellular-genetic set-up, laws and principles of motion, sexual differences in the brain and the effects of x and y chromosomes, oceanographic phenomena, geological formations of mountains, gravity, crop-science agronomy, chemical composition of milk, and, of course, embryology and astrophysics.[10] Apart from the appallingly low standards of these contributions, they add nothing to the sum of our knowledge. They amount to little more than post-facto rationalizations: they do not expand the frontiers of science or increase our understanding of the Quran. However, Bucaillism does equate Quranic truth with the mathematical truth and makes the Quran appear more and more like a contemporary data-base. From here, it appears, the next logical step ought to be to present the Quran as a scientific textbook. And Afzalur Rahman has obliged us with exactly that.[11] Rahman asserts that 'the Quran provides a *complete* picture of the material universe and what is beyond in a scientific and rational manner, appealing to the scientific mind as well as to the ordinary layman', and finds almost every secondary school science subject, from heat, light, sound, even to electricity, in the Quran, and presents them as a long list of subject headings with appropriate Quranic quotations. The book is meant to be used in schools (and probably is) and to prepare the next generation of Muslim scientists!

The only thing now left for Bucaillism is to be institutionalized in the school curricula. Mohammad Abdus Sami and Muslim Sajjad have produced a plan to accomplish this goal.[12] Every chapter of every textbook on physics, chemistry, biology and zoology should contain the appropriate verses from the Quran. But unlike Rahman, the two Pakistani scientists foresee some problems: for example, how are we going to treat the theory of evolution? 'This theory seeks to provide essentially a rational justification for those who do not believe in God'.[13] Perhaps there are, after all, a few things in science that do not tally with what the Quran tells us! And what do they propose as a solution to the problem of evolution? Replacing nature with God.

> wherever nature is now portrayed in textbooks as the originator of the causes for the effects and actions (of evolution), we ought to highlight the concept of God and that whatever happens in the universe is entirely due to His wisdom and guidance.[14]

However, the contents of what is taught remains more or less standard fare.

One of the main strengths of the conference on scientific miracles of the Quran and Sunnah was the number of scholars who argued for caution and emphasized the importance of following the well-established rules of interpretation when studying the scientific content of the Quran.[15] Indeed, opposition to reading science into the Quran has a long and distinguished history. The eighth-century classical scholar, Abu Ishaq al-Shatbi, for example, complained that most of those who engaged in reading science in the Quran 'exceeded the proper bounds in their claims over the Quran and they attributed to it, all that they found in the works of old or new scholars; no matter whether it was physics or logic or something else'. Commenting on the Quranic verse, 'nothing we have omitted from the Book' (6: 38), al-Shatbi says that the verse does not mean that 'all the sciences and humanities' are to be found in the Quran: 'It is not permitted to add to the Quran that which is not required by it, and it is not permitted as well, to deny a thing which is required by it.'[17]

More recently, the noted Egyptian scholar, Sayyed Qutb, also opposed the tendency to discover modern science in the Quran. He argues that the whole exercise 'to link the general Quranic indications to changeable and renewable theories arrived at by science' involves a basic methodological error, based on the assumption that science is all-powerful and that the Quran is subsidiary to it, hence the efforts to strengthen the Quran by science or find scientific facts in the Quran. The exercise involves equating the eternal with the relative: while the Quran is absolute, science is 'not final or absolute because it is tied to man's environment, mind and tools, all of which, by their nature, are not capable of giving one final and absolute truth'. A second assumption which leads to this methodological error concerns the nature of the Quran itself. Since the Quran is absolute and eternal, the argument goes, it must provide all the facts that man needs to be a good trustee to God. The purpose of the Quran, asserts Sayyed Qutb, is not to provide basic information on science and nature—this is to be achieved by work and thought. The Quran is a book of guidance, and revelation of some scientific fact in the Quran is a means of this guidance.[17]

However, warnings against Bucaillism have clearly not been heeded, because of the strong psychological value. For some Muslim scientists, scholars and intellectuals, Bucaillism reinforces their faith in the Quran and Islam on the one hand, and confirms their belief in the superiority and universal validity of Western science, on the other. Their naiveté is well reflected by Candide: 'all is well in this best of all possible worlds'.

However, the dangers inherent in Bucaillism are very grave. There is the obvious fact that it generates a strangely dumbfounding theology—as all scientific knowledge is contained in the Quran, simply studying the Quran from a scientific perspective will reveal everything and lead to new theories and discoveries. While the Quran obviously contains some passing references to natural facts, it is by no means a textbook of science. It is a book of guidance. It provides motivation, and only motivation, for the pursuit of knowledge. Knowledge begins with the Quran and does not end with it.

But, more important, by equating the Quran with science, Bucaillism elevates science to the realm of the sacred and makes Divine Revelation subject to the verification of Western science. Apart from the fact that the Quran needs no justification from modern science, Bucaillism opens the Quran to the counter argument of Popper's criteria of refutation: would the Quran be proved false and written off, just as Bucaille writes off the Bible, if a particular scientific fact does not tally with it, or if a particular fact mentioned in the Quran is refuted by modern science? And what if a particular theory, which is confirmed by the Quran and is in vogue today, is abandoned tomorrow for another theory that presents an opposite picture? Does that mean that the Quran is valid today but will not be valid tomorrow?

Moreover, by raising science to the level of sacred knowledge, Bucaillism effectively undermines any criticism of science. Because the pursuit of knowledge is so strongly emphasized in the Quran, most Muslim scientists already possess a sense of reverence towards modern science. Bucaillism takes this reverence to a new level: a whole generation of Muslim scientists do not just accept all science as good and true, but attack any one who shows a critical or sceptical attitude towards science. Furthermore, the belief in a universally beneficial science leads to a pestiferous kind of fatalism: since science is universal and for the benefit of all humankind, it will eventually make its way to Muslim societies and serve their needs!

Nonsensical Numerology

Apart from reading science *in* the Quran, there are also attempts to read the Quran *with* science. More appropriately, discovering new meanings in the Quran by statistical analysis and computer manipulation. The doyen of this undertaking is the Egyptian engineer Rashad Khalifa, who originally set out to prove the divine nature of the Quran by showing its remarkable mathematical nature. The jacket to Khalifa's first book, *Miracle of the Quran*, proclaims, 'using the ultimate in scientific proof, namely, mathematics, this book puts in your hands physical, examinable evidence that the Quran is the word of God. Undoubtedly, it will strengthen the faith of the faithful, and it will provide those who are seeking the truth with an unprecendented opportunity to find it'.[18]

What is this scientific evidence? Khalifa alleges that the Quran consists of an elaborate mathematical pattern whose basic element, building block as it were, is the prime number 19. This number is contained in the first verse of the Quran, Bismillah ir Rahman ir Rahim ('In the name of God, the Beneficent, the Merciful'), which consists of nineteen letters. The twenty-eight Arabic letters can be given numerical values. When number 19 is written corresponding to its alphabet it spells 'wahid', one of the names of God, that also means 'God is One'—and this is the message of the Quran. The Quran consists of 114 suras or chapters and this figure is a multiple of 19. The first Quranic revelation (96: 1–5) consists of nineteen words. This first revelation also consists of 76 letters which is a multiple of 19; and the whole chapter itself consists of 96 verses which is also a multiple of 19. The number 19 is also mentioned by the Quran itself.

Armed with his personal computer, Khalifa focuses on Quranic initials—letters that appear at the beginning of some suras (chapters)—and feeds the frequency of occurrence of each letter into his computer. The letters are: Alif (A), Ha (H), Ra (R), Sin (S), Sad (S), Ta (T), Ayn (A), Qaf (Q), Kaf (K), Lam (L), Mim (M), Nun (N), Ha (H) and Ya (Y). His additional data includes the total number of letters in each of 114 suras and the number of verses in each sura. He manipulates the data to calculate the percentage value and average frequency of occurrence for each of the fourteen letters in each verse of the Quran. For the multi-lettered Quranic initials, such as Ta Ha, Ta Sin and Ya Sin, he calculates the absolute frequency of occurrence, percentage of the frequency value for each of the 114 suras, and the average occurrence per verse for each of the multi-lettered Quranic initials in each sura. Finally, he arranges all the suras of the Quran in the ascending order of the absolute frequency of occurrence of each Quranic initial and percentage frequency of occurrence for each of the fourteen sets of Quranic initials. What does Khalifa find? That the chapters which begin with the Quranic initials also contain the highest frequency of the specific letter(s) used at the beginning of the sura. For example, sura Qaf contains a higher frequency of the letter Qaf than any other sura of the Quran, or there is not one sura in the Quran where all three values of Nun are higher than their counterparts in the Nun-initialed sura, al-Qalam. The analysis for Quranic initials Alif, Lam, Mim, which occur in four Meccan and two Medinan suras, shows that the four Meccan suras are superior to all Meccan suras in the overall frequency of Alif, Lam, Mim. So what can we conclude from this? In Khalifa's own words:

> The Quranic initials, as a whole, have shown us that every word, indeed every letter, in the Quran was carefully calculated. The Quran itself states this fact very clearly in the first verse of sura Hud . . . Placement of the Quranic initials in their specific locations proves the existence of advance knowledge of the distribution pattern of the alphabet throughout the Quran. No one can claim that such advance knowledge is attainable by man; any man. To translate this into physical, tangible evidence, the computer was asked to calculate the number of manipulations one should master in order to write a mathematically controlled book such as the Quran. The composition of (the) Quran involves 114 chapters where 14 alphabet letters were distributed according to specific combination. According to the well-known mathematical formula, the number of manipulations involved in this case equals 114 . . . This value, 626,000,000,000,000,000,000,000,000,000 (626 septillions) is certainly beyond the capacity of any creature, including today's most sophisticated computers. When we look at this number we can readily appreciate the divine statement in sura *Al-Isra* (The Night Journey), verse 88 (Say, if all

the humans and all the jinns banded together in order to produce a verse like this, they will surely fail). Furthermore, this is the number of controlled manipulations for a specific distribution pattern of the alphabet, without placing them in useful sentences. To place these mathematically distributed alphabetic letters in useful sentences is another complete job . . .[20]

On the basis of his analysis, Khalifa can also prove that the present order of recording the Quranic chapters is divinely inspired, the locations of revelation of the Quranic chapters, whether Meccan or Medinan, can be proved to be correct, the Quran's specific way of dividing each sura into verses is divinely prescribed ('the average per verse value is a highly significant property throughout the Quran'), that the opening statement 'Bismillah-ir-Rahman-ir-Rahim' ('In the name of God, the Compassionate, the Merciful') is an integral part of each sura, except sura al-Tawba, and even the particular way of spelling certain words in the Quran has mathematical significance. In his *Quran: Visual Presentation of the Miracle*, Khalifa produces fifty-two 'physical facts' to prove his number 19 theory. In the preface to the book, he boldly declares:

> There now exists physical evidence for a message from God to the world. This marks the advent of a new era in religion; an era where faith is no longer needed. There is no need to 'believe' when one 'knows'. People of the past generation were required to believe in God, and uphold His commandments on faith. With the advent of the physical evidence reported in this book, we no longer believe that God exists; we know that God exists.[20]

So there we have it! Khalifah's numerological analysis proved contagious. Within a short period he had followers everywhere. The famous Muslim preacher, Ahmad Deedat, for example, used Khalifa's analysis extensively in his lectures and confrontations with evangelical Christians.[21] In Malaysia, one of Khalifa's disciples, Kassim Ahmad, established a group devoted to following and promoting Khalifa's declaration. In addition, Khalifa eventually acquired a devoted following in Bangladesh, India, Pakistan, Egypt and the United States.

Slowly, Khalifa became a bit too drunk on his 'discovery'. To begin with he showed only mild signs of derangement: he began to denounce the codes of Muslim ethical behaviour and announced that he had calculated the exact date of the Day of Judgement.[22] Then he began to find 'evidence' of fabrication in the Quran: the computer had discovered nine violations of the theory of number 19 revealing that the last two verses of sura at-Taubah (chapter 9) had been tampered with.[23] On the basis of adjustment to these verses, he put a new interpretation on them and declared that Prophet Muhammad, the recipient of the Quranic revelation, had no role to play in Islam: 'when we seek "religious" instructions from Muhammad or any other source beside God, we support Satan in his claim that God needs a partner'.[24] At least one of his followers, Kassim Ahmad of Malaysia, promptly wrote a pamphlet denouncing the traditions and declaring them null and void.[25] Then, perhaps fuelled by a mention in *Scientific American* which found his work 'ingenious',[26] Khalifa went completely overboard: he declared himself to be a Prophet of God. Considering that Khalifa was the one to discover 'the secret that has remained hidden for 1,400 years', it was only natural for God to bestow further mercy on him and provide him with direct revelation! 'My commission as God's messenger to you', he writes in 'God's Message to the World', the flyer announcing his claim, 'is supported by a computer-age miracle that leaves no doubt whatsover in your mind. You will know that God is speaking to you'.

It is interesting to note that during the two decades and more that Khalifa has been propagating his message, it occurred to no one actually to examine his evidence and check his statistical work. Apart from emotional swipings, the theory of number 19 is still accepted by many devout Muslims as valid.

To lie with statistics is not a difficult task. Indeed, when Khalifa's 'physical evidence' is examined for statistical accuracy, it reveals numerous errors, distortions, half-truths and downright fabrications. His opening statements are quite correct: there are nineteen letters in the Bismillah, and the first revelation. But beyond that the evidence of number 19 embeded in the Quran as a secret code does not stand up to scrutiny.

To begin with, there is a great deal of inconsistency in Khalifa's letter counting. He claims that all the twenty-nine suras which begin with the Quranic initials contain these initials in multiples of 19. In fact, at least twelve of them are not multiples of 19 and have to be combined with the totals of up to six other suras for their grand total to become multiples of 19. For example, of the seven suras which begin with the letters Ha Mim, none of them contain Ha Mim in the multiples of 19. Moreover, Khalifa is not a good observer. He asserts that sura 42 is initialled with three letters—Ain, Sin and Qaf—but, it is initialled with five letters—Ha, Mim, Ain, Sin, Qaf—and the occurrence of these letters in this sura is not a multiple of 19 either (it is in fact, 562). The letter Ha occurs as a Quranic initial in sura Ta Ha (chapter 20) and sura Maryam (chapter 19), but in neither sura is the occurrence of this letter a multiple of 19. The occurrence of the letter Kaf which is found as a Quranic initial only in chapter 19 is not a multiple of 19 in that chapter. These are only a few examples.

Khalifa undertakes all sorts of juggling to produce his magic multiples. For example, sura Sad (chapter 38) begins with the letter Sad—but the occurrence of this letter in this chapter is not a multiple of 19. To get the required multiple, Khalifa adds the Sads that occur in sura al Araf (chapter 7)—which is prefixed with Alif, Lam, Mim, Sad—and sura Maryam (chapter 19)—which is prefaced with Kaf, Ha, Ya, Ain and Sad.[27] In certain cases he produces a letter out of thin air to come up with the required figure: for example, he tabulates eight Alifs in chapter 2, verse 10, to produce a total of 4,502 Alifs in this chapter, which when added to 3,202 Lams and 2,195 Mims produces a grand total of 9,899 which is a multiple of 19.[28] But there are only seven Alifs in that verse, which would make his total 9,898, a rather nice symetrical figure but not a multiple of 19. When he can add, he can also subtract: in 30:21, Khalifa calculates seven Lams;[29] in fact, there are eight Lams in this verse which makes his 'physical fact number (41)' a blatant lie. On numerous occasions, that is when it suits him, he counts Hamzahs as Alifs, when it does not he simply ignores them! Similarly, he ignores the well-established rules of Arabic grammar and counts the words as it suits him.

However, the most obnoxious of Khalifa's manipulations concerns the actual doctoring of the Quranic text to yield his required figures. His 'physical fact number (28)' claims chapter 68, which is initialled with the letter Nun, contains 133 occurrences of that letter. In fact, there are only 132 occurrences of Nun in that chapter. However, to get the required figure, Khalifa actually adds an extra Nun by spelling out the letter Nun, hence gaining an extra nun![30] In other places he invents his own spelling of the words: to prove his 'physical fact number (29)' he rewrites the word 'Bastatan' which is actually written with a Sad with a Sin, thus losing a Sad and producing the right magic number.[31]

All this is a very brief indication of the nature of 'evidence' produced by Rashad Khalifa, Ph.D., to prove his theory of number 19.

That such an absurd enterprise could command such a huge following in Muslim intellectual circles is a reflection of the quality of these intellectuals.

Grotesque Gnosticism

Numerology has ancient roots in Islamic history. When Greek writings began to be translated during the Abbasid period, Pythagorean numerology began to make an impact on Muslim mystical and secret circles. As early as the ninth century, Ismaili Shia sects had incorporated numerology as part of their theology. The Ismaili mystic Ibn Hawshab al-Kufi, for example, produced the number 19 in a way analogous to Rashid Khalifa and used it to justify seven Imams (who have personal mastery over the community) and twelve Hujjahs (who have the authority of decision-making).[32] It is not surprising then that numerology is also an important part of certain mystical approaches to Islamic science, along with astrology, alchemy and other forms of occultism. Here, the confusion is produced largely by the particular approach of Seyyed Hossein Nasr and his followers, who have had a major impact on contemporary discussions on Islamic science. Indeed, many Muslim thinkers and scientists know only Nasr's interpretation of Islamic science. To differentiate Nasr's approach from Sufism, the conventional form of mysticism in Islam, I have deliberately chosen to refer to his strand of thought as gnosticism since it derives its intellectual foundations largely from the gnostics of classical Greece.

The concern about the secular nature of science among certain scholars with Sufi tendencies is understandable. No one, for example, would quarrel with Syed Ali Ashraf's assertion that the emphasis of science on reason is excessive and epistemologically too exclusive or 'that we can never arrive at religious truths with the help of scientific discoveries',[33] or that scientism, that breeds an 'attitude of mind according to which nothing can be or should be accepted as true unless and until that thing is rationally proved',[34] is undermining religious values in Muslim societies. Such warnings and analyses have a positive role to play in the debate on Islamic science.

Indeed, Sufi analysis has produced profound insights for the development of a contemporary philosophy of Islamic science. An example is Syed Muhammad Naquib al-Attas's suggestion that, as the Quran describes the material and natural world as a great open book,

Islamic science should study various elements of natural and material worlds as words.[35] Just as words do not have an independent reality of their own, to know them is to know what they mean, what they symbolize, what they stand for, so 'the study of nature, or anything, any object of knowledge in creation', should be undertaken to seek meaning and to understand what it represents. And the meaning of things is 'determined by the Islamic vision of reality and truth as projected by the Quranic conceptual system'.[36] In other words, scientific inquiry should be sought within the framework of the Quranic conceptual system, that would give the results of this inquiry meaning and significance. Quite clearly, a sound philosophy of science can be developed from this suggestion—and this philosophy can actually lead to policy guidelines.

The confusion arises when mysticism is actually equated with Islamic science. In Hossein Nasr's framework there is no difference between Islamic science as such and gnostic mysticism. For Nasr the kernel of Islamic science is his particular variety of Islamic cosmology which is an amalgam of 'such diverse elements as Quranic symbolism, concepts and symbols drawn from the doctrinal formulation of Sufism (itself developed to a large extent from the Quran and Hadith), theosophical and philosophical descriptions of the cosmos, numerical symbolism and traditional astronomy'.[37] In this hotchpotch, Islam and the Quran figure only tangentially. It is theosophy, Greek philosophy and magic, numerology, and the occult which are the actual foundation of this 'Islamic cosmology'. Nasr limits the boundaries of Islamic science to this cosmology in such a way that Islamic science becomes synonymous with gnostic esotericism. For Nasr, the methodology of Islamic science is the methodology of gnosis. It is based on an epistemology and psychology which considers the accessibility of ultimate knowledge through the personal and subjective experience of gnosis and makes esoteric exegesis the methodology of Islamic science *par excellence*. All objectivity is thus sacrificed at the altar of mystical experience and inner satisfaction. Nasr is so deeply entrenched in Greek gnostic doctrine and methodology that he sees Greek gnosticism wherever he looks when surveying the work of Muslim scientists and scholars over ten centuries, and devotes much of his book to such topics as astrology, alchemy, occult sciences, and gnostic ideas on the position of man in creation. Some of this material is of dubious nature, some clearly outside the world-view of Islam, and some belongs to the very narrow interpretation of Ismaili thought that

Nasr endorses. The link between Islamic science as it existed in history, and gnosticism is a purely artificial creation: the vast majority of Muslim scientists who flourished during the golden age of Islam were not mystics, neither were they gnostics in the Greek tradition. They were Muslims; and what shaped their science was their worldview and its values.

A detailed analysis of Nasr's ideas are undertaken in the final chapter of this book. Here it suffices to point out that Nasr's representation of Islamic science makes it appear as an esoteric activity, a nebulous enterprise concerned not so much with solving physical and material problems as with acquiring mystical insights and enlightenment. Yet, even in the philosophical framework of a Sufi like Naquib al-Attas, there is nothing magical, occultish or supernatural about Islamic science; one does not have to be a gnostic to appreciate that man is a natural part of the environment, that his right to live on the earth is not exclusive and that his internal and external environment is sacred— these are part of the basic teachings of Islam. Moreover, the methodology of gnosis is limiting and suffocating: it cannot be allowed to become an all pervasive method as its domain is confined to inner fulfilment and mystical realization. To equate Islamic science with gnosticism is to do gross injustice to Islam as well as science and the historic achievements of Islamic science.

The confusion generated in the debate on Islam and science, and the efforts to contemporize Islamic science by Bucaillism, statistical analysis of the Quran and the imposition of the gnostic framework on Islamic science, has produced stilted discussion and suffocated genuine inquiry. Science is not the pursuit of truth, and its discoveries and facts do not, and cannot, have the same validity as the verses of the Quran. To read science in the Quran as though it were a scientific textbook reveals a lack of understanding of science. To justify the Quran by showing the scientific nature of some of its verses reveals a twisted form of inferiority complex. While statistical analysis can be used to produce insights into trend, developments and natural phenomena, its use in attempts to prove the divine origins of the Quran is a futile exercise. There are no magical mathematical codes buried in the verses of the Quran; and even if there were such codes, our discovery of them would not enhance our understanding of the message of the Quran. Science is a problem-solving enterprise: it is a method, a technique, for solving problems within a given paradigm and worldview. But its methodology cannot be the methodology of gnosis: while scientific work may be intellectually, socially and even spiritually fulfilling, it is not an exercise in mysticism. Conversely, gnosis does not solve physical and material problems; it may enrich one spiritually, but it does not fill one's stomach: gnosis is not going to solve the problems of famine, shelter, health, hygiene and transport. Given the confusion generated by Bucaillism, the theory of number 19 and gnostic interpretations of Islamic science, it seems that the Muslims have used the Quran to justify every kind of tendency, every excess, every banal idea—but that they have never actually looked at its message, actualised its ethical framework in a living, dynamic form, or attempted to build a civilization around its worldview. It's like a starving monkey with a coconut, who uses it as a hammer, football, pillow, but never actually eats it to save himself from starvation.

All these confusing tendencies actually end up mystifying science. Nasr's activities actually give science magical and supernatural qualities; and despite his concern for mystical enlightenment he actually believes in the objective, value-free nature of mathematics. Yet, there is nothing mystical, or mythological about science. There is nothing magically objective and neutral about the scientific method or mathematical formulations; to believe this is to be victim of a cruel hoax. Bias-free observation is a myth. Nothing 'out there' can be perceived without filtering it through our worldview and culture. Scientists often modify their observation with their own ideas and prejudices, the values and norms of their society. Not just observation but experimentation also cannot be undertaken in a cultural vacuum, and have meaning and significance solely in the framework of a theory itself set in the conceptual picture of a worldview. Putting a theory into a mathematical code does not strip the value content of a proposition of modern science. On the contrary, the nature of mathematics is such that its application to the world through science is purely fortuitous. Mathematical propositions, including the geometric propositions of Euclid, are *a priori* analytical—that is to say, their status is determined merely by analysing the terms of the proposition. That one plus one equals two can be determined as conforming to the principle that one plus one means two. That some theories can be codified in mathematical expression is a matter of scientific convenience. The laws of nature are not expressed in mathematical formulae, in indelible ink across the heavens; they are manufactured in ball-points in laboratories and institutes.

The fact that some of these manufactured laws and theories agree with what the Quran says is not in itself of any significance. It is a non-statement. Whether we can prove the divine origins of the Quran by codifying its verses in mathematical terms is irrelevant. The Quran promotes the pursuit of knowledge within a framework of values: it is these values which should be the focus of our attention and which should shape our scientific activity. Only by turning these values into a living reality can Muslims be truly honest to the Quran and fulfil their obligations to it.

References

1. *BIMA*, **6** (1), 1–2 (April 1985).
2. Moore, 'Highlights of human embryology in the Quran and the Hadith'.
3. The Supreme Council of Islamic Affairs, 1961.
4. *Ibid.* p. 21–2.
5. *Ibid.* p. 336–7.
6. Sher Ali Akhtar, Karachi, undated.
7. *The Bible, the Quran and Science*, p. 7.
8. 'The Quran and modern cosmology'.
9. 'Creation and the cosmos', in *Islamic Scientific Thought and Muslim Achievements in Science*, proceedings of the International Conference on Science in Islamic Polity, Islamabad, 1983, vol. 1, p. 96–113.
10. *Abstracts of Papers Presented at the First International Conference on Scientific Miracles of the Quran and Sunnah*, Islamabad, October 18–21, 1987, International Islamic University, Islamabad and Muslim World League, Makkah al-Mukkaramah.
11. See his *Quranic Sciences*, The Muslim Schools Trust, London, 1981.
12. *Planning Curricula for Natural Sciences*.
13. *Ibid.*, p. 68.
14. *Ibid.*, p. 69.
15. See, for example, the contributions of Mohammad Amin Al Shaikh, 'The scientific interpretation of Quran: views of those who permit it and those who object,; al Sayed Riaq al-Taweel, Hamouda Muhammad Daoud Sanad and Mohammad Khair Hassas Al Rassoul Ahmad who have the same titles for their papers, 'Rules of writing about scientific miracles of the Quran and Sunnah'; and Saud Yildirm, 'Principles of harmonizing Quranic texts with true scientific discoveries'.
16. *Al-Muafaqat*, vol. 2, pp. 55–6.
17. *Fi Zalalal al-Quran*, Daral-Shuruq, Beirut, 1973, vol. 1, p. 182.
18. Islamic Productions International, St Louis, Missouri, 1973.
19. *Ibid.*, pp. 183–4.
20. Preface to *Quran: Visual Presentation of the Miracle*.
21. See Ahmad Deedat's pamphlet, 'Al-Quran: the ultimate miracle', not dated, and his video, 'Al-Quran: a visual miracle', Islamic Centre International, Durban.
22. Rashad Khalifa, *Quran: The Final Scripture*, Islamic Productions

International, Tucson, Arizona, 1981, p. 177.
23. *Muslim Perspective*, Masjid, Tucson, March, 1985, p. ii.
24. Rashad Khalifa, *Quran, Hadith and Islam*, Islamic Productions International, Tucson, Arizona, 1982, p. 88.
25. Kassim Ahmad, *Hadis: Satu Penilaian Semula*, Media Intelek, Petaling Jaya, 1986.
26. *Scientific American*, September 1980, pp. 22–4.
27. *Quran: Visual Presentation of the Miracle*, p. 90.
28. *Ibid.*, p. 193.
29. *Ibid.*, p. 209.
30. *Ibid.*, p. 90.
31. *Ibid.*, p. 98. A detailed analysis of Khalifa's theory has been undertaken by Abu Ameenah Bilal Philips. His 'The theory of 19: hoax and heresy', to be published, notes this and other misspellings.
32. Translated by Kamil Hussein, Leiden, 1948.
33. S. A. Ashraf, 'Islam and modern scientific attitudes', *The Islamic Quarterly* **23** (3), 137–45 (1979), p. 141.
34. S. A. Ashraf, 'Foreword', *Muslim Education*, **1** (2), 4–6 (1982), p. 5.
35. Al-Attas, *Islam, Secularism and the Philosophy of the Future*.
36. *Ibid.*, p. 213.
37. Nasr, *Islamic Science: An Illustrated Study*, p. 31.

Three

Islamic Science or 'Science in Islamic Polity'?

Contemporary Muslim scholars appear to have little inclination for value or ethical analysis. Indeed, in the discipline Islamic studies, specific discussion of values and ethics is conspicious only by its absence. Only one contemporary Muslim scholar, Fazlur Rahman, has realized the significance of the ethical study of the Quran for solving the contemporary problems of the Muslim ummah.[1] It is hardly surprising then, particularly when most Muslim writers on science subscribe to the 'value-free and universally objective' model of science, that all discussion on scientific ethics and values in science has been shunned.

For most Muslim scientists the term 'Islamic science' itself is objectionable. Since science is value-free, how can it be labelled Islamic, or for that matter, Christian or Jewish? From a historical perspective, this objection can be readily met. In almost any introductory text of the history of science, one would find chapters on Greek science, Egyptian science, Babylonian science, Roman science and Chinese science. So at least in this respect, we are justified to talk about 'Islamic science'—being a science which was practised within Muslim civilization during the period 650 to 1500 C.E. It is in this sense that George Sarton speaks of Islamic science: as a localized affair, 'even though its locality was the best part of the world', undertaken in a local, religious context.[2] Some scholars have put Islamic science into an even more local context. Thus, the first issue of the *Journal for the History of Arabic Science* justifies the use of the term 'Arabic-Islamic science' in these words:

> Our efforts are focused on studies and investigations to rediscover and evaluate scientific and technical activities, most of which were carried out and recorded under Islamic patronage and aspiration. By and large, it was

the Muslim rulers who sought scholars of various backgrounds and religious convictions, and encouraged and sponsored their intellectual pursuits and productivities. More than any other rulers of their times, they generously supported education, and created interests and incentives in support of scientific activities and technical skills among all their subjects, regardless of ethnic origins or religious affiliations. The vehicle of communication in learning, trade, politics and religion, however, was Arabic, the language of the Quran, the holy book of Islam. . . . Thus . . . to respect both the language of the media as well as the civilization, it seems appropriate to use such terms as Arabic (Persian, Turkish or Urdu)—the Islamic legacy.[3]

Similar considerations led to the efforts of the Istanbul Technical University to organize regular conferences and seminars on 'the history of Turkish-Islamic science and technology'.[4]

At least in historical sense, it would seem, we are justified in the use of the term 'Islamic science'. However, when we speak of Islamic science, Chinese science or Babylonian science, we are talking about distant civilizations. Even if we were to accept that the development of science is linear, we could still discover differences in character, style and content among the sciences of these civilizations, giving them a specific space-time flavour. But what about more recent times? For example, would the twentieth century history of science in America and Europe be all that different, or would both continents simply be an integrated part of the history of science in Western civilization? What is the difference between science in America and American science? If we are to believe the contributors to the first volume of the revived journal, *Osiris*, it is the context within which science is done that gives science its unique, local character.[5] The consensus seems to be that there is something called American science which is different in character and style from science done elsewhere in Western civilization. For example, stratigraphic evolutionary geology is a science not merely done in America but American. Moreover, there are disciplines and times when the Americans have been at the forefront of a science; for example, genetics in the early twentieth century, and since this science was only being done in America, at least at that particular period, it is American. Furthermore, there have been approaches to science, such as Baconianism, which were popular in America and less so or not popular at all elsewhere. There are also a number of structural factors which give a unique flavour to science in America: the fundamental nature of entrepreneurship, politics and funding, the emphasis and importance of pluralism and local circumstances. It is not possible to distinguish the worldview and the social and political needs of America, as well as the perception of science in American society, from the science that is actually done in America. The history of American science is an integral part of American history and, in many respects, just as unique and national:

> 'All history is local history', because without the specifics of setting, the events and ideas are meaningless. 'All local history is social history', because without players and interaction between them nothing occurs. 'All social history is intellectual history', because social interaction is only understandable when we see the mindset and worldview behind it. 'All intellectual history is local history', because belief systems are far more apt to the 'tribal behaviour' than universal. Context is the linchpin that holds together the concept of American science.[6]

Context is also the linchpin on which the notion of a contemporary Islamic science is based. If it is possible to distinguish the style and characteristics of American science of the early twentieth century, then it is possible to distinguish the unique features of contemporary American science. If this is so, surely it is also possible to construct a contemporary Islamic science with a distinctive character and style that evolves from the worldview of Islam and the needs, requirements and perception of Muslim societies.

To a very large extent, accepting the notion of a contemporary Islamic science involves appreciating the value-bias and ideological character of science. And the major stumbling block here is the faith of most Muslim scientists in the value-free, universal character of science. It is this faith which has produced such notions as 'science in Islamic polity' which is particularly favoured by scientists in Pakistan. The thesis behind the notion is that while science itself is neutral and universal, it has a particular role in an Islamic polity. I intend to discuss this notion in some detail; but first, we ought to have some understanding of what is meant by science.

Science has been notoriously difficult to define. The conventional view of science as being pure and unsoiled by cultural, political and ideological concerns and the concept of 'the scientist' after the Renaissance as being a dedicated lone researcher, a quasi-religious figure analogous to a saintly hermit, is now dangerously obsolete. In the West, such a vast body of literature has been produced against this view that entire new disciplines that study the subjective nature of science, such as 'science and society', 'sociology of science', 'anthropology of science' and 'science policy', have emerged. In Muslim societies, this view of science would be detrimental to the work of those scientists who are seeking Islamic solutions to contemporary problems.

In pinning down science, definitions such as 'by weighing, measuring, and making experiments, you try to describe nature in mathematical terms, that is science'[7] do not really help since they leave out a host of other activities that scientists often find themselves involved in. For example, scientists are always speculating and making assumptions which cannot be proved. In elementary particle theory, there is the assumption that there is a reality outside the observer, and *those* assumptions cannot be proved objectively. Moreover, in certain cultures there are no words for science: in Hindu thought, for example, the pursuit of a Platonic Truth is not recognized as a valid form of inquiry. When faced with such difficulties, we can fall back to Lord Rutherford's definition that science is what scientists do. Essentially, science is a human activity and as such it is subject to the strength and weaknesses of all human activities. More generally, we can say that science is a unified system of research and application—a system on which our daily lives depend. Scientists do not seek after truth or collect facts, they solve problems. The choice of the problem, who makes the choice and on what grounds, may well be more important than the solution. The choice is the principle point of influence of society, worldview, political realities of power, prejudice and value systems on even the 'purest' science. Reliable statements about the world and its phenomena are facts, but these come to be recognized as such by the action of social processes and values after the completion and publication of the research on which they are based. In a basic model of science, it might be said that research leads to facts which in turn lead to application. Research is stimulated by curiosity on the part of the scientists, and the applications of the results of research fulfil perceived social needs. The perception of certain social needs could also provide the stimuli for research. Science needs both motivations. Pure curiosity leads to ivory-tower science, with only coincidental applications to human needs, while excessive concentration on the applications of science can lead to trivialization of research. A combination of the two was first called for by Francis Bacon when he asked for experiments 'of fruit and light' to provide the stimulus for a balanced approach to societal needs and scientific curiosity.

But scientific endeavour can be blocked by dogma and superstition which do not have to come from traditional religion, but can come from science itself. Most scientists are fundamentalists in the sense that they believe all science to be true and good. The belief in the pure objectivity of science and its absolute truths are no less superstitions for being modern, and the Darwinian Theory of Evolution is no less a dogma for it being a fundamental tenet of belief for biologists. These beliefs, rationally speaking, are analogous to the beliefs, say, in Jesus Christ being the 'son of God' or the belief in 'life after death'. Belief systems in science often parallel belief systems in religion.

When I refer to Western science, I mean the entire system and process of research and applications, with its power structures and underlying values, concern for capitalist economics and domination of nature, which is a vogue in our times. The roots of this system lie in the Enlightenment.

Enlightenment and After

The Enlightenment was the intellectual and scholarly tradition which is responsible for shaping the character and style of contemporary Western science and technology. The Enlightenment was the work of the *philosophes*—the intellectuals who conceived and perfected it. The philosophes looked at science and exploration not just for new knowledge, but also for new attitudes towards knowledge. From science they acquired the sceptical attitude of systematic doubt, and from exploration a new relativistic attitude towards belief, using them as ammunition against traditional norms and values. Montesquieu's tolerant Persians, Voltaire's sage Chinese, Diderot's virtuous Tahitians, coming after Fontenelle's plurality of worlds that was designed to reduce man in his pride, all served excellently as weapons to knock down European society and for suggesting a better one. Curiously, the effect of such scepticism and relativism was to glorify and magnify man in general and European man in particular.

When the Enlightenment wanted to characterize its power in one word it called it 'reason', which became the verifying force of the eighteenth century, expressing all that it strives for and all that it achieves. Reason, after all, is the same for all cultures, all epochs.

The methodological concerns of the Enlightenment derived from the seventeenth century. The intellectual spokesmen of that century—Bacon, Descartes, Hobbes, Locke, Newton—appealed for a rational standard of truth. The philosophy of the Enlightenment, particularly the methodological pattern of Newtonian mechanics, began to generalize it, becoming the basic epistemological framework of the Enlightenment. However much individual scholars agree or disagree with the end results, they are all unified in their framework of knowledge. The new tools of reason and analysis however, were not only for mathematical and physical knowledge but they were also used by the philosophes to dissect all branches of human endeavour. Such traditional disciplines as politics, ethics, metaphysics and religion were analysed on the basis of reason with a view to ending their perplexities once and for all. The principles which the philosophes attempted to apply were the new scientific canons of the seventeenth century: there was to be no *a priori* deduction from natural principles without concrete experimental evidence. 'This use of observation and experiment', writes Isaiah Berlin,

> entailed the application of exact methods of measurement, and resulted in the linking together of many diverse phenomena under laws of great precision, generally formulated in mathematical terms. Consequently only the measurable aspects of reality were to be treated as real—those susceptible to equations connecting the variations in one aspect of a phenomenon with measurable variations in other phenomena. The whole notion of nature as compounded of irreducibly different qualities and unbridgeable 'natural' kinds, was to be finally discarded. The Aristotelian category of final cause—the explanation of phenomena in terms of the 'natural' tendency of every object to fulfil its own inner end or purpose—which was also to be the answer to the question of why it existed, and what function it was attempting to fulfil—notions for which no experimental or observational evidence can in principle be discovered—was abandoned as unscientific, and, indeed, in the case of inanimate entities without wills or purposes, as literally unintelligible. Laws formulating regular concomitances of phenomena—the observed order and conjunctions of things and events—were sufficient, without introducing impalpable entities and forces, to describe all that is describable, and predict all that is predictable, in the universe. Space, time, mass, force, momentum, rest—the terms of mechanics—are to take the place of final causes, substantial forms, divine purpose, and other metaphysical notions.[8]

This conviction—that reason and analysis can bring man knowledge of all reality—gained footholds in the most varied fields of eighteenth-century culture. The celebrated quote from Lessing, that the real power of reason is to be found not in the possession but in the acquisition of truth, has its parallel everywhere in the intellectual history of the eighteenth century. This fundamental idea of the Enlightenment was the adhesive which united the Christians and non-Christians, theists and atheists, concrete materialists and romantic poets. Even the calmest and most discrete thinkers were swayed by this movement. They were helpless, they could not escape, and they thought, as well as felt, a trend towards a new future for mankind.

The Enlightenment separated knowledge from values without giving an adverse judgement on either. The philosophes were in favour of reason; but they did not throw intrinsic values overboard. Kant, for example, clearly saw in Newtonian mechanics knowledge of the law of the physical universe, but he did not submit the autonomy and sovereignty of man to deterministic mechanics. He separated the domains of physical knowledge and intrinsic values by proclaiming 'the starry heavens above you and the moral law within'. The philosophes who followed the Enlightenment took the divorce of knowledge and values further.

The nineteenth century heralded the true triumphs of reason in the unparalleled spread of materialism. Logical positivism and materialism (of which Marxism is a part) and their twentieth century counterpart, logical empiricism, threw values overboard. In their epistemological framework values are not considered proper knowledge. Utilitarianism declared that the goal, the ideal, of all moral endeavour is the greatest happiness of the greatest number of people. What came to be practised, in fact, was the greatest number of material goods for the largest possible number of people. Industrialization, which also became the main agent of the environmental devastation, had produced this reality.

Besides economics, there were also a number of political and technical causes that prompted the myth of the neutrality of science. A key one of these was the legacy of imperialism with its subjection of the less developed world by the European powers. This subjection was not just an economic and political phenomenon; it also had an overt cultural goal. Western political and technological power led to the subjugation and self-abnegation within the developing societies of all aspects of indigenous culture. This was specially true of science and technology. Glyn Ford argues,

> it was here that cultural clash was most direct, and most weighed in favour of the West. Western military technology decisively proved its superiority again and again as the European nations painted the globe in their various national hues. The result was that Western technical advisors began to litter the court circles of the Middle East and elsewhere. In many cases, the

courts wanted their influence strictly contained with the military sphere. But this was a barrier that was impossible to hold. The technology itself required a skilled workforce, and it was therefore necessary to send suitable candidates abroad to receive appropriate technical training. When these neophytes returned from the Imperial homeland and took their place as junior officers they began to want to generalize the application of what they had learnt outside the military sphere.[9]

And that meant promoting science as 'the pursuit of objective truth' and ensuring that 'Western science—and who was to deny its claims—took precedence over all other realms of knowledge'.

This is where matters stood until recently. As the religious-based *weltanschauung* of the European and other occidentalized people lost its quality of enchantment with the natural world, it became the common-place view that only science was really safe. Effects could only be proportionate to their material causes. The idea of a non-linear synergistic reaction, of an ecological system, was effectively absent from mainline scientific thinking until well into the 1960s. The environmental crisis and the associated predicament of what the Club of Rome described as the *world problematique* came as a rude surprise.[10] Suddenly, wherever one looked, there seemed to be problems concerning the interactions of science and technology with the natural environment. Political and environmental constraints began to limit increasingly the practical solutions which previous experience and methods led one to believe might be eminently suitable ways out of the complex and growing labyrinth of problems that mankind created for itself. Perhaps the most significant aspect of the contemporary predicament of mankind is the widespread bewilderment that so many problems and dilemmas should come together at once.

Science and Values

The mid-twentieth century doubts about the inevitability of progress touched science over three decades ago. For many it was Thomas Kuhn's *The Structure of Scientific Revolutions* which was crucial. Kuhn in a survey of the history of science claimed that two very different and alternating types of scientific practices were to be found. These he termed 'normal' and 'revolutionary' science respectively. Normal science is characterized by a refined articulation of ideas within a framework of accepted practices and beliefs about nature. This matrix determines both the kinds of problems investigated and the manner in which solutions are offered. This framework of fundamental beliefs and accepted practices Kuhn termed a paradigm, and by definition during periods of normal science the ruling paradigm of the time remains inviolate.

However, eventually progress within the template falters, resulting in a crisis developing within normal science. This situation, if not speedily overcome, forces scientists to call into question the paradigm itself. This is then what he termed revolutionary science. The crisis acts like rain in a desert: a blooming of alternative paradigms takes place, all of which threaten to cast into oblivion much of the immediately preceding normal science. But it is not long before scientists start to group themselves behind one of the alternatives and with great speed the options start to narrow, until to remain a scientist one must subscribe to the new paradigm within which normal science recommences. For Kuhn, most scientists do normal science and nothing but. It is only a few who, on rare occasions, cross the boundary into revolutionary science.

Most important, Kuhn contended that paradigm choice, when revolutionary science is in the process of resolving its options down to one new, underpinning schema, is not free from the influence of personal and partisan considerations on the part of scientists. It is at this point that the belief that science is objective, neutral and value-free collapses. If personal and partisan considerations influence paradigm choice, science loses its claimed unique character over other disciplines.

Since the publication of Kuhn's book in 1962, several other studies have appeared supporting the thesis that science is not neutral and value-free. Notable among these is J. R. Ravetz's *Scientific Knowledge and Its Social Problems*, where he describes the industrialization of science and argues that contemporary social problems are a direct product of the nature and content of science; Ian Mitroff's *The Subjective Side of Science*, in which some interesting evidence is presented concerning the analysis of moon rocks by eminent scientists and how their findings supported their own pre-conceptions; and the two-volume *Ideology of/in the Natural Sciences*,[11] edited by Hilary and Steven Rose, in which a group of Marxist scientists and critics of science show how values infringe almost every aspect of science from selection of problems, delineating the areas of research, development of science syllabus to the construction of scientific theories and the development of experiments to test these theories. These and other studies show that as soon as we come away from accomplished facts and look at the processes of decision and choice, then the presence of values in science is undeniable.[12]

However, the proponents of the neutrality of science would argue that even if our knowledge is selected by values, that which scientists find is essentially value-free. However, even this last reculade is untenable. As Ravetz argues, values impinge upon even the experimental methods. Consider, for example, the design of statistical tests:

> If one wishes to test a correlation between two factors or variables, it is not simply a case of getting a yes or no answer—yes they do correlate or no they don't—rather one will get a certain number indicating the degree of correlation but that will always be modified by an estimate of the significance of the correlation, roughly speaking the odds against that particular correlation being purely chance. Now what we find is that when we are designing a statistical test, we must decide in advance on what significance level we wish to work to. If you wish to have a higher significance level, which is then a more rigorous test, you must have a larger size of sample, a more lengthy and laborious and careful testing procedure. In many fields testing is done to 95 per cent significance, in other words one in twenty chance. In other fields it must be done to 99 per cent significance, that is 100 to 1 odds against a result being spurious. The choice of significance level determines the design of the experiment and then we say, from what derives this choice of significance level? And that, the source of the selection of the significance level is the value assigned to the different sorts of errors that might arise in the taking of the test. I cannot go into full details here, but roughly speaking, you can see that if you are testing for something very, very dangerous then you want a higher significance level to be sure that you have missed nothing bad. If you are doing something which is rather straightforward then it is alright to have a lower significance level and save money on the test. That is speaking in a very loose way. And so deep in the heart of our quantitative techniques, we have value loadings put on, which derive from the intended functions of a result and which then shape the hard experimental quantitative work that is done.[13]

If we were to take issue with this analysis and argue that the influence of values on the contents of scientific knowledge can be debated, we will still have to concede the overpowering influence of values in the limits of our knowledge. Scholars of the sociology of science have been arguing that scientific knowledge is socially constructed. We can also argue, perhaps more powerfully, that our ignorance is also socially constructed in terms of values and political and ideological forces which determine that which is desirable to know and that which is undesirable, and therefore, unnecessary to know.

Social Responsibility of Muslim Scientists

In the face of such powerful arguments, the plea of such scholars as Ahsan Jan Qaisar that 'the Muslim scientists must realize that, as far as processes and methodology are concerned, science and religion are two separate worlds', sounds almost pathetic. If values are as deeply entrenched in science as Kuhn, Ravetz, Mitroff, Rose and Rose and a host of other scholars argue, then how can religion, the prime source of values, be separated from science? In this context, Qaisar's paper 'On the Definition of a "Muslim Scientist" and the Parameters of His Role Within the Ummah' is worth examining for the confusion that such naive thinking causes in Muslim scholarly circles.[14]

Qaisar sets out to answer a vital question: in what manner can a Muslim scientist be different from a non-Muslim scientist? The first segment of his answer is that 'no radical demarcation seems to be possible between a Muslim and a non-Muslim scientist solely on the basis of methodology'. He quotes the work of ibn al-Haytham and al-Biruni to support his hypothesis. But neither al-Biruni nor ibn al-Haytham actually supports his case; both of them had a very different approach to the methodology that is prevalent today. And if Muslim scientists want to stand out from the crowd, it is precisely the methodology of science that they need to sort out and Islamize. The Enlightenment raised the method of science to the level of a demi-god. For a Muslim scientist, the method of science is only one method of inquiry. The most significant aspect of al-Biruni is that he never became servant of one particular method or accepted the tyranny of methodology so characteristic of Western science. For al-Biruni, the answers we receive from science depend on the nature of questions, the area we decide to study and the way the questions are formed. And we know that he used a number of different methods himself in conformity with the nature of the science in question. Where he felt it necessary he used deduction, observation or experimentation, induction, or had recourse to intellectual intuition.[15] For him reason and scientific method were not the supreme authority, a view that must hold true for other Muslim scientists. If this is the case, then the methodology of science does not play the same role for Muslim and non-Muslim scientists.

But, more than that, the method of science is reduction; and reduction has never been the dominant mode of enquiry in the history of Islamic science. It is precisely reduction that has been isolated by scholar after scholar as the prime cause of the crisis of science and the contemporary predicament of mankind. Even such a strong pillar of the international scientific community as physicist John Ziman has been forced to acknowledge this truth. 'Think of physics simply as the "fundamental science" ', he writes,

> and it is over-subscribed almost to bankruptcy. But describe it as the science whose aim is to describe natural phenomena in the most mathematical and numerical language, and you will understand its past and have confidence in its future. In the past this programme has demanded *reduction*. To discover the mathematical sermon in store, reduce the agglomerate to its tiny crystals; analyse its crystal to molecules; each molecule, still too complex for precise mathematical description, is broken into atoms; from the atoms draw an electron or two, from the nucleus its constituent nucleons and other 'elementary particles'; only the submicroscopic building blocks dance perfectly to the tunes of quantum electrodynamics, group theory and relativistic invariance. But Reduction = Destruction. In separating out parts which behave so properly, we kill the collective spontaneity of the many body assembly of which they are elements. The interaction is where the action is, not in the individual actors.[16]

If reduction equals destruction, how can Muslim scientists continue to work ceaselessly with the same method and claim an Islamic identity? It requires intellectual courage to acknowledge that it is the very method of science that the Muslim scientists need to tackle, that they need to develop a new mode of doing science that balances reduction with synthesis.

Qaisar's second assertion is that 'it is only in the matter of approach/attitude that the use of the term Muslim scientist gets validated'.[17] He acknowledges that 'science and technology are not value-free' and as such 'a Muslim scientist must exercise extreme care and caution in selecting/accepting the type of research he plans to perform.' Moreover, 'he must assure himself that his work falls within the syndrome of Islamic values and ideals, especially with reference to the social, economic and cultural consequences of his research.'

Who could disagree with this? But, unfortunately, Qaisar does not tell us how Muslim scientists could do just that. He simply offers 'intermediate/appropriate technology' as the ultimate solution as though it was the panacea of all our technological problems.

The system and processes that constitute science nowadays are so complex and interconnected with politics and ideology that to say simply, 'I am a Muslim and therefore I have a different attitude and approach to science' is the ultimate in intellectual blindness. Within a dominant paradigm one cannot take a different approach. One either works within it or outside it. Research priorities and emphases are set not by individual scientists but by national governments, external influences—like the military–industrial complex—aid agencies and the international culture of science. There is no way for an individual scientist working in his laboratory safely to conclude that his particular piece of research will not serve a socially disruptive purpose.

Finally, Qaisar argues that the epistemologies of al-Farabi, ibn Tufail, ibn Rushd and al-Ghazzali were ultimately responsible for the decline of science in Islamic cultures. He particularly singles out al-Ghazzali and argues that his epistemology will 'lead all scientific investigations into a cul-de-sac'. In order 'to wriggle out of some philosophical predicament, perhaps his own, al-Ghazzali threw out the baby with the bath water'. Here, Qaisar is blaming the entire tradition of Islamic science for being non-rationalist. This is, of course, blatant nonsense. First of all al-Farabi, ibn Tufail and ibn Rushd were Mutazilites, they actually believed in reason and science, although like Qaisar they did not have an over-belief in science, seeing science as the only true knowledge and neglecting other forms of understanding. As such, al-Farabi, ibn Tufail—whose story of Hayy ibn Yaqzan, on which Daniel Defoe based his *Robinson Crusoe*, sets out to demonstrate that it is possible for a man stranded on an island to realize that there is a Creator simply by appropriate use of his reason—and ibn Rushd would not, however, subscribe to the Enlightment notion of reason. Al-Ghazzali was an Asharite, who believed that rational inquiry can be just as value-laden as non-rational inquiry. Qaisar actually wants to preserve not just science, but scientism for he realises that once science is separated from scientism it loses its universal validity. But his venom is actually directed towards al-Ghazzali.

The fact is that al-Ghazzali is unique among classical Muslim scholars for foreseeing the course that rationalism, untamed by a framework of values, could take and for developing an epistemology which cannot be surpassed even today for its intellectual rigour and relevance. Al-Ghazzali's *Book of Knowledge* is essential reading for all Muslim scientists. For despite his concession that science and technology are not value-free and neutral, Qaisar and others like him still have absolute faith in science; for them the belief that all science and knowledge is good is an article of faith. This is precisely why they want scientific inquiry unpolluted from religious concerns. The belief that knowledge *per se* is virtuous goes back to Aristotle. But al-Ghazzali rejects this axiom. He relates *Fard-ul Kifayah*, that is socially requisite knowledge, to its social function and divides it into praiseworthy and blameworthy categories. For scholars like Qaisar, it is unthinkable that knowledge can be blameworthy. Yet, blameworthy science—mostly related to social control and violence, either domestically by repressive regimes against their own populations, or externally as war—is now estimated to absorb approximately half the community of scientists worldwide. It is not just a question of weapons of mass destruction, the production, development, and refinement of chemical and biological weapons, and other instruments of war such as napalm and tools of torture, but more a system, intricately and intrinsically connected to the industrialized countries' war machines, that is blameworthy.

Within this system one cannot take an Islamic approach or argue that the reductive methodology of science will lead Muslim scientists, by virtue of their religion and beliefs, to make environmentally sound and socially beneficial contributions to Islamic societies. Nor, indeed, can one take refuge in academic isolation and blame others who have soiled the fair name of science by applying its results to evil deeds. Such breathtaking disregard for the ways in which the total, unified system of Western science works is a major reason why genuine problem solving methods and socially relevant research and development work has never taken root in Muslim countries.

So where does all this leave the social responsibilities of the Muslim scientist? The Muslim scientist has three basic responsibilities: to God whose pleasure he must seek at all times; to the ummah whose needs, requirements and problems must be the focus of his attention; and to himself for making the best of his life in this world and the hereafter. If there is one principle that unites these three responsibilities it is this: for a Muslim scientist science must not only be clearly directed towards Islamic goals but its processes and methodologies should also promote Islamic values and concerns.

Surely, devout Muslim scientists would argue, science in an Islamic polity would do just that.[18] The Islamic polity would produce a framework that would ensure that science promotes cherished Islamic values and fulfils the needs and requirements of Muslim societies. But, if one accepts the arguments presented above that the entire unified system of science that exists today is so deeply entrenched in Western values and culture that even the experimental and quantitative techniques cannot escape the onslaught of these values, then the practice of this science in an Islamic polity, far from promoting Islamic ideals, would, in fact, undermine the goals of Muslim societies. Indeed, there will always be conflict and tension between the goals of this science and Islamic polity. As such, it is nonsensical to speak of 'science in Islamic polity'. A science that shares and promotes the goals of an Islamic polity, a science whose processes and methodologies incorporate the spirit of Islamic values, a science that is geared to the needs and requirements of Muslim societies, a science that is done not for its own sake but for the pleasure of Allah, is a completely different entity in nature and style. And such a science is most appropriately called 'Islamic science'. Islamic science describes the total system of scientific enterprise in the Islamic civilization.

Restructuring Islamic Science

No civilization is possible without its own science. Seats of learning, discourse, debate, research and development are the springs that supply a civilization with the dynamic dimension around its axioms. If we accept, as we must, that every civilization must have two dimensions—the self-evident truths requiring no proof, and a dynamic and volatile body of scientific knowledge—then a relationship must also exist and must be demonstrable.

The Muslim position is that the greater the stability of the axioms supporting a civilization the wider will be the field of the dynamic and volatile body of knowledge that the civilization will generate and develop. Islam provides the most stable set of axioms man could possibly need in his great scientific enterprise of exploration, speculation and shaping the future. This has been demonstrated by the emergence of the Muslims during the European Dark Ages with a set of beliefs provided by revelation and prophetic experience. And this is the prime reason why this civilization spread within a remarkably short time over three continents (Europe, Africa and Asia); there is evidence that there were even settlements in America and Australia. It gave rise to a body of scientific knowledge, and great seats of learning emerged at places as far apart as Cordova, Istanbul, Baghdad, Cairo, Damascus, Tashkent, Bukhara, Delhi, Champa, Bandar Abbas, Kotabaru, Java, Guangdong and Beijing. Their contribution to physics, chemistry, medicine, astronomy, navigation, mathematics, geodesy, geography, botany, zoology, sociology and philosophy is well known to the historians of science and human development.

However, despite the fact that contemporary science owes an enormous debt to Islamic science, the point is that science as it is practised today is Western science. Western civilization has few axioms. Those it has are negative, derived from the Reformation, Renaissance and the Enlightenment. Deprived of axioms, Western science has had to provide its own, thus effectively reducing the range of scientific enquiry and enterprise. Western science has developed to a point where the inner contradictions are becoming self-destructive as regards the discipline, and actually harmful to man and his environment. The revival of Islamic science in our time means that contemporary science will get a much-needed ethical base. The reconstruction of Islamic science is one of the formidable challenges facing Muslim intellectuals today. But it is a challenge that has to be met if a dynamic, thriving civilization of Islam is to emerge in the future. The process of reconstruction of Islamic science begins with the realization that modern science is only a science of nature and not *the* science. It is a science making certain assumptions about reality, man, the man–nature relationship, the universe, time, space and so on. It appears universal because it is the only science that is being practised in our times. The basic assumptions of this science that reason is supreme, nature is there to be dominated, the purpose of science is to solve all problems and that only science can do this, are those of the Enlightenment. As such they are, in Arnold Toynbee's phrase, embodiments of the post-Christian Western actions and intellectual traditions that developed principally in seventeenth, eighteenth and nineteenth century Europe and were stimulated by the rabid anti-clericalism that arose with the French Revolution. As these very assumptions and this intellectual tradition have created the contemporary predicament of mankind and the crisis in science, the basic values of this science are manifestly inadequate for ensuring a safe and viable future for mankind.[19]

The reconstruction of Islamic science can only be achieved in a systematic manner. We need to work on three different fronts simultaneously: the philosophical and sociological bases of Islamic science need to be delineated; science policies which are an embodiment of Islamic goals, values and ideals need to be shaped; and alternative modes of research and development work have to be discovered.

While working on these fronts we ought to remember that we are not throwing western learning overboard—we are simply extracting that which is good and promotes our ideals, and synthesizing it with Islamic values and norms. At the same time we are discovering, conceiving, developing Islamic alternatives. For example, while acknowledging the pragmatic benefits of research in reducing human suffering, we need to find alternatives to vivisection and use of live animals in biological experiments—that is, an alternative mode of research. We would reject scientific and technological developments pursued with an intent to perpetuate certain bigotry, such as sociobiology, but would promote environmental research and technology assessment, and so on.

It is a truism that Islamic science could only provide a fully operational model within a social context that had truly assimilated and internalized its paradigms. But we need to begin somewhere: if we can develop a clear philosophical framework for Islamic science it will help us shape appropriate science policies and, perhaps the hardest task of all, guide us in the discovery of alternative modes of doing science.

Such a vision can come only from the ethical and conceptual teachings of the Quran. And it was to the major conceptual values of the Quran that a meeting of Western critics and philosophers of science and Muslim scientists and intellectuals, mostly from the West, turned to develop a contemporary philosophical and sociological framework for Islamic science. Entitled 'Science and Values in Islam and the West', the seminar was held in Stockholm during September 1981 under the auspices of the International Federation of Institutes of Advanced Studies (IFIAS).[20] The debate deduced that to be significant, issues of science and values in Islam must be treated within a framework of Quranic values that shape the goals of a Muslim society. These concepts generate the basic values of an Islamic culture and form a parameter within which an ideal Islamic society progresses. The seminar identified ten such concepts, four standing alone and three opposing pairs: *tawheed* (unity), *khilafah* (trusteeship), *ibadah* (worship), *ilm* (knowledge), *halal* (praiseworthy) and *haram* (blameworthy), *adl* (social justice) and *zulm* (tyranny), *istislah* (public interest) and *dhiya* (waste). When translated into values, this system of concepts embraces the nature of scientific enquiry in its totality: it integrates facts and values and institutionalizes a system of knowing that is based on accountability and social responsibility. But what do these values really mean and how do they shape scientific and technological activity?

Usually, the concept of *tawheed* is translated as unity of God. It becomes an all-embracing value when this unity is asserted in the unity of mankind, unity of man and nature and the unity of knowledge and values. From *tawheed* emerges the concept of *khilafah*: that man is not independent of God but is responsible and accountable to God for his scientific and technological activities. The trusteeship implies that man has no exclusive right to anything and that he is responsible for maintaining and preserving the integrity of the abode of his terrestrial journey. Thus the heroic concept of science, the lone scientists out to dominate nature at all costs, has no place in this framework.

Now, if man is not to seek knowledge for the outright exploitation of nature, is he simply reduced to being a passive observer? On the contrary, contemplation (*ibadah*) is an obligation, for it leads to an awareness of *tawheed* and *khilafah*; and it is this very contemplation that serves as an integrating factor for scientific activity and a system of Islamic values. *Ibadah*, or the contemplation of the unity of God, has many manifestations, of which the pursuit of knowledge is the major one.

But is the pursuit of all knowledge *ibadah*? The concept of knowledge, *ilm*, which is a value when it is pursued within an Islamic framework, is one of the most written about and discussed concepts of Islam. There are more than 1,200 definitions of *ilm*; and almost all Muslim classical authors from al-Kindi (d. 373), al-Farabi (d. 950) and al-Biruni (d. 1048) to ibn Khaldun (d. 1406) have produced major classifications of knowledge. Al-Ghazzali divided *ilm* into two categories: revealed, which provides the ethical and moral framework, and non-revealed, the pursuit of which is an obligation under the dictates of *ibadah*.

Non-revealed knowledge is further sub-divided into two categories: *fard-ayan*, such as ethics and morality, which is essential for individuals to survive and *fard-kifayah* which is necessary for the survival of the whole community. The pursuit of knowledge for the benefit of the individual or the community is *ibadah*. The notions of science for science's sake and science as a means to an end are rejected.

What determines the social responsiveness and non-utilitarian nature of science? Here the concept of *halal* and *haram* come into play. When closely examined, haram includes all that is destructive for man as an individual, his immediate environment and the environment at large. The word destructive should be understood in its physical, mental and spiritual sense. On the other hand, all that is beneficial for an individual, his society and his environment is halal. Thus an action that is halal brings all-round benefit. But an action that may bring benefits for the individual may have harmful effects either on society or the environment or both. This is why halal operates on the premises of the distribution of *adl* (social justice). Haram propagates *zulm* (tyranny). Within the framework of Islamic values, *zulm* is of three categories: between man and God, between man and man, and between man and nature. Thus, scientific and technological activity that seeks to promote adl is halal, while that science and technology which promotes alienation and dehumanization, concentration of wealth in fewer and fewer hands, unemployment and environmental destruction is *zalim* (tyrannical) and therefore haram. A major charac-teristic of zalim science and technology is that they destroy human, environmental and spiritual resources and generate waste. Such science is therefore categorized as *dhiya* (wasteful). Scientific and technological activity that promotes adl—distributive technologies, science for the people—draw their legitimacy from *istislah* (public interest) which is the chief supplementary source of Islamic law.

It was just such a consideration of key Islamic concepts that enabled the Stockholm seminar to produce a simple contemporary model of Islamic science: the paradigms of Islamic science are the concepts of *tawheed*, *khilafah* and *ibadah*. Within these paradigms, Islamic science operates through the agency of *ilm*, to promote *adl* and *istislah*. Thus the accountability of a Muslim scientist is both social and spiritual. A natural science that develops within this framework would also promote God-consciousness, harmonize the means and ends in the production of knowledge, and emphasize social relevance in both the pursuit and the application of knowledge.

It is clear that this model of Islamic science needs a considerable amount of further work. For it to become acceptable to a wide cross-section of Muslim scientists—as well as to Western ones—Islamic science has to prove itself both theoretically and practically. Specific science policies based on the model must be devised and specific proj-ects which would highlight the nature and content of Islamic science ought to be developed. Considering the vast array of issues—from food, water, housing, transportation, medicine to public health and safety problems—that now confront the Muslim world, there is no shortage of problems to work on. From the viewpoint of the West, such an exercise could be a useful stimulus for devising a new direction for occidental science: a convergent teleology of late twentieth-century scientific development might well emerge. The Muslim scientists, philosophers and sociologists of science, on the other hand, should be articulate in emphasizing not only the desirability of Islamic science for the Muslim world, but also their belief that it is the only Kuhnian revolutionary option that can become the normal science of the future.

References

1. See his brilliant study, *Major Themes of the Quran*, Bibliotheca Islamica, Chicago, 1980.
2. Sarton, 'Islamic Science'.
3. Sami Hamarneh, 'Arabic-Islamic science and technology', *JHAS*, 1 (1), 3–7, 1977.
4. The first of these conferences was held 14–18 September 1981 in Istanbul and produced five volumes of proceedings, published by the Institute of History of Science and Technology, Istanbul Technical University, Istanbul.
5. *Osiris*, second series 1, 1985.
6. The cycle of definitions is from Nathan Reingold, quoted by Elizabeth Barnaby Keeney, 'Science in America or American science?'.
7. *Lund Letter on Technology and Culture*, No 1., June 1981, p. 3.
8. Berlin, *The Age of Enlightenment*, p. 17.
9. Glyn Ford, 'Is Islamic Science Possible?' in Sardar, *The Touch of Midas*.
10. The environmental crisis and the predicament of mankind is discussed in a host of books of which the various reports to the Club of Rome have become quite famous. See D. Meadows, et al. *The Limits of Growth*, Potomac Associates, New York, 1972; Mihajlo Mesarovic and Eduard Pestel, *Mankind at the Turning Point*, Hutchinson, London, 1974; Amilcar O. Nerrera et al., *Catastrophe or a New Society?*, International Development Research Centre, Ottawa, 1976. For a summary of various attempts to analyse *world problematique*, see chapter 4 of Ziauddin Sardar, *The Future of Muslim Civilization*, Mansell, London, 1987.
11. Macmillan, London. 1976.
12. See Lakoff, *Science and Ethical Responsibility*; Lakatos and Musgrave, *Criticism and the Growth of Knowledge*; Whitley, *Social Processes of Scientific Development*; Morley, *The Sensitive Scientist*; Holton and Blanpied, *Science and Its Public*.
13. J. R. Ravetz, 'Science and values'.
14. In the proceedings of the International Conference on Science in Islamic Polity, *S & T Potential and its Development in the Muslim World*, Ministry of Science and Technology, National Hijra Centenary Committee and Organization of Islamic Conference, Islamabad, 1983, vol. 2 pp. 236–44.
15. For an introduction to al-Biruni's work, see Said and Khan, *Al-Biruni*.
16. *Physics Bulletin* **25**, 280 (July 1974).
17. Translated in 1708 by Simon Ockley as *The Improvement of Human Reason Exhibited in the Life of Hai Ebn Yokdhan*, Georg Olms Verlag, 1983.
18. This position has led to the establishment of a 'Research Unit for Science in Islamic Polity' at the National Science Council of Pakistan, which

Sardar: Explorations in Islamic Science

organized the International Conference on Science in Islamic Polity, held in Islamabad, November 1983, and now publishes the quarterly journal, *Science and Technology in the Islamic World*.

19. The classic paper presenting this view is Lynn White, 'Historical Roots of our Ecological Crisis' *Science* **155** 1203 (1967). He writes: 'Today, around the globe, all significant science is western in style and method, whatever the pigmentation or language of the scientist'.

20. The discussion at Stockholm is fully reproduced in Sardar, *The Touch of Midas*. An analytical report on the seminar appears in Ziauddin Sardar, 'Why Islam Needs Islamic Science', *New Scientist* **94**, 25–8 (1982).

Four

Arguments for Islamic Science

Whether Islamic science can be accepted as the 'normal' science of the future, at least by the majority of Muslims, depends to a large extent on the arguments proponents of Islamic science can produce to justify the whole enterprise. Of course, it also depends on the practical utility of such a science; but at this stage of the debate, there are numerous theoretical issues that need to be settled and cogent arguments produced to show that the contemporary realization of Islamic science is both theoretically necessary and practically possible.

Here, I intend to produce four arguments to justify the need for a contemporary Islamic science which is a true embodiment of the values, culture and worldview of Islam. I intend to show that science has had a different identity and has played a specific role in various civilizations, inlcuding that of Islam. Moreover, I argue that Western science is inherently destructive and does not—cannot—fulfill the needs of Muslim societies.

Argument One
Different civilizations have produced distinctively different sciences

A civilization is an embodiment of its total spiritual and material culture. It is an open, and to some extent, self-perpetuating interchange between man, the values and norms inherent in his worldview and cosmology in their numerous dimensions and orders. Human history has seen a number of civilizations each seeking the realization of its own values within the framework of its worldview. Behind each civilization there is a vision of man's place in creation which motivates its attitude towards Nature and promotes the search for its specific problems and needs. Whitehead regards this vision, or worldview, as the central element that shapes the main characteristic of a civilization, 'in each age of the world distinguished by high activity, there will be found at its culmination, and among the agencies leading to that culmination, some profound cosmological outlook, implicitly accepted, impressing its own type on the current springs of action.'[1] It is this cosmological outlook, or *Weltanschauung*, that shapes the value structure of a society and political, social and problem-solving activities of a civilization.

Thus, at the centre of any civilization is a worldview that acts as a fulcrum on which the society flourishes or falls. The other parameters of a civilization—namely, culture, values and norms, social and political organization and science and technology—derive their legitimacy from the worldview (Fig. 1). The way the society is organized, the dominant values which shape its political structure and social organization, how its material problems are solved, and how the individual members, as well as the society as a whole, seek its cultural aspirations all stem from the worldview.

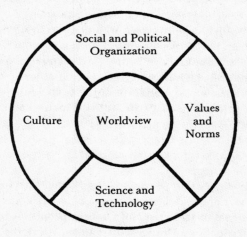

Figure 1. Components of a Civilization

As the worldview of different civilizations tends to be different, the associated parameters also tend to be different. For example, the Chinese worldview based on Confucianism, which dominated China for nearly twenty-five centuries, has produced a civilization distinctively different from Greek civilization. In essence, the worldview of Confucianism, which was later developed by Mencius and Hsun Tzu, is characterized by humanism, occupying itself mainly with human relations subtleties and the supernatural. The bases of Chinese worldview are the concepts of *jen*, humanity, *tao*, the doctrine of harmony, and *yin* and *yang*, the cosmic principles of male and female. *Jen* is the central thesis of the whole system of Chinese thought. The ethics, the politics, the social organization of the Chinese civilization all flow from the doctrine of *jen*.

Jen is defined as the 'perfect virtue' and expresses the Chinese ideal of cultivating human relations, developing human faculties, sublimating one's personality and upholding human rights. Its basis is to be found first in one's duties towards one's parents and brothers. In the *Analects*, two other concepts, *hsiao*, filial piety, and *ti*, fraternal love, express the idea of *jen*: *hsiao* signifies a state of spiritual communion with the eternity of time, and *ti* signifies a state of spiritual communion in the infinity of space. Hence, these virtues have become the foundations of Chinese social structure. Mencius claimed that for the cultivation of virtue, *jen* should be supplemented with *yi*. 'What one upholds in one's heart is *jen*; what one upholds in one's conduct is *yi*.' Thus *yi* is the virtuous principle for guiding external conduct. Hsun Tzu recommends *li* as the norm of social conduct. *Li*, a code of ritual embodied in ancient Chinese culture, is also a set of general rules of propriety, the regulating principle in a well-ordered society. It has often been translated as 'social order', 'social institutions and conventions' or 'all regulations that arise from the man-to-man relations'.

The worldview of *jen* is a major force in unifying China and shaping the temperament of the Chinese people. The major characteristics of the Chinese people is that everyone, rich or poor, educated or illiterate, male or female, has profound respect for life. There is an insistence in Chinese culture that in order to live well, one must try to get the best out of life and enjoy what one has. The passionate love of life, the national characteristic of Chinese people, is coupled with a corresponding notion of rational happiness. 'Rational happiness', a unique characteristic of the worldview of *jen*, is not based on worldly riches or external, circumstances, but on one's own virtues. As Confucius said, 'the wise are free from doubts; the virtuous from concerns; the courageous from fear'. . . . 'The noble man is completely at ease; the common man is always on edge.'[2] Virtue lies in living with total harmony, in developing a sense of justice and fairness, a spirit of tolerance, a readiness to compromise, and a firm determination to enforce the observance of these virtues against egoism and altruism. Exaggeration, or total absence of *jen*, would upset the social order, and both altruism and egoism are too extreme and could lead to calamities. The way of *jen* is a way of action that avoids extremes, and leads to a state of mind that combines human reasoning and feeling to reach perfect harmony. Only harmony can bring about balance, and only balance can lead to progress. Harmony is obtained by fulfilling one's duties in one's relationships with oneself, with one's family, with the community, with the nation and with the world. Hsun-tzu symbolized *li* with five characters—Heaven, Earth, Emperor, Ancestors and Tutors. The ethics of *jen, yi* and *li* stresses the moral importance of human relationships in politics. In the last analysis, virtue alone constitutes the ultimate goal of man.[3]

In contrast, the Greek worldview saw rational knowledge as the ultimate goal of man. Formal religion in Greece revolved around Olympian gods under their leader, Zeus, who was dominant. Although Zeus was supreme, the Greeks did not regard him as the creator of the world but only as a ruler. Indeed, his supremacy was qualified by the fact that the other gods had independent wills and functions. Important among them were Apollo, whose concerns covered medicine, the care of animals, music, and the Delphic Oracle; Hera, Zeus's consort and protectress of marriage; Poseidon, the sea-god and bringer of earthquakes; Athene, patroness of Athens and of the arts; and Aphrodite, goddess of love. Dionysus gained importance over time as a vegetation deity and as the focus of ecstatic cults. The gods spent most of their time fighting with each other and, in particular, with Titans, the gods of evil. Greek religion was at its most personal and ecstatic in the worship of Dionysus who gained a mystical significance when Orphism, a movement that became influential in the sixth and fifth centuries B.C., adopted his worship. The legend was that Dionysus, under the name of Zagreus, was son of Zeus by the earth goddess Semele, but was eaten by the Titans. Zeus, in anger, burned up the Titans with thunderbolts and from their ashes the human race was formed. Hence, man is a combination of evil (he is Titanic) and good (for he contains an element of the divine Zagreus). The Orphics believed that the body was a tomb that imprisoned the soul; they taught reincarnation and in this and other ways influenced the thinking of Plato and other philosopher-scientists.

As the city-state developed, religion was increasingly integrated into political and civic life. The cult of the hero or patron of the city expressed the unity of the state as an expanded form of the clan or family. The former Greek religions shunned mystical cults such as those of the Orphics who practised their rituals in secret. From the worldview of many gods looking after different aspects of the world emerges the central political notion of a city-state; the Greek civilization consisted of many city-states that, like the gods, had individual outlooks. The Greeks could seldom agree to act in common.

Order was the main notion of the Greek worldview. A measured balance of forces in society produced a well-ordered state. Order in society meant that every one knew his or her position and the task to be performed. Order was to be found in rational knowledge. In ethical order, goodness comes from the pursuit of reason, and evil from ignorance. The Greek way of life was mainly secular, dividing functions into various compartments—indeed, reductionism was the cornerstone of the Greek worldview and culture.

For example, Socrates, the father of Greek philosophy, believed that the soul has, in descending order, a rational part, an emotional part, and an acquisitive part. In the just soul these are properly ordered, each attending its own business and obeying the parts above it. Reason, at the top, rules emotion. Emotion, in turn, helps to inspire the actions that reason dictates. When the parts are so ordered that a subordinate part gains an upper hand, the soul is sick. Because the soul is ruled by reason, it is akin to the realm of Form—the eternal, unblemished objects of knowledge over which the Form of the Good is supreme. Similarly, Socrates divided the city-state into three types of citizens: first, the common people, the workers, the artisans and the merchants; second, the military, whose task was to protect the city-state from outside dangers and keep the order within; third, the rulers and the guardians, who govern and legislate. To ensure the stability of this kind of system, the three orders are kept separate, and each is given training in its appropriate function: the people in their various skills, the soldiers in the art of war and the rulers in government.

As in the Chinese worldview, the Greeks considered that the good life is attained by conforming to the goal or purpose of human existence. But here the purpose of life is seen not as the pursuit of *jen, ye* and *li* but as the pursuit of reason. Aristotle, for example, sees the principal occupation for a man who would aim at goodness as the virtuous exercise of reason. Happiness is a virtue called reason. 'If happiness is activity in accordance with virtue, it is reasonable that it should be in accordance with the highest virtue; and this will be that of the best thing in us. Whether it be reason or something else that is this element which is thought to be our natural ruler and guide and to take thought of things noble and divine, whether it be itself also divine or only the most divine element in us, the activity of this in accordance with its proper virtue will be perfect happiness.'⁴

We see from this brief description, that the worldviews of Chinese and Greek civilizations are distinctively different: for Greeks reason is the supreme, almost divine, virtue; for the Chinese *jen*, the Confucian ideal of cultivation of human relations, developing human faculties, sublimating one's personality, and upholding human rights are the supreme virtues. While the Greeks emphasize individualism, separation of function and roles in society and the religious from the rational; the Chinese stress synthesis, a balance in inner and outer life. In the Greek framework, order comes from Form and separating the individuals and various aspects of social and political life; in Chinese thought, people are interrelated so that order may be maintained. Needless to say, the two worldviews produced two distinct cultures, values and norms, and social and political organizations.

The key question is: did the two civilizations also produce two distinct and unique systems of science and technology? Or, if science and technology is a neutral, value-free and universal system, as the conventional wisdom would lead us to believe, are the Chinese and Greek sciences identical? Even a casual examination of Chinese and Greek sciences reveals that they are two distinct ways of knowing and solving problems.

In Chinese science, as indeed in the worldview of *jen*, unity of man and nature is a predominant positive value. The Chinese way of thinking and knowing is organic where the interconnections between various facts of material reality and spiritual needs are emphasized. The fundamental ideas and theories of Chinese science revolve around the theory of Five Elements (*wu hsing*) and the Two Fundamental Forces (*Yin and Yang*). The theory of Five Elements goes back to Tsou Yen, the real founder of Chinese scientific thought, who flourished around 350 and 270 B.C. While basically naturalistic and scientific, the theory of Five Elements also served a political function, as it frightened the feudal masters and kept them on an appropriate path. Tsou Yen describes the theory in the following words:

The Five Elements dominate alternately. [Successive emperors choose the colour of their] official vestments following the directions [so that the colour may agree with the dominant element].

Each of the Five Virtues [Elements] is followed by the one it cannot conquer. The dynasty of Shun ruled by the virtue of Earth, the Hsia dynasty ruled by the virtue of Wood, the Shang dynasty ruled by the virtue of Metal, and the Chou dynasty ruled by the virtue of Fire.

When some new dynasty is going to arise, Heaven exhibits auspicious signs to the people. During the rise of Huang Ti [the Yellow Emperor] large earthworms and large ants appeared. He said, 'This indicates that the element Earth is in the ascendant, so our colour must be yellow, and our affairs must be placed under the sign of Earth.' During the rise of Yu the Great, Heaven produced plants and trees which did not wither in autumn and winter. He said, 'This indicates that the element Wood is in the ascendant, so our colour must be green, and our affairs must be placed under the sign of Wood . . . ' During the rise of the High King Wen of the Chou, Heaven exhibited fire, and many red birds holding documents written in red flocked to the altar of the dynasty. He said, 'This indicates that the element Fire is in the ascendant, so our colour must be red and our affairs must be placed under the sign of Fire.' Following Fire there will come Water. Heaven will show when the time comes for the *chhi* of Water to dominate. Then the colour will have to be black, and affairs will have to be placed under the sign of Water. And that dispensation will in turn come to an end, and at the appointed time, all will revert once again to Earth. But when that time will be we do not know.[5]

The Chinese conception of the elements was not so much in terms of fundamental matter but more in terms of fundamental processes. The theory was an attempt to classify the basic properties of material things when they undergo change. But the significant point is that by concentrating on relation rather than substance, Chinese thought emphasized the interconnectedness of man and nature as well as individual and society. Consider, for example, this passage from the *Ta Tai Li Chi* (Record of Rites of the Elder Tai), a compilation made between 85 and 105 C.E., Where the insistence of seeing man and nature in a unified framework is so clear:

Tseng Tzu said, 'That to which Heaven gives birth has its head on the upper side: that to which Earth gives birth has its head on the under side. The former is called round, the latter is called square. If heaven were really round and the Earth really square the four corners of the Earth would not be properly covered. Come nearer and I will tell you what I learnt from the Master [Confucius]. He said that the Tao of Heaven was round and that of the Earth square. The square is dark and the round bright. The bright radiates *chhi*, therefore there is light outside it. The dark imbibes *chhi*, therefore there is light within it. Thus it is that Fire and the Sun have an external brightness, while Metal and Water have an internal brightness. That which irradiates is active, that which imbibes radiation is reactive. Thus the Yang is active and the Yin reactive.

The seminal essence (*ching*) of the Yang is called *shen*. The germinal essence of the Yin is called *ling*. The *shen* and *ling* (vital forces) are the root of all living creatures; and the ancestors of [such high developments as] rites and music, human-heartedness and righteousness; and the makers of good and evil, as well as of social order and disorder.

When the Yin and Yang keep precisely to their proper positions, then there is quiet and peace . . .

Hairy animals acquire their coats before coming into the world, feathered ones similarly first acquire their feathers. Both are born of the power of Yang. Animals with carapaces and scales on their bodies likewise come into the world with them; they are born by the power of Yin. Man alone comes naked into the world; [this is because] he has the [balanced] essences of both Yang and Yin.

The essence [or most representative example] of hairy animals is the unicorn, that of feathered ones is the phoenix [or pheasant;] that of the carapace-animals is the tortoise, and that of the scaly ones is the dragon. That of the naked ones is the Sage.[6]

Yin and *Yang*, the two fundamental forces of Chinese scientific thought are ever present in the Heaven as well as man, each one dominating the other in a wave-like succession. The Chinese classic, *I Ching* (The Book of Change), contains a mathematical exposition of the *Yin* and *Yang* theory. The book contains a series of sixty-four symbolic hexagrams, each of which is composed of six lines, whole or broken, corresponding to the *Yang* and the *Yin*. Each hexagram is primarily *Yin* or primarily *Yang*, and by a judicious arrangement it was found possible to derive all the sixty-four in such a way as to produce aternating *Yin* and *Yang*, while the *Yin* and *Yang* components never become completely fragmented and separated; however, at any given stage, in any given fragment, only one is manifested. In one respect, the *I Ching* provides a practical demonstration of the principle of *Yin* and *Yang*.

Within this theoretical framework, Chinese science achieved tremendous heights. While at first sight it may appear that empirical and pragmatic work is not possible in such a framework, it would be a very misleading conclusion. Even in contemporary terms, the Chinese theoretical framework has many parallels: the Yin and Yang principle in genetics and the theory of Five Elements correspond to what might be called the five fundamental states of matter—'one could think of Water as implying all liquid, and Fire all gaseous states; similarly,

Metal could cover all metals and semi-metals, and Earth all earth elements, while Wood could stand for the whole realm of the carbon compounds, that is, organic chemistry'. However, to look at Chinese science with the perspective of Western science is to miss the point: Chinese science was aimed at meeting the practical and spiritual needs of the Chinese civilization and not of Western society.

Within its framework, Chinese science was as empirical as was demanded by Chinese society. The Chinese produced major achievements in hydraulic science and engineering. They excelled in mathematics: the earliest indication of the abacus arithmetic (*suan-p'an*) appears in the work of Hsu Yo who lived around 150–200 C.E. Much Chinese arithmetic originates from the classic treatise of Chang Ts'ang (d. 152 B.C.), entitled *Chiu Chang Suan Shu* (The Arithmetical Rules in Nine Sections) in which there is the earliest-known mention of the negative quantity (*fu*), and the tradition was maintained through several centuries, being noticeable in the Arithmetical Classic of Hsia-Hou Yang (600 C.E.). In the second century C.E., the solution of indeterminate equations of the first degree, and a decimal system appear in the work of Sun-Tzu; an elaborate treatment of fractions and further work on indeterminate equations occurs in the Arithmetical Classic of Chang Chiu-chien (650 C.E.); and by the early seventh century Wang Hsiao-tung had solved simple cubic equations in connection with the volumes of solids, to be followed by further contributions to the study of indeterminate equations by I-hsing (683–727); so that the body of knowledge in the *Chiu Chang Suan Shu* was gradually augmented. Medicine too was a major science in China and the Chang Chung-ching, the Chinese Galen, led the field at the end of the second century with two treatises, one on dietetics and the other on fevers. It had many branches, including theoretical studies of health and disease; macrobiotics or the theory and practice of longevity techniques; pharmacognosy, the study of *materia medica* veterinary medicine: and acupuncture, a minor branch of therapeutics. Because the Chinese science clearly incorporated value considerations it has been assumed to be somewhat less scientific. For example, Joseph Needham classifies geomancy—the sciene of wind and water which decides the auspicious placement of houses and tombs with respect to features of the landscape and aesthetics of land-use—as a 'pseudo-science' simply because empirical and precise work has been made subservient to value and aesthetic judgement. Experiments and theory-building were an important part of Chinese science although they did not have paramount importance as in Western science. Consider the probability of sticking pins in a human body randomly, without a theory, and hitting all the acupuncture points and the absurdity of the suggestion that Chinese science lacked a theoretical and experimental base becomes all too obvious. Indeed, Chinese experimental work led to the discovery of the three great inventions which became crucial to the transformation of European society from the Dark Ages to the Industrial age: the magnetic compass, gun-powder, and the printing-press.

From this rather brief and sketchy description of Chinese science, it can be seen that it not only has a Chinese flavour but a distinct Chinese identity. Within its given framework, it was objective and rational and met the needs and solved the problems of Chinese society. Its priorities reflected the values of the Chinese worldview and its products enhanced the Chinese culture.

In contrast to Chinese science, which showed the overwhelming tendency to argue and analyse phenomena in terms of dialectical logic where rigid 'A or not-A' categorizations were avoided, Greek science was based on a linear logic and emphasized reduction. The foundation of Greek science is Aristotelian logic: here two general principles of proof are recognized—the law of contradiction (nothing can both have and not have a given characteristic) and the law of excluded middle (everything must either have or not have a given characteristic). The Greeks, in particular the Pythagoreans, saw the world as a vast mathematical pattern; and to seek mastery of this world one had to seek the numbers in things. Hence the emphasis in Greek science on mathematics and deductive logic.

The Greek emphasis on mathematics is personified by the Pythagorean thought. Pythagoras blended his science with his religious worldview and his politics. The Pythagorean community was a religious brotherhood for the practice of asceticism and the study of mathematics. The sect practised a severe discipline which included secrecy, respect for the authority of the master, ritual purification, memory exercises, examination of conscience, and various taboos concerning food. Pythagoras taught a cosmology that gave a special place to numbers, which were represented by points juxtaposed to form square, triangular and rectangular figures. 'Things are numbers' was the Pythagorean motto. Pythagoras himself discovered the relation of simple numbers (2/1, 3/2, 4/3), which determine the principal intervals of the musical scale (fourth, fifth, octave), and thought that the distances separating the heavenly bodies observed the same proportions.[7]

Many Greek philosopher-scientists were concerned with questions of life and ethics. Thus Aristotle's interest in the natural and human world led him to biology and a taxonomy of a 'scale of nature'. Aristotle considered mathematics as an abstraction from natural reality, which for him was a complex, self-regulating system. He saw natural phenomena in terms of cause and effect and introduced the principle of teleology which led his biological studies to the problem of generation and the transmission of form between separate bodies. Aristotle explained why animals and plants grow into whatever they happen to become as though growing was like pursuing a goal. In physics and astronomy, he explained the first cause of all phenomena, through the realization of its purpose in the celestial cycles.

The Aristotelian doctrine that first principles are required for rational science was challenged by the Skeptic philosophers like Pyrrho of Elis (fourth century B.C.) who made doubt the central theme of their philosophy. Pyrrho's follower, Timon, criticized the logicians because of their inability to arrive at sound starting points for their deductions. Sextus Empiricus (second century B.C.) attacked the doctrine of syllogism for being empty since it is based on circular argument: the conclusion is presupposed in the premise. He also dismissed the theory of causality, arguing that only events that happen at the same time can be linked, whereas causes precede effects. The causal relation is thus merely a mental construction. Skeptics did not believe in divine providence and tried to be detached, refraining both from judgement and action.

Despite the various stances of Greek philosopher-scientists, on the whole Greek science is deeply entrenched in linear mathematical logic and the supremacy of deduction. Despite the powerful influence of the Pythagorean cult, it is thoroughly secular and exhibits a certain degree of rational arrogance. The Greeks were generally irreverent and disdainful, had a great opinion of themselves and despised all other people. All those outside their city-states were barbarians. Thus they called the great funeral monument of Egypt *pyramids*, which is Greek for 'wheatcake'. Greek scientists were preoccupied with theory and pure mathematics, and largely shunned experimental and empirical work because they had a prosperous economy and a comparatively simple political structure which gave them a certain amount of stability. Indeed, when they were faced with a social problem, it immediately reflected in their scientific thought. Thus, faced with an ever increasing number of beggars in Greece, Isocrates made a special study of the problem and suggested that they should be enlisted, drilled and hurled against the Persian Empire. If they could not conquer it outright, they could at least tear enough off its territory to provide living-space for themselves. The alternative was unthinkable: 'If we cannot check the growing strength of these vagabonds', wrote Isocrates, 'by providing them with a satisfactory life, before we know where we are they will be so numerous that they will constitute as great a danger to the Greeks as do the Barbarians.' Isocrates's social remedies are reflected in the scientific thinking of his contemporary, Plato. Just as Isocrates sought to liquidate the vagabonds in Greece, Plato set out to liquidate the five disorderly vagabonds (planets) in the heavens. He set a problem to all earnest students to find 'what are the uniform and ordered movements by the assumption of which the apparent movements of the planets can be accounted for?'. This problem had to be solved if Plato's astronomical ideas were to work, especially when he had turned it into a theology by which he wanted to reconstruct society.[8]

Greek science, it can be seen, is different from Chinese science. Not only are the emphases of the two sciences different, but also the nature, characteristics and, indeed, the logic and methodologies. Now, can one generalize from this and argue that all civilizations have their distinct, unique styles of doing science that gives them particular characteristics and shapes their contents according to the culture and value structure of their specific worldview?

On the basis of pure logic, it seems unreasonable to assume that two civilizations with different societal problems and perceptions of reality should produce identical systems for solving problems. Schematically, the logical inconsistency in the conventional view that science is the same for all mankind can be demonstrated quite clearly. Figure 2 represents two distinct civilizations, A and B; and W, C, V, PS and S represent worldview, culture, values and norms, political and social organization and science, respectively. Now if $WA \neq WB$, $CA \neq CB$, $VA \neq VB$, and $PA \neq PB$, what logic is there which suggests that $SA = SB$?

As I have tried to show in the case of Chinese and Greek sciences, the two are different yet equally valid ways of looking at reality and solving problems. If we look at other civilizations, such as

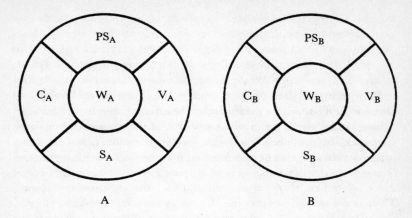

Figure 2. Two Civilizations

the Romans, the Hindus, the Aztecs or the Mayans, we see that these
civilizations, too, had their individual ways of knowing and solving
problems. As an activity of human beings, science manifests itself as a
process which occurs in time and space and involves human actors.
These actors live not only in science, but in wider cultures, societies
and civilizations. And each civilization stamps the unique characteristics of its worldview on the nature, style and content of the science of
that civilization.

Argument Two

*Islamic science in history had a distinctive identity expressed in its
unique nature and characteristic style*

Islamic science flourished during the zenith of Muslim civilization, a
period of some seven hundred years from 700 to 1500 C.E. The
science that evolved has a distinct Islamic identity, manifested in
terms of an epistemology that shaped the outlook and the goals of
science, and in terms of methods that affected the ways of doing, as
well as the content of, science.

The epistemology of Islam emphasizes the totality of experience
and promotes not one but a number of diverse ways of studying

nature. The Islamic concept of knowledge, *ilm*, incorporates almost every form of knowledge from pure observation to the highest metaphysics. Thus *ilm* can be acquired from revelation as well as reason, from observation as well as intuition, from tradition as well as theoretical speculation. While the various ways of studying nature are equally valid in Islam, all are subservient to the eternal values of Quranic revelation. As such, Islamic epistemology emphasizes the pursuit of all forms of knowledge within the framework of eternal values which are the cornerstone of the Islamic civilization.

Besides diversity, the epistemology of Islam also emphasizes interconnectedness. All forms of knowledge are interconnected and organically related by the ever-present spirit of the Quranic revelation. Thus Islam not only makes the pursuit of knowledge obligatory, but also connects it with the unique Islamic notion of worship: *ilm* is a form of *ibadah* (worship). As such, knowledge is pursued in obedience to, and for the pleasure of, Allah. Moreover, *ilm* is not just connected to *ibadah* it is also connected to every other Quranic value such as *khilafah* (trusteeship), *adl* (justice) and *istislah* (public interest). While the connection between *ilm* and *ibadah* means that knowledge cannot be pursued in open transgression of Allah's commands, the connection between *ilm* and *khilafah* transforms nature into the realm of the sacred. Man, as the trustee of God, as the custodian of His gift, cannot pursue knowledge at the expense of nature. On the contrary, as the guardian of nature he seeks the understanding of nature not to dominate it but to appreciate the 'signs' of God. The study of nature, therefore, leads to two outcomes: an understanding of the material world as well as reflection of spiritual realities. The interconnection between *ilm* and *istislah* ensures that knowledge is pursued to promote equality, social justice and values that enhance the well-being of Muslim society and culture.

Its emphasis on diversity and interconnectedness gives a very unique character to the epistemology of Islam. It provides a middle path for the pursuit of knowledge, ensuring that no individual form of knowledge or method of knowing becomes the sole criteria of truth or is pursued to the exclusion of all others. It is for this reason that a predilection for systematic classification of knowledge is so noticeable in Muslim civilization, which was the prime occupation of many Muslim scholars of the classical age.[9] It provided a method indispensable to genuine scholarship and proved extremely fertile in the history of Muslim intellectual endeavour. Moreover, the insistence of

Islamic epistemology on giving equal status to all forms of knowledge within a single matrix of values meant that Muslim scholars were able to accept the existing sciences of various civilizations which they inherited. Once it became part of the framework of eternal Islamic values, it was transformed into a new substance. However, while Islamic science, like Greek and Chinese science before it, had its own unique identity, unlike them, it was truly international because of the geographical spread and the cosmopolitan nature of Muslim civilization.

It was their concern with the classification of knowledge that enabled Muslim scholars, first, to appreciate the intellectual output of other civilizations and then to synthesize it with the worldview of Islam. Thus, right from the beginning, Muslim scholars agreed on the fundamental division of sciences into Arabic (that is indigenous) and foreign (that is, predominantly Greek) sciences. However, as the process of synthesis proceeded, knowledge was classified on more sophisticated basis that reflected the worldview of Islam. Thus, al-Farabi's (d. 950) classification of knowledge follows the Aristotelian pattern but gives more emphasis to the linguistic sciences and to *fiqh* (jurisprudence) and *kalam* (speculative theology). But his younger contemporary, al-Khwarizmi (writing c. 976) already offers a classification that is more adequate and incorporates a hierarchy giving prominence to religious knowledge which provides the value structure within which all other forms of knowledge are sought. In the *Rasail Ikhwan as-safa*, an encyclopaedia compiled in the tenth century by a group of scholars who called themselves the 'faithful friends', metaphysics is placed on the same level as mathematics, logic and natural sciences. In ibn Hazm's treatise *The Categories of Sciences (Maratib al-ulum)* we find a perfect fusion of knowledge and values. While establishing a hierarchy of sciences, ibn Hazm also insists on their interdependence. For ibn Hazm knowledge is the certainty (*tayaqqun*) of a thing as it is. He associates knowledge with four cardinal virtues: justice (*adl*), understanding (*fahm*), courage (*najdah*), and generosity (*jud*). This brings the intellect and knowledge close to each other in the pursuit of virtue. Knowledge is a multi-faceted thing, but the noblest knowledge is that which brings the individual closer to his maker. A. G. Chejne summarizes ibn Hazm's perception of knowledge, 'Knowledge, like faith, is a passport to happiness in this life and in the hereafter. As depositories of knowledge, faith and reason—although differing in nature—have an identical aim in ibn Hazm's thinking, that is, the attainment of virtues (*fadail*)'.[10] This approximation with faith and reason becomes more evident in his broad conception of knowledge. In as much as knowledge is related to the state of individual happiness on earth as well as in heaven, it should be sought incessantly and disseminated; its seeker, however, should not boast about it, because it is a gift from God.

He should always be humble with whatever knowledge he may have, because someone else could have more knowledge than he. Finally, knowledge should be put into practice, otherwise the ignorant person would appear better off than the scholar. In fact, knowledge and action (*al-ilm wa-l-amal*) are inseparable, particularly with regard to the performance of religious duties. In consequence, the greatest virtue along with the practice of goodness is to teach and implement knowledge.

Ibn Hazm emphasized the middle path in the pursuit of knowledge in numerous statements found throughout his *Akhlaq*. For example:

> The one who is greedy with his knowledge is more blameworthy than the one who is greedy with his money.
> Intellectual inquiry will be useless if it is not supported by the good fortune of religion and by that of (the sciences) the world.
> Recondite sciences are like strong medicine; they help people with strong constitutions, but destroy those with weak bodies. Similarly, they will greatly enrich and purify the vigorous intellect, but they will destroy the weak one.
> True science unveils the ignorance concerning the attributes of God—may He be glorified and exalted.
> The utility of knowledge in the practice of virtue is enormous, for through it one will be able to know the beauty of virtue which will never escape him; he will also be able to know the ugliness of vices, avoiding them except on rare occasions; he will take heed of nice praise and will wish something like it for himself; he will also take heed of damnation and will attempt to avoid it. On these grounds, it is necessary to conclude that knowledge has a great deal to do with every virtue, and that ignorance has its share in every vice. Moreover, no one will ever achieve virtue without learning the sciences, excepting those who possess pure natures and virtuous constitutions. To this category belong the prophets (may God's prayer and peace be upon them); this is so because God Almighty has taught them all goodness (*khayr*) without the intervention of man.[11]

The concern of such classical Muslim scholars as ibn Hazm to synthesize values with knowledge, and knowledge with action and virtue led to the classification of certain branches of knowledge as 'blameworthy'. It was clear to scholars and scientists of the 'Golden Age of Islam'

that the pursuit of all knowledge did not necessarily lead to virtue; that
not all *ilm* can be connected with *ibadah* and the pleasure of Allah. The
basis of the distinction is clearly set forth by Hujwiri:

> Knowledge is obligatory only in so far as is requisite for acting rightly. God
> condemns those who learn useless knowledge, and the Prophet said, 'I take
> refuge with Thee from knowledge that profiteth naught'. Much may be
> done by means of a little knowledge and knowledge should not be separated
> from action. The Prophet said, 'The devotee without divinity is like a
> donkey turning a mill' because the donkey goes round and round on its
> own tracks and never makes any advances.[12]

Much has been said by orientalists and contemporary Muslim
scholars of how such a distinction limits inquiry and suffocates science.[13] The subtlety in the Muslim classification of knowledge and
divisions of knowledge into those which promote human welfare and
eternal values, and those which squander resources or promote injustice and myths, cannot really be appreciated by those who measure the
achievements of Islamic civilization by alien scales and by methods
designed to show the almighty supremacy of reason. Only when one
appreciates the value of synthesis, the connection between reason and
revelation, can one really appreciate the deep insight shown by
Hujwiri and other Muslim philosophers. Behind the division of
knowledge by al-Ghazzali, for example, into individually and socially
requisite, and praiseworthy and blameworthy, is a deep commitment
to maintain a social balance in society and promote the values of the
worldview of Islam. The classical scholars of Islam were concerned
that in the pursuit of knowledge the needs of the community should
not be lost sight of, that *ilm* should not create undesirable social effects,
that it should not tend to such a level of abstraction that it leads to the
estrangement of man from his world and his fellow men, or to confusion rather than enlightenment. In this framework science is guided
towards a middle path. While it should be socially relevant, the idea of
a purely utilitarian science is rejected. Moreover, there is no such
thing as science for science's sake; yet the pursuit of pure knowledge
for the perfection of man is encouraged. Science, far from being
enjoyed as an end in itself, must be instrumental to the attainment of a
higher goal.

These special features of the epistemology of Islam gave rise to a
unique tradition of science. For the classical Muslim scientists all
experiences are real and therefore worthy of investigation. To exclude

any one of them is to exclude reality itself. Thus, Muslim scientists did not believe in a single, all-encompassing method of inquiry, but used a number of methods in conformity with the object of study. This is a major feature of the style of Islamic science. Consequently, we find scientists in the classical period working with different methodologies, each as rigorous as the other, and accepting all methods as invaluable in themselves. They defined a particular method or sets of methods for each clearly defined discipline and considered these methods not as contradictory but as complementary. Of course, there were incidences of tension, philosophers arguing with theologians, each accusing the methods of the other as being unreliable, but by and large harmony prevailed and the principles of diversity and interconnectedness of Islamic epistemology ensured that the multiplicity of methods were integrated into a totality. Thus it was possible to have several sciences dealing with the same subject, each using its particular methods. A tree, for example, could be studied from the point of view of botany, hence observed and described; or medicine, hence its products tested and turned into drugs, or physics, hence its form and matter analysed; or even sufism, hence contemplated.[14] Indeed, it was not uncommon for an individual scientist, for example al-Biruni, to have access to all these methods, which he used to arrive at coherent interpretation of reality. In all this he is always *partial* to the truth and never loses sight of the worldview and the framework of values in his working—a practical demonstration of the pragmatic epistemology of Islam.

The hallmark of Islamic science in history is partiality to truth in all its multidimensional manifestations: Muslim scientists were well aware that objectivity reveals only part of the truth, that truth can also be found by other modes of inquiry. We can well illustrate this point by looking at the work of such a representative of Islamic science as al-Biruni.

In al-Biruni we find a scientist who has integrated a number of methods in his very being; there is no such dichotomy as the 'two cultures' of C. P. Snow here. Al-Biruni never fails to remind his readers that there is more than one method of reaching the truth. He starts one of his treatises with the words, 'I pray for God's favour and spacious bounty to make me fit for adopting the right course and help me in perceiving and realizing the truth and facilitate its pursuit and enlighten its courses (methods) and remove all impediments in achieving noble objects.' Thus for al-Biruni there are a number of courses towards the truth, a vital, living assimilative force which permeates every aspect of his scholarly outlook. Al-Biruni derives his emphasis on the truth from the Quran, which he quotes often. In his preface to *India* he quotes, 'Speak the truth, even if it were against yourselves'. And it is in the pursuit of truth, not of reason, that al-Biruni uses a number of methods.

Mathematics is central to al-Biruni's scientific research. He considers it natural that man should count the objects around him and establish a quantitative correlation among them. But he also repeatedly stresses usefulness of knowledge as an important motive for his own research and promotion of science in general. In a purely technical book, *The Determination of Co-ordinates of Positions for the Correction of Distances between Cities*, he gives the following reason for pursuing knowledge:

> We look around and we see that man's efforts are directed only towards earning a living, and for this purpose he endures hardships and fears, though he needs his food only once or twice a day for his life in this world. But he pretends ignorance and neglects what he must not fail to do for his soul in the hereafter, five times in every day and night, thinking that his ignorance is a valid excuse, though he has the opportunity and the power to know it (what is good for his soul).
>
> The Jews also need a direction, because they turn in their prayers to the Temple in Jerusalem which is of known longitude and latitude . . . The Christians need the (direction of) true east because their elders, whom they call fathers, prescribed to them that they should turn to Paradise in their prayers.[15]

Yet he is not a complete utilitarian. Truth, in itself, is also beautiful for al-Biruni: 'It is knowledge, in general, which is pursued solely by man, and which is pursued for the sake of knowledge itself, because its acquisition is truly delightful, and is unlike the pleasures desirable from other pursuits.'[16]

It is the synthesis of the approaches to knowledge into a middle path which is the hallmark of al-Biruni's science. It was this outlook that led to his theory of solar apogee, considered to be one of the most original accomplishments in the history of science. In his *al-Qanun al-Masudi* al-Biruni starts his investigations by recounting the work of previous scientists and then presents and evaluates the results of his own observation. He finds the solar apogee to be situated at 84° 59' 51'', 9' ''. But his results are arrived at by applying a method of his own, consisting of three essentially different variants, all three of which he shows to lead to the same numerical result. He bases his investigation, on a theorem set forth first by Archimedes of which al-Biruni provides twenty different proofs. Briefly stated, the theorem reads: if a broken line is inscribed in a circular arc, and if the perpendicular is drawn from the point bisecting the arc on the (major part of the) broken line, then the broken line too is bisected by the perpendicular. Of course others before al-Biruni introduced new concepts and methods into astronomy, but what is unique to al-Biruni is the systematic consideration of the criteria according to which preference is to be given to one method over another. His investigation leads al-Biruni to infer that there undoubtedly exists a continual motion of the apogee in the direction of increasing longitudes. He goes further to demonstrate that the apogee and perigee are the points at which the apparent velocity reaches its extreme values and that, in passing from one to the other, a continual increase or decrease of velocity will be observed—- thus, making for the first time, the concept of accelerated motion the subject of mathematical analysis. All this leads him to establish a value for the motion of procession: he states that the longitudes increase by one degree in 68 years and 11 months (the modern values is c. 71m 7.5m).[17]

Al-Biruni was aware of the limitations of the methods he used to develop his theory of solar apogee. For one thing it could not be used to equal effect in his study of India: 'To execute our project, it has not been possible to follow the geometrical method which consists in referring back to what has been said before and not what has been said later'.[18] In *India* al-Biruni uses methods nearer to those developed by Muslim jurists and the scholars of hadith. The truth here demands a different method but one which is just as systematic, rigorous and critical as the 'geometric method'. The methodology used in *India* is field work and is based on three cardinal principles: 'hearsay does not equal eye witness', 'written tradition is the most preferable', and 'the tradition regarding an event which in itself does not contradict either logical or physical laws will invariably depend for its character as true or false upon the character of the reporters'. Combining these principles with field work and partiality towards truth, al-Biruni was able to produce one of the first and most detailed sociological analyse of India —an achievement that alone would have placed him among the great scholars of the world.

The ability to synthesize different methods in his work was not unique to al-Biruni. It was a general rule, rather than an exception. Ibn Sina, for example, was a master of integrating scientific research in a logical and metaphysical framework and developing different methods for different disciplines. In his *al-Qanun fil Tibb* (Canons of Medicine), ibn Sina argues that both speculative method as well as empirical observation and practice have a role in medicine. The *Canons* is a monumental work which shows ibn Sina's power of observation and ability for empirical work. Just the breakdown of the canons reveals the scope of ibn Sina's medical researches: the first book presents a general introduction, dealing with physiology, nosology, aetiology, symptomatology and the principles of therapy. In the second book, the samples from the three realms of nature are presented, the strength, effect and use being given exactly. Special pathology covers the whole of the third book, with diseases enumerated in the order of where they occur in the body. Illness involving the whole body—fevers, ulcers, fractures and poisonings—are covered in the fourth book. The final fifth book deals with the mixing of drugs. In the *Canons*, ibn Sina also developed a method for discovering whether a particular drug has curative properties. A clear description of this method is given by Abul-Barakat al-Baghdadi who followed ibn Sina's lead in this matter.

> As for experience, an example is provided by the following judgement: scammony purges human bodies of yellow bile. In this [example] the frequency of the phenomenon puts out of court [the notion] that it might be due to chance. Because of the frequency of the experience these judgements may be regarded as certain, even without our knowing the reason [for the phenomenon]. For there is certain knowledge that the effect in question is not due to chance. It must accordingly be supposed that it is due to nature or to some modality thereof. Thus the cause qua cause, though not its species or mode of operation, is known. For experimental science is also constituted by a knowledge of the cause and by an induction based on all the data of sensation; whereby a general science is reached . . . But in the cases in which the experiment has not been completed, because of its not having been repeated in such a way that the persons, the time and the circumstances varied in everything that did not concern the determining cause, whereas this cause [remained invariable], the experiment does not prove certain knowledge, but only probable opinion.[19]

Despite the fact that ibn Sina formulates a similar method in a more abstract form in some of his philosophical treatises, he is well aware of its limitation. It is in fact a close description of the experimental method which, ibn Sina believed, was more suitable to medicine and did not constitute an all-embracing method of intellectual inquiry.

Empirical observation and experimentation was only one method of knowing which method had its uses in particular disciplines.

Consider, for example, ibn Sina's method of providing evidence for prophecy. In answer to someone afflicted with doubts about prophecy, he writes:

> You have asked—may God set you right—that I sum up for you the substance of what I said to you for the purpose of eliminating your misgivings about accepting prophecy. You were confirmed in these misgivings because the claims of the advocates of prophecy are either logically possible assertions that have been treated as the necessary without the benefit of demonstrative argument or even dialectical proof, or else, impossible assertions on the order of fairy tales, such that the very attempt on the part of their advocates to expound them deserves derision.[20]

What follows is not an empirical demonstration of prophecy, but a carefully constructed, elaborated *psychological* proof of prophecy. Despite its inherent difficulties, the philosophical method is just as valid for ibn Sina as empirical observation. Similarly, in his work on linguistics, law, philosophy, astronomy and Quranic exegesis, ibn Sina had recourse to different methodologies, all of which were considered by him to be equally valid.

Even when a Muslim scientist, for example ibn al-Haitham, placed a high level of confidence on observation, experimentation, and empirical analysis, he did not lose sight of philosophical and metaphysical methods. Ibn al-Haytham has been described by many Western historians of science as the most secular of Muslim scientists because of his unquestioned commitment to science for science's sake. For example, his programme of methodological criticism has been compared to that of Descartes:

> Truth is sought for its own sake. And those who are engaged upon the quest for anything that is sought for its own sake are not interested in other things. Finding the truth is difficult, and the road to it is rough. For the truths are plunged in obscurity. It is natural to everyone to regard scientists favourably. Consequently, a person who studies their books, giving a free rein to his natural disposition and making it his object to understand what they say and to possess himself of what they put forward, comes (to consider) as truth the notions which they had in mind and the ends which they indicate. God, however, has not preserved the scientist from error and has no safeguarded science from shortcomings and faults. If this had been the case, scientists would not have disagreed upon any point of science, and their opinions upon any (question) concerning the truth of things would

not have diverged. The real state of affairs is however quite different. Accordingly, it is not the person who studies the books of his predecessors and gives a free rein to his natural disposition to regard them favourably who is the (real) seeker after truth. But rather the person who is thinking about them is filled with doubts, who holds back with his judgement with respect to what he has understood of what they say, who follows proof and demonstration rather than the assertions of a man whose natural disposition is characterized by all kinds of defects and shortcomings. A person, who studies scientific books with a view to knowing the truth, ought to turn himself into a hostile critic of everything that he studies. . . . He should criticize it from every point of view and in all its aspects. And while thus engaged in criticism he should also be suspicious of himself and not allow himself to be easy-going and indulgent with regard to (the object of his criticism) If he takes this course, the truth will be revealed to him and the flaws . . . in the writings of his predecessors will stand out clearly.[21]

But presenting al-Haytham's partiality for truth in a secular mould is a gross injustice to the celebrated scientist.[22] The fact that he demands an exacting standard of criticism is not particularly original to al-Haytham; it simply reflects the methodological concerns of Muslim jurists and scholars of hadith. Where al-Haytham emphasized the pursuit of science for its own sake, he also emphasized the fact that it should be pursued within a framework of philosophy and theology. Al-Haytham's reputation undoubtedly rests on his mathematics and physics—in particular his vast researches on optics which make Newton's achievements look decidedly pale—but he was equally versed in metaphysics, philosophy, medicine and Islamic theology. Science and theology played an equal part in his philosophy; moreover, despite his belief in science *per se* he sought to serve his society. In a letter dated some thirteen years before his death, al-Haytham wrote:

There are three disciplines which go to make philosophy: mathematics, physical sciences, and theology. I (have) discovered that duality and controversy are natural to human beings, and man is mortal; so that, while in his youth man can ponder over these three disciplines which govern his existence on earth, he cannot do so when he grows old. So I thought over these three philosophical disciplines so far as my ratiocinative and intellectual faculties could allow me and summarized and explained them and their branches. . . . I have three objects in adopting this view: first, to be of service to those who are in search of truth; second, that the disciplines which have been able to understand to some extent should be extended and studied; and, third, the knowledge that I possess may turn out to be the wherewithal of my old age.[23]

Thus, for al-Haytham theology was just as real as science. He believed that reality was a unitary entity which could be studied by both objective and subjective methods. For him knowledge and wisdom went hand in hand: 'I have always been haunted by the desire to seek knowledge and wisdom, and it has also dawned on me that there is nothing better than these two things to bring man closer to God', he writes.[24]

For al-Haytham the pursuit of science without an ethical framework is inconceivable. And ethics, for al-Haytham, is a pragmatic concern not some abstract philosophical notion. He equates every action with accountability on the Day of Judgement. His ethical system is based on three main points: (1) beautification and perfection of morality are not possible without the quest for knowledge; (2) truth, knowledge, and realization of self depend for their acquisition on (a) a clear and thorough understanding of theology, (b) acquirement of good through noble deeds, and (c) avoidance of evil; and (3) the main object of beautification and perfection of morals is to enjoy a happy, eternal life in paradise in the hereafter. It is this ethical edifice that forms the base of al-Haytham's works.[25]

Here then in al-Haytham is a scientist from the classical period of Islam who introduced the inductive method and who is an arch believer in rationality—a belief that has led many orientalists and western historians to dub him a secularist, an Aristotelian, even a scientist in the tradition of the Enlightenment, but whose rationality is subservient to his ethical system, so much so that al-Haytham was against the Mutazilites, the founders of the rational school of thought in Islam, and wrote several treatises against them. It is in fact an irony of fate that Basra, where the Mutazila movement had its origins, was also the birth place of one of the greatest physicists of Islam, indeed, of entire mankind, whose other major field of interest was the refutation of the rationalist doctrine of the Mutazilites.

Al-Haytham, ibn Sina and al-Biruni are just three classical Muslim scientists in whose works we can show a synthesis of knowledge and values in operation. Modern Muslim historians have tended to study these and other scholars of early Islam largely from the perspective of their achievements and their intellectual and scientific output, and all too readily have accepted the interpretation of Western historians that their contributions neatly fit the linear progress of science from the days of the city-states of Greece. Yet, even a casual examination of their methodologies reveals an entirely different system of science: a system which believes not in a single, all-pervasive method but in methods, giving due importance to all; a system that believes in rationality but in a rationality that is subservient to an ethical code; a system that is based more on synthesis and integration than on reduction and isolation; a system that is essentially interdisciplinary, that refuses to place different disciplines in watertight compartments; a system that draws its legitimacy from a worldview based on social and personal accountability; a system that draws its strength from a matrix of Quranic concepts and values which it seeks to promote. How can such a system fit an imagined slot in the 'linear progress of science'?

It was its emphasis on synthesis and interdisciplinary investigations, multiplicity of methods and social function and accountability before God, which produced an institution that is largely unique to Islam and is unparalleled by any other civilization: polymathy. The Islamic civilization of the classical period was remarkable for the number of polymaths it produced, a natural outcome of the nature of Islamic science. The emphasis of Islamic science on a whole array of methods meant that Muslim scholars were led by the system to study, write about and contribute to many, if not all, of the different branches of learning recognized in their day. They sought to master, if not the whole field of knowledge in all its details, at least the principles of every branch of learning which then existed. One can fill volumes with the names of Muslim polymaths of early Islam; the fact that al-Jahiz (d. 868), al-Kindi (d. 873), al-Razi (d. 925), al-Idrisi (b. 1166), ibn Bajjah (d. 1138), Omar Khayyam (d. 517), ibn Zuhr (d. 1162), ibn Tufail (d. 1185), ibn Rushd (d. 1198), al-Suyuti (d. 1505) and thousands of other scholars of this period were polymaths is not an accident; it is a clear demonstration of the unique nature of Islamic science.

The existence of the polymath as a permanent feature of classical Islam is an indication of an intellectual attitude radically different from the dominant attitude of Western civilization. As M. J. L. Young points out, 'what a contrast between this (Western) disconcerting prospect of two mutually incomprehensible areas of human experience, and the possibility of being literate in one and totally illiterate in the other, with the homogeneity of culture which we find symbolized in the career of an Avicenna (ibn Sina), who, among his many other books, wrote a concise survey of the science of medicine in verse, consisting of 1,326 stanzas; or which we find in perhaps its most striking form in Omar Khayyam, whose immortal quatrains have, at any rate in the West, overshadowed his achievements in the very different field of mathematics.'[26]

The motives and the driving force behind polymathy was the paradigm that the physical universe was not inferior to the spiritual, that both, as manifestations of Allah's bounty and mercy, were worthy of study and equally valid. Moreover, the methods of studying the vast creation of God—from the mystic's ecstasy to a mother's love, to the flight of an arrow, the circumference of the earth, the plague that destroys an entire nation, the sting of a mosquito, the nature of madness, the beauty of justice, the metaphysical yearning of man—were all equally valid and shaped understanding in their respective areas of inquiry. Every creation of God is equally important as the subject of study, and each step forward in understanding and appreciating His creation brings man closer to God. In no other civilization has there been a more complete synthesis of science and religion.

It is this all-embracing emphasis on the unity of science and religion, knowledge and values, physics and metaphysics, which gives Islamic science its unique character. And, it is its insistence on multiplicity of methods which gives it a characteristic style with synthesis as its main feature. This unique nature and characteristic style means that while Islamic science values a systematic, rigorous search for truth, it is not 'objective' in a clinical sense—it does not kill off all it touches. Concern for social welfare and public interest, promotion of beauty and a healthy natural environment, as well as systematic observation and experimentation and rigorous mathematical analysis are hallmarks of Islamic science in history. As such, Islamic science is *subjectively objective*; that is, it seeks subjective goals within an objective framework. The subjective, normative goals include seeking the pleasure of Allah, the interests of the community, promotion of such eternal Islamic values as *adl* (justice), *ibadah* (worship) and *khilafah* (man's trusteeship.). This contrasts sharply with naive inquiry that is based on emotions, dogma and prejudices. Islamic science has nothing to do with the magic and the occult: it does not seek to introduce anarchy and dogmatism into the pursuit of knowledge, neither does it seek to impose the method of one discipline on to another. It simply seeks to give equality to all methods of inquiry, and promote research and development within a framework of ethics and values which by nature are subjective. It therefore also contrasts radically with Western science which excludes all other branches of knowledge and is based on a single method which is considered to be outside human values and societal concerns. Islamic science, on the other hand, seeks a *total understanding of reality*. It is thus a very holistic enterprise.

Our brief historical analysis shows Islamic science to have an entity different from that of science as it is practised today. We can summarize the nature and style of science of classical Islam as a set of norms. Table 1 gives this summary and also compares it with the idealized norms of 'conventional science' as developed by Ian Mitroff.[27]

Table 1. A comparison between Western and Islamic science

Norms of Western Science	*Norms of Islamic Science*
1. Faith in rationality.	1. Faith in revelation.
2. Science for science's sake.	2. Science is a means for seeking the pleasure of Allah; it is a form of worship which has a spiritual and a social function.
3. One all-powerful method the only way of knowing reality.	3. Many methods based on reason as well as revelation, objective and subjective, all equally valid.
4. Emotional neutrality as the key condition for achieving rationality.	4. Emotional commitment is essential for a spiritually and socially uplifting scientific enterprise.
5. Impartiality—a scientist must concern himself only with the production of new knowledge and with the consequences of its use.	5. Partiality towards the truth: that is, if science is a form of worship a scientist has to concern himself as much with the consequences of his discoveries as with their production; worship is a moral act and its consequences must be morally good; to do any less is to make a scientist into an immoral agent.
6. Absence of bias—the validity of scientific statement depends only on the operations by which evidence for it was obtained, and not upon the person who makes it.	6. Presence of subjectivity: the direction of science is shaped by subjective criteria: the validity of a scientific statement depends both on the operation by which evidence for it was obtained and on the intent and the worldview of the person who obtained it; the acknowledgement of subjective choices in the emphasis and direction of science forces the scientist to appreciate his limitations.

Table 1 continued.

7. Suspension of judgement—scientific statements are made only on the basis of conclusive evidence.

7. Exercise of judgement—scientific statements are always made in the face of inconclusive evidence; to be a scientist is to make expert, as well as moral judgement, on the face of inconclusive evidence; by the time conclusive evidence has been gathered it may be too late to do anything about the destructive consequences of one's activities.

8. Reductionism—the dominant way of achieving scientific progress.

8. Synthesis—the dominant way of achieving scientific progress, including the synthesis of science and values.

9. Fragmentation—science is too complex an activity and therefore has to be divided into disciplines, sub-disciplines and sub-subdiscipines.

9. Holistic—science is too complex an activity to be divided and isolated into smaller and smaller segments; it is a multi-disciplinary, interdisciplinary and holistic enterprise.

10. Universalism—although science is universal, its primary fruits are for those who can afford to pay, hence secrecy is justified.

10. Universalism—the fruits of science are for the whole of humanity, and knowledge and wisdom cannot be bartered or sold; secrecy is immoral.

11. Individualism—which ensures that the scientist keeps his distance from social, political and ideological concerns.

11. Community orientation; the pursuit of science is a social obligation (*fard kifaya*); both the scientist and the community have rights and obligations on each other which ensure interdependence of both.

12. Neutrality—science is neutral, it is neither good nor bad.

12. Value orientation—science, like all human activity is value-laden; it can be good or evil, 'blameworthy' or 'praiseworthy', science of germ warfare is not neutral, it is evil.

13. Group loyalty—production of new knowledge by research is the most important of all activities and is to be supported as such.

13. Loyalty to God and His creations—the production of new knowledge is a way of understanding the 'signs' of God and should lead to improving the lot of His creation—man, wildlife and legitimacy for this endeavour and therefore it must be supported as a general activity and not as an élitist enterprise.

14. Absolute freedom—all restraint or control of scientific investigation is to be resisted.

14. Management of Science: science is an invaluable resource and cannot be allowed to be wasted and go towards an evil direction; it must be carefully managed and planned for, and it should be subjected to ethical and moral constraints.

15. Ends justify the means—because scientific investigations are inherently virtuous and important for the well-being of mankind, any and all means—including the use of live animals, human beings and foetuses—are justified in the quest for knowledge.

15. Ends do not justify the means—there is no distinction between the ends and means of science, both must be *halal* (permitted), that is, within the boundaries of ethics and morality.

We now move on to my third argument for Islamic science; that Western science carries within it seeds of its own and global destruction; and unless it is replaced by a more enlightened mode of knowing, mankind will throw itself into an infinite abyss. Let us then look at the inherent nature of modern science.

Argument Three

Western science is inherently destructive and is a threat to the well-being of mankind

It is a common belief, aggressively perpetuated by Western historians and apologetic Muslim scholars, that today's scientists stand on the shoulders of their predecessors, especially on Greek and Muslim scientists, to place new bricks on the pyramid of knowledge. To some extent this is true: Newton did build on the work of al-Haytham, Harvey plagiarized ibn Nafis, and Kepler drew heavily from the studies of al-Battani, al-Biruni and other noted Muslim astronomers. But, as I have just argued, Muslim scientists operated within an entirely different worldview: the nature and style of their science was different from the way science is practised today, even if some of their results became cornerstones for the development of Western science. The major difference is in the belief system: while Muslim scientists believed in revelation and regarded reason as one instrument for moving toward God, Western scientists believe in rationality and dismiss all other forms of knowing as nonsense.

Western science is a product of this belief. In the Islamic perspective, science is one tool for the realization of religious goals; in the Western purview, science itself is a universal religion. Thus David Landes in his classic book, *The Unbound Prometheus*, makes the point explicit: 'This world, which has never before been ready to accept universally any of the universal faiths offered for its salvation, is apparently prepared to embrace the religion of science and technology without reservation.'[28] When science passed from Islam to Western Europe in the Middle Ages, the Christian ethos and the Protestant ethic, with its concern for industrial and mercantile enterprises, its military rivalries and expansive tendencies, was able subtly to transform science. The rather pathetic and sometimes violent conflict that ensued between science and religion led to the old authorities—largely the dominant irrationality of an institutionalized Church—being challenged and ultimately replaced by a cynical view of authority in all its forms. The traditional, cyclic view of life was replaced by a linear sense of time and a belief in progress. And in the advance towards ever greater achievements it became axiomatic that Man could and would win an Empire over Nature, as Francis Bacon graphically expressed it. Science now became a quest for domination, a search for new social institutions and new meanings, and for more aesthetic and orderly structures of cognition. In its early days it was science which predominated. In sixteenth and seventeenth century Europe, the scientist was claiming the right to search for another truth and adopt another mode of self-realization. But that was left-over romanticism from the classical period; by the end of the nineteenth century, science had developed a formidable organizational base and the romantic goals had given way to more pragmatic objectives of domination and control. Western science had now become an ideology.

The idea of domination has a distinguished lineage in Western civilization, and its deepest roots are to be found in the dominant religious tradition of that civilization.[29] Only in the modern period, however, was this idea transformed into a socially significant ideology, that is, a conscious principle of legitimacy for a particular phase of Western civilization—capitalism. Science became an ideology when its method became an exclusive way of knowing reality, the only valid entry into the entire realm of objective understanding, and when it assumed the character of instrumental rationality with an exclusive focus on the rationality of means, that it is techniques for attaining a given objective in the most efficient manner. It thus, in a multitude of conceptual forms, promoted the interests of a part of society, a particular class, as the interests of the whole society.

The ideology of instrumental rationality treats its object of study (both human and non-human) as mere stuff that can be exploited, manipulated, dissected and generally abused in the pursuit of scientific progress. Thus, in the attitudes of such champions of Western science as Descartes and Boyle that animals are automata are the origins of the revolting experiments that take place in modern laboratories. Once again, the legitimacy for such dehumanizing actions of modern science are derived from Christian theology where, in medieval times, the idea of beast–machine was well established. It was simply carried over into the Western philosophy of science because, in ontological terms, the relation between spirit and nature in the dominant Judeo-Christian theology is analogous to the Cartesian conception of the relation between ego cognito and the realm of matter.

The inherent logic of instrumental rationality has reduced Western science into a problem-solving enterprise. It is an endless process of solving problems, of freezing or 'fixing' a subject for study, and of placing it at a 'distance' to evaluate. In its more extreme form, for example in biological reductionism, it has become what Fromm calls necrophilia, the passion to kill so as to freeze and love. Munawar Ahmad Anees summarizes the inherent destructive logic of reductionism:

> Reductionism, by virtue of its technique and approach, invariably leads to the disappearance of certain attributes peculiar to a given form of life. As a corollary of this, the inter-relationship established through a value structure may crumble. This is precisely what seems to be happening with modern science. Its alleged objectivity and neutrality spring from its adherence to the dictates of reductionism wherein it creates an illusion that at micro level the observations are the same as those at the macro level. It is at this critical point that the organismic holistic attributes are sacrificed at the altar of 'objectivity'. The net products of reductionism are, therefore, a methodological illusion that blurs the social significance of human science and technology, and a 'picture' of life without attributes of life is developed.
>
> The havocs caused by the pursuit of reductionist science in the recent past are only beginning to make their impact on our lives. For example, for the first time in history, we are losing control of human reproduction. Birth control has become a misnomer, for genetic engineering has reached a stage where life at its molecular level can be tampered with. Motherhood has now become a saleable commodity for we can buy eggs or even rent a

uterus. In its euphoria for 'perfection' of techniques or celebration for the recombinant DNA technology, reductionists have utterly neglected the social upheavals that will certainly be triggered by such hot pursuits of mindless scientific activity.

Is there an end to reductionism? And is there an alternative to reductionism? The argument that reductionism should be allowed to take its logical course is now dangerously untenable. Moreover, the stand that reductionism is by itself a good thing because the pursuit of knowledge can only bear beneficial fruits for mankind is naive—there is no indigenous self-correcting methodology in reductionism that will stop it from the path of oblivion.[30]

The logic of reductionism reduces objectivity to objectification. Behaviourists such as J. B. Watson and B. F. Skinner have only taken to its logical conclusion this process of objectification. How far they derive their legitimacy from the promise of scientific control over human fate is obvious from the fact that behaviourism remains the official ideology of both Western modernism and Soviet Marxism.

The objectification of a phenomenon yields a mythical illusion of progress. This illusion has been used to justify blatant injustice and authoritarianism: Western science, as it is widely believed, is not an *ally against* authoritarianism; on the contrary, it has an in-built tendency to be an ally of authoritarianism. It is in science that justification of oppression and domination is sought. The excesses of Western civilization, colonialism and racism, class hatred and sexism, and a host of social problems that have been generated by Western society, are now attributed, by the magical processes of objectification, in the fixed interaction of humanity's biological nature. Inequalities of wealth and power, violence and aggression, competitiveness and xenophobia, it is claimed, far from being socially and politically determined, are being reduced to being merely the inevitable products of the human genome and the process of biological evolution.[31] It is noteworthy how authoritarian ideologues of the new Right, from Reagonite militarists to Thatcherite monetarists to the facists of France, Britain and Israel, have seized upon and reiterated scientific ideologies which emphasize the fixity and 'naturalness' of human nature: for instance, see the works of such sociobiologists and proponents of I.Q. theory as Robert Ardrey, Desmond Morris, Edward Wilson, Richard Dawkins, Hans Eysench and Arthur Jensen.

These are not accidental developments: they are a logical outcome of the nature and style of Western science. Most scientists, particularly in the Muslim world, have a textbook, fairy-tale image of how science works. Most textbooks which have a chapter on scientific method have various ideas about what this includes, but all of them are equally dogmatic about the three or four points they mention: observation, hypothesis, experimentation, conclusion and the like. This story book image is taken further by presenting a linear model of 'autonomous science'

Research→Fact→Application

At best the textbook version falsifies science. In real science one works to propagate a particular hypothesis and does not start with it. Observations are often selective; experiments are carried out to support conclusions; it is often considered highly praiseworthy to be unwilling to change one's opinion in the light of latest evidence; lack of humility is highly valued; often the application of results have already been worked out; bias is freely acknowledged; and there is a great deal of emphasis on the importance of intuitive judgement.

Therefore, research activity does not always produce results leading to the true and the good. Of course, we know at least that there are other factors that play a part in the process of scientific research: curiosity and social need. Sometimes a perceived social need stimulates research which produces results that satisfy the need. The process may throw up new problems which excite curiosity and the process repeats itself.

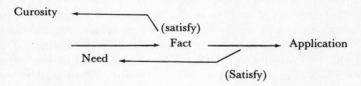

It is to the credit of some social critics of science who argue that both motivations are necessary for a healthy growth of science: pure curiosity leads to 'ivory tower' science with only haphazard application to social needs; and excessive concentration on application leads to the trivialization of research.

To this largely dominant, but somewhat simplistic picture of how Western science works, Marxist philosophers of science, most notably J. D. Bernal, have added the elements that most distort the picture. First of all scientific curiosity can be clocked by dogma and superstition.

Up to the end of the nineteenth century, this dogma and superstition were generated by the institutionalized Church; today it is produced by secular institutions and the various ideologies of domination. More simply, applications of science can be distorted by commercial greed. Or science can be distorted by applications which are deformed and evil: the worst being war. War science now employs over half the scientists worldwide: all the major powers of the world spend a disproportionately large percentage of their natural resources on military science.

But this is as far as Marxist analysis of science takes us. Being a progeny of the Judeo-Christian heritage, Marxism's faith in science as the ultimate value and the arch force for goodness and truth is unshakeable—hence the role of 'scientific' revolutions and 'scientific' socialism in Marxist theory. Marx, as opposed to many latterday Marxists and champions of the New Left, was a complete prisoner of nineteenth-century scientism and instrumental rationality. As Ashis Nandy has put it, 'in spite of his seminal contribution to the demystification of the industrial society, he did not have a clue to the role modern science had played in the legitimation of such a society. The product of a more optimistic age, he faithfully put science outside history. That is why Stalin is not an accidental entry in the history of Marxism. He remains the brain-child of Marx, even if, when considered in the context of Marx's total vision, an illegitimate one.'[32]

Recent critics of Western science, including J. R. Ravetz, Theodore Roszak and Ian Mitroff have added four more factors to the picture of how Western science operates in the real world. First, is unfulfilled promises; that is, no matter how much research is done to find a solution for a pressing social need, the research remains ineffective. No matter what quantity of financial resources is poured into research, the Promethean promise remains unfulfilled. Perhaps the most obvious example here is the ever increasing, indeed maddening pursuit to conquer cancer.

Unfulfilled promises and misplaced optimism only lead to disappointments. But now we must face an even more serious outcome of the contemporary practice of Western science: the ever-present shadow of ecological catastrophe. We have learned recently that science not only has an intended outcome, but it can also have many unintended, unplanned, side-effects. Indeed, beyond the first order effect of science lies a whole minefield of second and third order consequences which a scientist never imagines. As Ravetz points out, most well-meaning scientists have been victims of what we can now see as an illusion, from which we only now are recovering; that is, that the conscious benevolent applications of science cannot do harm. This assumption, or rather faith, has a long history, back indeed to the seventeenth century. We can see it in Francis Bacon, who really believed that magic and the idea of 'powers too great to be revealed' were not merely sinful, because you were getting something for nothing, but also implausible, because things do not *really* happen like that. As the vision of the world (for European peoples) lost its quality of enchantment, it became commonsense that science was really safe—effects could only be proportionate to their (material) causes. The idea of a trigger reaction, of a non-linear, synergistic reaction, of an ecological system, was effectively absent from mainline scientific thinking . . . until well into the post-war period. In the absence of such ideas, one cannot imagine blunders, and cannot imagine some things with which we are now confronted as urgent problems of survival.[33]

One can plead innocence for the unforeseen outcome of one's research, however serious it may be. But one can also consciously conduct research into unethical areas and inhuman domains all in the name of curiosity. The lack of ethical control is a major factor in the destructive nature of Western science. If one considers science to be a pure, virtuous activity, it is only a short step to the illusion that scientists themselves are somehow purified by the activity of research. Western science refuses to treat the scientist as a human being with weaknesses and imperfections. Rather, it claims a special status for scientists as far as the goals of science are concerned. Yet, it refuses to acknowledge that the scientist may have a vested interest in science. When one considers that science refuses to allow criticism from the outside or admit ethical constraints, one can truly appreciate how the domineering presence of science in our society has made the whole of society the prisoner of a small group of professionals who, unlike the political élite in their position, are relatively exempt from the criticism, checks and values of society.

It is, however, always possible for an individual scientist to work according to his own conscience. However, much of Western science is 'big science' requiring organizations that are large scale, complex and have a tendency to take on a life of their own. There is not much scope here for an individual scientist to preserve his individuality. 'Big science' consists of hierarchically organized laboratories in which the individual scientist seeks solutions to minute segments of problems, often unaware of a connection between the overall jigsaw and the puzzle they are solving. Institutionalized science has now managed to do the impossible: it has become simultaneously a market place and vested interest. It has an organizational logic of its own; independent of the creativity of the individual scientist but dependent on, and observing, his material interest. It is this hierarchical organization of science, with its priests and clergy, which has pre-empted basic internal criticism in science. No scientist can now say anything about science policy and scientific choices which is not uncoloured by organizational interests of science or can be taken at its face value.

When we incorporate such factors as unrealism, the possibility of ecological blunders, the acute questions of ethics and the organizational structure of science into our picture of Western science, an altogether new beast makes an appearance. This system of science has its own internal dynamic which transforms every society it touches: indeed, the society of science cannot survive as an uncontaminated heaven of non-material values. If it continues on its present journey, its relentless logic will inevitably lead to the total destruction of man's terrestrial abode—the Promethean fire, stolen from Heaven by Man's quest for knowledge and power, burns just as fiercely as ever.

Argument Four

Western science cannot meet the physical, cultural and spiritual needs and requirements of Muslim societies

It is easy for us to overlook the inherent destructive nature of Western science for one very strong reason: it works. The glittering successes of Western science are many and diverse: it has enabled Western civilization to amass unimagined power and wealth; it has even relieved ordinary people of discomfort, pain, deprivation and squalor to a degree; it has made it easier for us to travel, communicate and manipulate information. These are by no means small achievements.

But the point is not that Western science works. The point is that it works in a particular way that is designed to fulfil the needs and requirements of a society and culture with a specific worldview. It is designed to fashion the image of the Western civilization wherever it operates. That's why, wherever and whenever its problem-solving techniques or its products are applied, the end result is an inferior reproduction of some segment of Western society. Thus promoting

the myth that both Western science and Western civilization—
implicitly implying their values and culture—are universal.

The prime concern of the system of Western science is its own
survival and extension. To do that it must give absolute priority to
itself, its own societal and civilizational roots. This it does in some
straightforward, mechanical way. The process, in fact, is very subtle.
Glyn Ford describes the main mechanics of the process:

> Science and technology depend heavily upon state finance and there is
> always more waiting to be done than resources available. That which is
> undertaken is done at the expense of alternative choices. Those who arbi-
> trate between options do so on the basis of their own ideological
> presuppositions. To expect otherwise is naive. Thus the choice of the
> trajectory of science and technology is partisan, although this is not to
> suggest that the work of contemporary scientists and technologists always
> neatly meshes with the requirements of contemporary Western society.
> Developments within science and technology emerge from an adversary
> process in which hypotheses compete for intellectual dominance. But the
> judging is rigged.
>   New scientific laws, for example, are not brought to society like the
> tablets from the mountain. They emerge from a field of competing alterna-
> tives, all of which reflect, to a greater or lesser extent, aspects of the
> multidimensional world of nature. The determination of which is to be the
> victor is not a simple one. It is not determined purely on grounds of truth
> content or to suit the implicit wishes of those in positions of authority.
> Rather it comes from a continuous and multiple series of interactions
> between science, scientists and society. Nevertheless, the choices that can
> be made are extremely limited. For mental slavery is as coercive as its
> physical counterpart. The values science and technology must always
> reflect are those material values of acquisition, unchecked and
> uncontrolled growth, and Darwinian competition. Spirit and compassion
> become marginal at best and ornamental at worst. There is an inevitability
> about the creation of technologies that are intensive, large-scale and highly
> centralized; in a word 'inhuman'.[34]

As the style and packaging of Western science reflects the needs and
priorities of an alien system, it can never meet the requirements of
Muslim culture and society. This is largely why Western science has
not taken social root in Muslim countries. And this is why, in the
Muslim world today, science is sporadic, isolated, largely
unconnected with local needs and interests and quite incapable of
self-sustenance. Most proponents of science decry the poor spending
on science in the Muslim countries: but that is only an external symp-
tom of a very deep malaise. And that malaise lies not just with Muslim

societies but also with the nature and style of science that is backed and promoted.

One of the most common examples of the wide gulf between what is needed in Muslim societies and what science offers, relates to capital and labour: much of Western science is geared to producing labour-saving, capital-intensive final products; yet, in the major part of the Muslim world there is an excess of labour and shortage of capital. What most Muslim people need are simple solutions to their basic problems of everyday living; what Western science is geared to is producing sophisticated solutions requiring massive inputs of energy. The most common killers in the Muslim world are diarrhoea and schistosomiasis; much of science-based modern medicine is looking for cures to lung cancer, heart disease and concentrating on trans-planting various bits of anatomy from one individual to another. Health problems in Muslim societies cannot be more basic: over-crowded and insanitary city life kills a high number of children and nurtures diseases such as cholera and malaria. Yet Western medicine is too preoccupied with herpes and AIDS, test tube conception and cryogenic freezing. In most Muslim countries obtaining energy to cook could be a major problem for a family; while Western science concerns itself with fast breeder reactors and development of nuclear missiles.

But it is not just a question of wrong priorities and emphasis, Muslim societies also have spiritual, cultural and environmental needs that Western science can never fulfil. Indeed, it can only aggravate such needs. The most blatant example of this is the imposition of solutions derived from Western science and technology on the hajj environ-ment. On the face of it the problem of the hajj environment is simple: meeting the accommodation, transport and material needs of pilgrims visiting Makkah and Madinah every year, while preserving the eco-logical and spiritual character of the holy areas. Since the early 1970s, almost every solution that modern technology can produce has been tried. The problems have not only become worse, but the very envi-ronment for which these solutions were sought has been destroyed. The entire environment has been turned into an extension of Western society.

The methodology of reduction cannot take into consideration cul-tural and spiritual needs. Neither can it grapple with social complex-ities. Schistosomiasis has been isolated from society and has been studied in Egypt and the Sudan for over fifty years, yet a solution to this problem is not in sight because its connection with irrigation, education, the play needs of children and rural development have not been taken into account. Reductive science approaches agriculture as though it were a problem and not a way of life: that is why agricultural research in Muslim countries has not borne much fruit; it has concentrated on crop yields, developing new strains of seeds, and the use of pesticide and high yield fertiliser. The social aspects of agriculture are beyond its scope.

One can go on listing the dichotomy between the physical, social, cultural and spiritual needs of Muslim societies and what modern science has and can deliver. But the record of Western science in Third World countries—including those which have developed a sophisticated infrastructure such as India and Brazil, and those which have tried to buy Western science and technology such as Saudi Arabia, Libya and pre-Revolutionary Iran—speaks for itself. I have documented and analysed it in considerable detail elsewhere.[35]

Islamic Science: The Way Ahead

The only true way of meeting the multidimensional needs of Muslim societies is to develop a science which draws its inspiration from the cultural and spiritual ethos of the worldview of Islam and is specially geared to meeting these needs. I have argued in this essay that different civilizations had different sciences reflecting their particular worldview. I have also tried to show that Islamic science in history had a unique nature and style and that Western science today also embodies within itself the Judeo-Christian intellectual heritage. Furthermore, I have argued that Western science is intrinsically destructive: the application of Western science and technology in Muslim societies is playing havoc with our values and culture and is not meeting our needs and requirements. Given this backdrop, the need for a contemporary Islamic science becomes imperative.

I have argued that the worldview of Islam maintains a unified structure through a matrix of eternal values and concepts which have to be lived and which give Islam its unique character. Because Islam is a total system, these concepts permeate every aspect of human life. Nothing is left untouched: whether political structures or social organizations, economic concerns or educational curricula, environmental outlook or framework for scientific enquiry and technological pursuits. These values shape the parameters of Muslim society and guide the civilization of Islam towards its manifest destiny.

Within the cordon of such values and concepts as *tawheed* (unity of God), *khilafah* (man's trusteeship of God's creation), *akhirah* (man's accountability in the hereafter), *ibadah* (worship of one God), *ilm* (the pursuit of knowledge), *adl* (social justice) and *istislah* (public interest), Muslim individuals and societies are free to express their individuality and meet their needs according to their wishes and resources. And, indeed, throughout the history of Islam, different Muslim societies have realized these values and concerns in different ways according to their time and place. It is by this mechanism that the Islamic civilization adjusts to change, yet retains its unique and eternal characteristics.

Contemporary Muslim societies have particular needs which have to be met within the purview of Islam. Some of these needs, like food and shelter, are common to all men. Others, such as the need to overcome dependency and technological exploitation, are a product of the particular historic situation of Muslim societies. Still others are an outcome of Muslim culture: the type of dwellings that are most suited for an Islamic way of life, cities that express the cultural and aesthetic concerns of Islam, and a natural environment that exhibits the Islamic relationship between man and nature. All these needs have to be fulfilled within the value structure of Islam. They have to be fulfilled with the full realization that Islam is a total system in which everything is interlinked, nothing compartmentalized or treated as an isolated problem. Such methods, processes and tools for meeting these needs and solving the problems of contemporary Muslim societies must be an embodiment of the culture and values of Islam. And this applies also to science, one of the most powerful tools for solving man's problems and meeting his needs.

As the history of Islamic science teaches us, a science that operates within an Islamic value structure has a unique nature and style. It is essentially a *subjectively objective* enterprise: objective solutions to normative goals and problems are sought within an area mapped out by the eternal values and concepts of Islam. In Islamic science, both the ends and means of science are dictated by the ethical system of Islam: thus, both the objectives of science as well as its tools, processes and methods have to conform to Islamic dictates. These dictates have nothing to do with dogma; but everything to do with ethics. Islamic science is beyond dogma and does not degenerate to the level of naive inquiry. It is a systematic, rigorous pursuit of truth, a rational and objective problem-solving enterprise that seeks to understand the whole of reality. It is holistic and is founded on synthesis. It seeks to understand and preserve the object of its study. It treats scientists as human beings who have weaknesses and who are part of the community and not outside it. It seeks to fulfil the needs of the vast majority and not a select few. It reflects the hopes and aspirations of the entire Muslim ummah. We need Islamic science because Muslims are a community of people who 'do good and forbid evil', and to show that science can be a positive force in society. We need Islamic science because the needs, the priorities and emphasis of Muslim societies are different from those that science has incorporated in Western civilization. And, finally, we need Islamic science because a civilization is not complete without an objective problem-solving system that operates within its own paradigms. Without Islamic science, Muslim societies will only be an appendage to Western culture and civilization. In short, we have no viable future without Islamic science.

References

1. A. N. Whitehead, *Adventures of Ideas*, CUP, 1938, pp. 13–14.
2. Chu Cahi and Winberg Chai (eds. & trans.), *The Essential Works of Confucianism*, Bantam Book, New York, 1965, p. 13.
3. *Ibid.*, p. 15.
4. From Aristotle's *Nicomachean Ethics*, W. D. Ross (trans.), R. Mckeon (ed.), Basic Books, New York, 1941.
5. Quoted in Colin A. Ronan's abridgement of Joseph Needham, *The Shorter Science and Civilization in China*, Vol. 1, CUP, 1978, p. 144.
6. *Ibid.*, p. 158.
7. Farrington, *Greek Science*, pp. 50–2.
8. *Ibid.*, p. 97.
9. For a detailed description of various Muslim classification schemes, see Rosenthal, *Knowledge Triumphant*.
10. Chejne, *Ibn Hazm*, p. 64.
11. *Ibid.*, pp. 64–5.
12. *Kashf al-Mahjub*, R. A. Nicholson (trans.), Brill, Leiden, p. 11.
13. Particularly G. E. Von Grunebaum has been very hostile to Muslim interpretation of knowledge. See his *Islam: Essay in the Nature and Growth of a Cultural Tradition*, Barnes and Noble, New York, 1961.
14. This example is taken from Seyyed Hossein Nasr, 'Reflections on methodology in the Islamic science', *Hamdard Islamicus*, 3(3), 1980, pp. 3–13.
15. Al-Biruni, *The Determination of the Co-ordinates*, p. 175.
16. *Ibid.*, p. 2.
17. For a detailed analysis of how al-Biruni came up with this figure and the theory behind his calculations, see Willy Hartner and Matthias Schramm,

'Al-Biruni and the theory of solar apogee: an example of originality in Arabic science', in A. C. Crombie (ed.), *Scientific Change*, Heinemann, London, 1962.

18. Quoted by Roger Arnaldez, 'The theory and practice of science according to Ibn Sina and al-Biruni', in Said, *Al-Biruni Commemorative Volume*, p. 431.

19. See S. Pines, 'La conception de la conscience de soi chez Avicenne et chez Abul Barakat al-Baghdad', *Archives d'histoire doctrinale et litteraire du Moyen Age XXI*, 1955, p. 97.

20. Ibn Sina, *Tis Rasail*, Cairo, 1908, p. 120.

21. S. Pines, 'Ibn al-Haytham's Critique of Ptolemy', in *Actes du Xe Congres internationale d'histoire des sciences*, Paris 1, 1964, p. 574.

22. In particular, see Anton Heinen, 'Al-Biruni and al-Haytham: a comparative study of scientific method', in Said, *Al-Biruni Commemorative Volume*, pp. 501–13.

23. Quoted by Naseer Ahmad Nasir from al-Haytham's *Tabaqat-ul-Attiba*, in his paper, 'Ibn al-Haytham and his philosophy', in Said, *Ibn al-Haytham*, pp. 80–93.

24. *Ibid.*, p. 80.

25. *Ibid.*, p. 84.

26. Young, 'Polymathy in Islam.'

27. Mitroff, *The Subjective Side of Science*, p. 79. Mitroff's table compares the norms of science with 'counternorms' which are considered by more radical scientists to form the basis of more enlightened paradigm of scientific research.

28. CUP, 1969, p. 554. For a really arrogant defence of untamed reason, see Gerald Feinberg, *The Prometheus Project*, Doubleday, New York, 1969.

29. See the classic paper by Lynn White, Jr., 'Historical roots of our ecological crisis'; see also William Leiss, *The Domination of Nature*, George Braziller, New York, 1972.

30. Anees, 'Islamic science: an antidote to reductionism.'

31. For a detailed account of how science is being used to justify oppression and inequality, see the brilliant work of Philip Green, *The Pursuit of Inequality*.

32. Nandy, 'Science severed from source'.

33. J. R. Ravetz, 'The Social function of science: a commemoration of J. D. Bernal's vision', *Science and Public Policy*, October 1982. I owe the diagrams to Ravetz. See also his classic, *Scientific Knowledge and its Social Problems*, OUP, 1982.

34. Ford, 'Liberating science with Islamic values'.

35. See Sardar, *Science, Technology and Development in the Muslim World* and *Science and Technology in the Middle East*.

Five

Where's Where? Shaping the Future of Islamic Science

Most concerned Muslim scholars agree that without some kind of science the future of Muslim civilization is grim. The debate on the kind of science Muslim societies need has now generated a body of ideas, criticisms, cherished positions and metaphysical expositions that need to be examined thoroughly if we Muslims are to understand the nature of a science that can take social, cultural and intellectual root in Muslim societies. In the final chapter of this book, I intend critically to examine the stock of accumulated ideas, look at the parameters within which the discourse on Islamic science has meaning, and study the direction towards which the discipline is moving. I shall do this by examining the ideas of various schools of thought taking part in this discourse and also by delineating my own and my colleagues' positions on Islamic science.

Ticket to Ride

In recent years Zaki Kirmani and M. Kaleemur Rahman have set out to develop a typology of positions within the discourse on Islamic science.[1] However, their typologies attributed beliefs by drawing similarities between the approaches of various authors without making their positions clear or developing appropriate correlation between their approaches. If we attribute beliefs simply by drawing superficial similarities between authors, we end up producing stange assimilations. For example, because Seyyed Hossein Nasr, Parvez Manzoor, Munawar Ahmad Anees and I consider Western science to be culturally biased and value-laden, Kirmani assumes that the approaches of Nasr and the other three are the same; in fact, the differences between these approaches are so fundamental that they constitute two totally different ways of looking at science, indeed even the notion of science in the two approaches is totally different. Again, Rahman assumes that because both Nasr and I have justified the use of the term 'Islamic science', we are talking about the same thing; not only do our justifications come from radically different perspectives, but the moulds in which we cast Islamic science are also totally different.[2]

The imputation of beliefs should be based on a critical examination of the entire *oeuvre* of an author, not just of a single work. Creative minds do not remain static; they grow; they learn, and not just from their own experience but also from the evidence brought forward by others. An *oeuvre* of an author, therefore, may reveal changes in position. However, much more interesting than attributing beliefs to individual authors is the imputation of beliefs to a group of authors.[3] Our imputation of beliefs to groups of scholars or schools of thought assumes that individuals express intellectual positions that are borne by the group to which they belong. While there is no such metaphysical entity as a group mind which thinks over and above the heads of the individual, or whose ideas the individual merely reproduces, nevertheless it would be false to deduce from this that all the ideas that motivate an individual have their origin in that individual alone and can be explained solely on the basis of that single life-experience.

Can we randomly attribute positions to a group of scholars or is there a more reasonable way of ascribing intellectual stands? One obvious criterion is where the members of the relevant group are willing to affirm the attributed position as their own and demonstrate the use of ideas in their work. This criteria is met by two groups of scholars who are active in the discourse on Islamic science. The first consists of Hossein Nasr and his followers, most notably Osman Bakr, who have produced a corpus of literature; I shall refer to them as the Guenon/Schuon school of thought because they derive most of their ideas from the scholarship of René Guenon and Fritjof Schuon. The second school describe themselves as the group of *Ijmal*—the root word *jml* conveys the ideas of beauty on the one hand and wholeness on the other, and *Ijmal* captures the substance of synthesis with the style of aesthetics. Three Ijmalis—S. Parvez Manzoor, Munawar Ahmad Anees and I—are active in the debate on Islamic science.[4] Four others are also familiar to those who are aware of the existence of a new trend in Muslim intellectual thought, first introduced in the now defunct journal, *Inquiry*: Gulzar Haider, Merryl Wyn Davies, Mohammad Iqbal Asaria and Ibrahim Sulaiman.[5] While the Ijmalis are a heterogeneous group, their intellectual position is united by a methodology of conceptual analysis, seen in all their works, that aims at synthesis and future-orientated expressions of the values of Islam in all aspects of contemporary thought and life.

Group identity is not fixed to declared intellectual positions, objective interests or stated goals. It may also arise by the connection of a group of scholars to a particular institution, where scholars may work on similar problems; even though their individual positions may be different, there is an overall unity that comes from the regular interchange of ideas and constant criticisms from colleagues. Thus, in the sociology of knowledge, there is the noted Edinburgh school of thought, attached to the University of Edinburgh, that bases its work on the relativist account of science, whereas at the opposite end is the historic Vienna Circle that produced the original logical positivist stance on science. In the area of Islamic science, the Aligarh school, based at the Centre for Studies on Science in Aligarh, India, has a adopted a similar loose grouping; its scholars contribute regularly to the *Journal of Islamic Science*. Positions within the group vary, but there is unity in the overall concerns and emphasis of the group: the Aligarh group is essentially a school of criticism of science, and most of its original ideas have emerged from criticisms of established positions, with a dominant concern for methodology. The group includes Mohammad Zaki Kirmani, Mohammad Riaz Kirmani, M. Kaleemur Rahman and Rias Ahmad.

Finally, group identity can also emerge as an outcome of discursive processes in the world at large. Different scholars may express their positions in different ways, articulate their thoughts using different concepts, may emphasize different areas of discourse, but their underlying, fundamental epistemological positions may be the same. As Foucault says: 'the frontiers of a book are never clear cut: beyond the title, the first lines, and the last full stop, beyond its internal configuration and autonomous form, it is caught up in a system of references to other books, other texts, other sentences: it is a node within a network'.[6] Many authors who have contributed to the discourse on Islamic science are part of the network of Western science. However they may couch their thoughts, whatever values they may seek to protect, whatever beliefs they may confess, they are essentially propagating the dominant, positivist and realist view of science, which sees science as a universal, objective pursuit of truth. Mohammad Abdus Salam, Ali Kettani, S. Waqar A. Husaini, Z. Rajib al-Nejjar and Jamal Mimouni belong to this school, along with most Muslim scientists.

I intend to examine critically the positions of each of these schools and then suggest some positive ways in which the discourse on Islamic science can move forward.

Nowhere Man

To understand where Nasr and his followers are taking the discourse and, through his prolific output, Islamic science itself, we must appreciate where he is coming from. We need to understand his worldview, not in order to make cheap sectarian points, but because his distinctive outlook permeates everything he writes; indeed, his whole work is an extended apologia for his own rather specific and circumscribed outlook.

I am not concerned here with Nasr's personal beliefs; the brand of Islam he follows is his own affair. I am concerned with his published views; and a reading of his oeuvre reveals that he is heavily influenced by Ismaili thought and is a strong—this is probably an understatement—supporter of the Guenon/Schuon school of thought. To understand Nasr, it is necessary to know both Ismaili thought and the Guenon/Schuon worldview which form the basis of his own *Weltanschauung*. I will explore them by looking at a representative segment of Nasr's work; where necessary I will provide background information essential to the argument.

Ismailism branched from the mainstream of Islamic thought in the latter part of the eighth century. Its principal dispute with mainstream Shia orthodoxy concerned Ismael, son of Imam Jafar Sadiq, the sixth Imam, who, his followers believed, should have been designated the seventh Imam of the Shia. The Ismailis emphasize the internal and symbolic teachings of the Quran, from which they derive a distinct body of esoteric teachings and a particular cosmology. As Hakim Mohammad Said and Ansar Zahid Khan point out:

> The Abbasid period saw this branch of Shiism developing regional and ethnic affiliations. It was able to gain Yemen and North Africa to its cause. At one stage coinciding with the decay of the Abbasids, the Ismaili beliefs nearly overwhelmed the whole Muslim world. The tenth century witnessed the greatest period of glory for these beliefs under the Fatimids

(A.D. 909–1171) with their new capital at Qahira (Cairo founded in A.D. 969).In the east their movement was characterized by two developments. In Iran and Transoxiana where the Abbasids had been successful, they developed a rational and philosophical style while in Sind they closely identified the idea of a redeemer with that of the awaited incarnation of Vishnu. The former gave birth to Ikhwan al-Safa, while the latter resulted in *Dasa-avtar*, one of the canons of modern Ismailis.[7]

Thus, Hindu philosophy, particularly the notion of reincarnation and cyclic time, became part of Ismaili doctrine at a very early stage.

The Ismaili doctrine has two main facets: the *zahir*, or the outwardly, which is similar to Shia theology and practices; and the *batin*, or the hidden, an esoteric system of philosophy and science, amalgamated with some notions of the Quran and serving as a guide to its inner content, providing religious prescriptions and, in its original formulation, intended to prove the divine origins of the institution of the Imamate and the exclusive rights of the Fatimids to it. The most prominent elements of this system are the gnostic traditions of the Greeks, including the mystical teachings of Pythagoras, the neo-Platonic philosophy, the natural philosophy of Aristotle, aspects of Hindu philosophy, and elements of Zoroastrianism. These heterogenous elements are combined with an Islamic gloss to produce an occult framework where gnosis circles around alchemy, angelology, numerology, astrology and other forms of esotericism.

Nasr fuses his Ismaili esotericism with the *religio perennis* philosophy of the Guenon/Schuon school of thought. This philosophy, based on the esoteric and sapiential teachings of Platonism, Vedanta, Sufism and Buddism, seeks a rediscovery of alchemy and other occult sciences and owes its formulation to the originator of the movement, René Guenon (d. 1951) and its main expositor, Fritjof Schuon. Guenon, a French mystic, attacked the modern world from a Platonic point of view in such works as *The Oriental Metaphysics* and *Reign of Quantity and the Signs of the Times*.[8] He considered all traditional forms to be various expressions of the one supra-formal truth, which he sought to illustrate with exposition of traditional symbols. Fritjof Schuon took Guenon's philosophy to the realm of *religio perennis* which he expressed in *The Transcendent Unity of Religions, Castes and Races* and *Light on the Ancient World*.[9]An important aspect of the philosophy of Schuon (who is now reliably reported to be having visions of the Virgin Mary) is that the ancient Orphic and Dionysian mysteries led to, in Nasr's words, 'a veritable Greek miracle' and such figures as Pythagoras, Plato,

Aristotle and Plotinus were associated with this miracle and thus had divine qualities. (Indeed, Nasr wants to believe that Plato was a Prophet—a Prophet who advocated oligarchy, eugenics, a dissolution of the family, controlled sexual relations between men and women, and who found homosexuality rather acceptable—and that 'Greek philosophers had learned their philosophy from the Prophets'.) Other members of the school include the Swiss Sufi, Titus Burckhardt (d. 1984), the Hindu mystic Ananda K. Coomaraswamy (d. 1947), the British mystic Martin Lings, Victor Danner and Jacob Needleman; Gai Eaton and Osman Bakr are new recruits, and other mystics such as Ali Ashraf and Hadi Sharifi are aspiring members.[10] (Lings and Eaton lean towards Islamic orthodoxy.) The writings of the group regularly appear in the British journal *Studies in Comparative Religion*.

In all his works, whether he is writing about art, science, religion, philosophy, history or the Islamic way of life, Nasr propounds the philosophy of Ismaili esotericism and *religio perennis*; this is why, whatever the context, he essentially says the same thing; this is also why he is so prolific (since he has nothing new to say). Almost all the references in his book are to the other members of the group or to two noted contemporary exponents of Ismaili gnosis: Louis Massignon and Henry Corbin.[11] And as befits the devotee, a great deal of his output is simply an exposition of the masters' philosophy: 'we wish to express our gratitude, especially to Fritjof Schuon, whose unparalleled exposition of traditional teachings is reflected, albeit imperfectly, upon many of the pages which follow'.[12] Not surprising, when 'Schuon seems like the cosmic intellect itself impregnated by the energy of the divine grace surveying the whole of the reality surrounding man and elucidating all the concerns of human existence in the light of sacred knowledge'.[13]

Having specified the context in which Nasr is writing, let us examine what he is actually saying. For Nasr, at a certain level of reality all religions are the same; this in fact is the basic thesis of *'scientia sacra* (which can be) expounded in the language of one as well as the other perspective. It can speak of God or the Godhead, Allah, the Tao, or even nirvana'.[14] When Nasr uses the terms 'knowledge', 'sapience', 'intelligence', 'science', 'consciousness', he means one and the same thing: Ismaili Guenon/Schuon version of gnosis.

In the beautifully illustrated, *Islamic Science*, the context in which Nasr is writing can be clearly seen. When setting out the cosmology of

Islam, Nasr takes particular care to ground it in his particular world-view. Islamic cosmology

> aims at providing a vision of the cosmos which enables man to pierce through the visible world to the higher states of existence and creating a science of the cosmic domain which acts as a ladder to allow man to mount to the 'roof of the cosmos', to use the well-known phrase associated with Rumi, and even beyond it to behold Metacosmic Reality which transcends all the planes of cosmic manifestation. The Origin of the Principle of the Universe is at once Being, Consciousness and Bliss (*wujud, wujdan* and *wajd* in Arabic) and these qualities flow in the arteries of the cosmos precisely because the cosmos is a manifestation of the Principle. Traditional cosmologies are means of gaining knowledge of this positive aspect of the cosmos; in the bosom of metaphysical doctrines and with the aid of appropriate methods of realization they enable men to gain access to that consciousness and experience, that bliss which is already a taste of paradise.[15]

Thus, in this highly reductive definition, Islamic cosmology is equated simply with mystical experiences; normal questions of cosmology such as origins and the structure of the universe, its ethical and value dimensions, are totally ignored. Furthermore, by mentioning Rumi, and then immediately bringing the notion of 'traditional cosmologies', Nasr makes it appear that 'traditional cosmologies' are an integral part of Islamic cosmologies. In Guenonite thought, the notion of 'traditional cosmologies' have a specific meaning, and that Nasr is referring to the Guenonite notion is borne out by the fact that there are no less than four citations to Schuon (as if Schuon is the only person who can enlighten us on this topic on a single page!).

What is the Guenonite notion of 'traditional cosmologies'? Two colour plates later, Nasr tells us: 'Islamic cosmology has made use of such diverse elements as Quranic symbolism, concepts and symbols drawn from the doctrinal formulation of Sufism (itself developed to a large extent from the Quran and Hadith), theosophical and philosophical descriptions of the cosmos, numerical symbolism and traditional astronomy'.[16] For 'Quranic symbolism', read the esoteric Ismaili interpretation of the Quran. The doctrinal formulation, even though it is based on the Quran and Hadith, must clearly be distinctively different from Islamic doctrines, otherwise it would not constitute one of the 'diverse elements'. And what 'theosophical and philosophical description of the cosmos' is Nasr referring to? He gives an example from the schemes found in the writings of Sayyid Haydar al-Amuli who:

had a particular love for geometric patterns and made use of them as symbols of his cosmological doctrines. He designed the mandalas to be contemplated by the adept, complicated patterns in which the twelve Imams of Shiism enter into the cosmic scheme to play a major role as so many epiphanies of the logos and reflections of the divine light. The number twelve naturally plays a central role in these patterns, which unify angelology, imamology and astronomy in grand schemes unveiling the contours of the Islamic cosmos with its particular Shiite colour.[17]

As to numerical symbolism, that comes from a combination of the

> Aristotelian doctrine of the three kingdoms and the Pythagorean philoso-phy of numbers with Islamic metaphysics while making use of the sciences concerned with symbolism of the Arabic alphabet as well as symbolism of certain words and phrases. In the case of the Ikhwan al-Safa, whose *Epistles* reflected the thought of certain circles within Shiism, especially Ismailism, and which are related in many ways to the Jabirean corpus, there is to be found more than anything else a Pythagoreanism combined with Aristo-telian natural philosophy and integrated into the matrix of Islamic esoter-icism, while in the works of such men as Shams al-din al-Buni certain Hermetic and also magical ideas enter into the picture.[18]

What is Pythagoreanism? And Hermeticism? And what aspect of Aristotelian natural philosophy are we concerned with? And why does Nasr insist on making them a central part of Islamic cosmology? The answer lies in the theology of Guenon and Schuon, in the religion of gnosis, what Nasr refers to as traditional cosmologies.

Gnosis emerged as a cult in Palestine in the first century B.C., although its exact origins are still disputed by scholars. At the end of the Hellenistic age, Greek philosophy fused with Persian dualism and orthodox Judaism in Egypt and Palestine to produce the lethal religion of gnosis—knowledge of the true nature of things. Pythagoreanism already provided a fertile ground for it. This esoteric cult was founded by the Greek mathematician whose name is associated with the famous theorem. Established in Croton about 530 B.C., this confraternity believed in the doctrine of reincarnation of the soul into the bodies of men and animals and even certain plants. Pythagoras had a very good memory which enabled him to recall his former lives. The sect practised a severe discipline which included secrecy, respect for the authority of the master, ritual purifications, memory exercises, examination of conscience and various food taboos. Pythagorean cosmology gave an essential place to numbers, which were repre-sented by points juxtaposed to form squares, triangular and rectan lar figures. 'Things are numbers', Pythagoras used to say. He believed that events in the heavens had earthly counterparts and that through appropriate disciplines men could become immortal gods. The last stanza of the golden verse of Pythagoras, which formed the basis of his creed, reads: 'And when, after having divested thyself of thy mortal body, thou arrivest in the most pure Aether, thou shalt be God, immortal, incorruptible, and death shall have no dominion over thee.'[19] Hermiticism, based on the treatises on alchemy and magic of Hermes Trismegistus, provided another impetus of the emergence of gnosis. In the *Asclepius*, the last and most advanced teachings of Hermes, one finds the bold claim that he who has grasped its meaning will have reached complete gnosis; he will see God, or be united with God.[20] Aristotle's theology, developed in *Physics* and *De Anima* added further fuel to the rise of gnosis.[21] It is from this Greek theological background that gnosticism derives its central notions: secrecy, authoritarianism from Pythagoras; the true nature of knowledge from Hermes Trismegistus; the notion that an improbable order reigns in the celestial domain while a large place is left to hazard and liberty in the sublunary domain from Aristotle; the ideas of oligarchy, purity and hierarchy from Plato. For example, a Gnostic–Platonist will explain the notion of hierarchy by stating that from the higher gods emanate lower gods in a vast hierarchy that stretches down from the One and the archetypal ideas to the demiurgic Jupiter, who made the planet we live on. The human soul, naturally a part of the higher planes, is sunk in matter and in ignorance, and its task is to journey laboriously upwards, leaving behind the world of substance to join its native star, or even to be subsumed in the very Absolute itself. Add Islamic terminology, and you have the gnosis of Nasr.

So where does Islam figure in all this? It is clear that there is little Islamic content, but as Greek gnosticism is able to fasten like a parasite on Islam, it is able to present the whole thing in Islamic terminology.

It is hardly surprising then when it comes to the actual history of Islamic science, Nasr presents it essentially as a history of esotericism and occult, interpretation and adaptation of Greek methodology by the Muslims, and takes every opportunity to glorify gnosticism. In the chapter on mathematics, he presents highly distorted and selected examples, constantly trying to read cosmological and magical schemes into Muslim mathematics. Thus 'Pythagoras was Islamized rapidly' because 'there already existed an "Abrahamic Pythagoreanism" in

Islam![22] Moreover, almost all of Muslim mathematics was concerned with and 'closely connected with the study of magic squares and amicable numbers, which were applied to various occult sciences from alchemy to magic'.[23] We *know* that algebra emerged to deal with the laws of inheritance, as is even evident in al-Khwarizmi's classical work from whence the discipline takes its name. But Nasr chooses totally to ignore the arithmetic of inheritance and describes algebra as 'closely related to certain metaphysical principles so central to Islamic doctrines'.[24] The implication is that algebra did not evolve from the physical necessity of dealing with the laws of inheritance, but was a natural outcome of the Greek mythological cosmologies that the Muslims were supposed to have adapted! Quite a few assertions of Nasr are simply statements of beliefs and have nothing to do with the history of Islamic science. Thus, because the Aristotelian system is an important part of both Ismaili and Guenonite theology, Nasr attributes the making of a meaningful model of the Aristotelian system to al-Biruni. No doubt al-Biruni would have made it if it were possible; but it is impossible, even with the help of gnosis, to make meaningful models based on the Aristotelian system.

When we come to astronomy, we discover that Nasr is not the least bit interested in the particularly Islamic aspect of Islamic astronomy: the determination of the visibility of the lunar crescent, the determination of astronomically defined times of prayer, the determination of the direction of the *qibla*—a task that occupied Muslim astronomers for over one thousand years and forms a vast corpus of the literature on Islamic astronomy. Instead we are presented with selected works of 'outstanding Persian' scholars to whom all sorts of things are attributed. For example, he attributes the calculation of the tables of tangent of the thirteenth-century Persian astronomer Nasir al-din al-Tusi, whom we know simply plagiarized them from the tenth-century Egyptian astronomer, ibn Yunus. He attributes the invention of the decimal fraction to Kashani, 'the outstanding Persian mathematician', when it has been established that al-Uqlidusi of Damascus wrote on decimal fractions five centuries ago. Similarly, the 'earliest astrolobe is from fourth/tenth century Isfahan', while at least six earlier ones can be traced back to Iraq. There is a great deal of emphasis on astrolabes because of their alleged astrological significance, but there is nothing on the two instruments which Muslims really developed: the sun-dial and quadrants. Instead, astrology, that most Islamic of Islamic science, gets appropriate attention:

It was the profound symbolism inherent in astrology which made its integration into Islamic civilization and especially into certain aspects of Islamic esotericism possible, despite obvious external differences between astrological attempts to predict future events and the Islamic emphasis upon the omnipotent character of the Divine Will. . . . But the branches of astrology among Muslims are the same as among the Greeks or ancient Persians. They include judicial astrology, dealing with the prediction of the future of events or institutions, genethliac astrology, dealing with the horoscope of individuals, and the cosmological aspects of astrology.[25]

But if Islamic astrology is the same as Greek and ancient Persian astrology, what is Islamic about it? Why adjectivize it with Islam, especially when it contradicts the Islamic notion of an omnipotent God? It is because of his fundamental belief in Greek esoteric mythology and its association with Islam, that Nasr demeans the formidable contribution of Muslims in this field. As David King points out, Nasr pays

perhaps the weakest tribute to the Islamic astronomical tradition. One of his final comments on p. 133 must suffice as an example: 'but perhaps the most enduring contribution of Muslims to the history of astronomy was their transforming the Ptolemic spheres from merely mathematical models to physical realities'. It happens that we know that Ptolemy's *Planetary Hypotheses*, which was the starting point of Muslim investigations of theoretical astronomy, is a description of the arrangements of the heavens based on the assumption that the models of planetary motions have a physical existence. And since modern astronomers no longer believe in the physical reality of the planetary spheres, this 'enduring contribution' of the Muslims (and the Greeks) is not generally recognized today.[26]

It is not just in mathematics and astronomy that occult, magic and Greek mythology is disguised as Islamic history of science. 'Science principles of physics are to be found solely in metaphysics and nowhere else'[27] (a statement of belief I find asburd) and we are launched into another magical, mystery tour. Nothing is spared: even animals and plants come in for occultish treatment. Thus, botany involved 'the study of the occult properties of plants, as well as their symbolic and spiritual significance in the cosmos',[28] although not a single example is given of the occult study of plants. Animals are symbols of cosmic qualities and spiritual attitudes.[29] And space itself has occult and sacred properties:

Cast within the worldview of Islam and centered most of all upon the vast confines of dar al-Islam, the science of geography drew from any sources, such as Babylonia, Greece, India and especially Persia. Pre-Islamic Persian geography had already influenced pre-Islamic Arabic geographical ideas, as the Arabic word *barzakh*, which comes from the Pahlavi *farsang*, reveals, and it played a central role in the early Islamic geography as well. The ancient Persian saw the earth as an angel and possessed a highly developed 'visionary geography'. Their division of the world into seven circular 'regions' (*kishwars*) was a terrestrial reflection of the sevenfold spiritual hierarchy and left its deep effect upon geographers of the Islamic period, who were fully aware of the symbolic significance of seven in both the Greek scheme of the climate and the Persian scheme of the *kishwars*. Likewise, the central cosmic mountain of the ancient Persians became transformed into the Mount Qaf mention in the Quran, and at least among a great number of Islamic geographers the central region of the world was conceived in a new fashion so as to encompass Mecca, the centre of the Islamic world and the point where, for Muslims, the heavenly axis touches the terrestrial plane. In 'Islamicizing' the natural world about it, Islam, in fact, incorporated much of the symbolic and sacred geography of the traditions before them, sanctifying them anew through the power of the new revelation. How many mountains, lakes and other distinct loci can be found today in the Islamic world which are of particular religious significance now and were also of special religious significance in the traditions which preceded Islam.[30]

None; with the obvious examples of the Haramain, including Jerusalem. But that does not give rise to a 'sacred geography' as a discipline!

Then, of course, there is the *piéce de résistance*: a whole chapter on occult sciences. Islamic sciences, we are told,

> include a category called the hidden (*khafiyyah*) or occult (*gharibah*) sciences, which have always remained 'hidden', both in the content of their teachings and in the manner of gaining accessibility to them, because of their very nature. . . . These sciences in their unadulterated form . . . deal with the hidden forces with the cosmos and the means of dealing with these forces. In a traditional world, these sciences were kept hidden in order to protect society from their being used, or rather misused, by the unqualified, much like esotericism itself, of which they are branches. . . . Moreoover, in the light of the esoteric dimensions of the Quranic revelation, these science, some of purely Semitic origin and others inherited from the Hellenistic, Egyptian, Babylonian and Iranian worlds, become like shining stars in the firmament, providing so many keys for the contemplative understanding of the inner processes of the natural order.[31]

This, of course, is a pure statement of belief: a description of the Ismaili doctrine of gnosis. It also happens to be one of the two chapters in the book containing a section of modern practices; physics does not deserve one; astronomy does not deserve one; even the chapter on environment does not discuss the contemporary work done by Muslim environmentalists and architects; but occult sciences deserve an 'Islamic alchemy today' section![32]

Even in his bibliographical work, Nasr's only concern is to propagate his Ismaili and Guenon/Schuon theology of gnosis. Science is said to 'embrace nearly all the traditional "intellectual sciences" ' with the exception of 'those elements which are not related either to the world of nature or mathematics'. But it includes all branches of philosophy except 'practical philosophy such as ethics, politics', and all areas of Sufisim and theology, including magic, folk medical practices and popular occult sciences.[33] Thus, once again in the guise of Islamic science, we are treated to Ismaili philosophy and theology, writings of Ismaili occultists and works on occult and Hermetic subjects. As a purely bibliographical work this is simply third rate, for it fails to differentiate between fundamental and trivial works, books and pamphlets; gives no indication of whether the book contains any illustrations, indexes, bibliographies; provides no distinction between important authors and minor figures; contains hardly any annotations, virtually no mention of reviews; has a daft classification, countless errors; is a reservoir of misinformation and contains important omissions. However, I am not concerned here with the questionable merits of the bibliography (those interested in this can read Robert Hall's assessment of volume 1),[34] but more its ideological orientation.

Nasr is concerned with an intellectual space called 'Islamic science' that he wants to define according to his own perceptions and worldview, and ultimately to control, and shape its content. Thus the notion behind the bibliography is that if 'Islamic science in history' can be equated with Ismaili gnosis and Greek traditional cosmologies, then the contemporary debate on the subject can be focussed on this arena. Thus, to ensure that the student using the bibliography does not discover the real content and nature of Islamic science, Nasr does not provide entries for established basic works in the area. Thus, Fuat Sezgin's *Geschichte des arabischen Schrifttums* does not get an entry;[35] it is not possible for a scholar trained in the history of Islamic science to overlook the basic bibliographical tool for Muslim scholars to C.E. 1040. Also ignored is the *Dictionary of Scientific Biography* that contains the standard accounts of Muslim scientists, many by noted Muslim historians of science. Noted serial bibliographies, such as *Abstraca Islamica*, are not mentioned either. Moreover, to ensure the

prominence of his particular notions of Islamic science, Nasr describes
his own book *Science and Civilization in Islam* in grandiose terms and
cites every chapter and section of the book!

In volume 2 we are treated to a long section on Greek mythology
and philosophy where all the favourites—Plato, Pythagoras,
Aristotle—appear in a very selected form. When we move to individual sciences, we are treated to a real hotchpotch of mysticism and
occultism. Under mathematics and astronomy, for example, we find
entries on 'the problems of the souls of the spheres from the Byzantine
commentaries to Aristotle through the Arabs and St Thomas to
Kepler', 'Arabic transmission of science' and 'the mercury horoscope of Marcantonio Michiel of Venice'.[36] We even get a special
treatment of Near Eastern, Iranian, Indian and Chinese varieties of
mysticism and gnosis in the guise of mathematics, cosmology and
medicine. In case we still have not got the message, there is a special
section on cosmology and cosmography with 'specific problems' such
as angelology, light (out of ten citations in this section eight refer to
Henry Corbin, one to Louis Massignon—needless to say talking
about Ismaili gnosis, p. 278) and time–space.

So there we have it: anyone ploughing through *An Annotated Bibliography of Islamic Science* may be forgiven for believing that Islamic science is another name for Ismaili gnosis, Greek mystery religions and
the occult.

Both in his *Bibliography* and *Islamic Science*, Nasr makes what are
essentially side issues and ideas and, on the whole, unimportant, the
main focus and hence the norm of Islamic science. Even if one accepts
Nasr's ideas as 'Sufism', which I do not, we know that Sufism was not
the only trend, nor indeed the dominant trend, in Muslim intellectual
history. Nasr's treatment is like writing a history of sexuality in Muslim civilization and making homosexuality (and homosexuals certainly existed throughout Muslim history,) the dominant and normal
sexual behaviour! This would be the case if one were to read Greek
notions of love in Islam, since homosexuality played a major part both
in Greek society and thought.[37]

It is worth noting that in contrast Ahmad Y. al-Hassan and
Donald R. Hill in their recent work, *Islamic Technology: An Illustrated
History*, do not consider Hermeticism, Pythagorian numerical mysticism, the occult, magic, astrology and alchemy as part of Islamic
science even though one finds that they are discussing many of the
same scientists and their works, and intellectual developments and

trends. Also, al-Ghazzali, who was himself a Sufi, rejected all the magical, mystical construction, labelling them blameworthy knowledge. Of astrology, he writes:

> . . . astrology is purely guesswork. . . Pronouncements in connection with it are the result of ignorance. Consequently astrology has been pronounced blameworthy because of its ignorance, not because of its knowledge. The rare cases in which the astrologer happens to be correct are coincidences . . . . For this reason, even the strongest-minded person has been forbidden to (practise) astrology. . . . The most that can be said on its behalf is that it is, at its best, an intrusion into useless things and a waste of time and life which are man's most precious belongings.[38]

Let us now look at the theological and practical aspect of Nasr's programme for Islamic science. In his forthcoming book, *Philosophy of Islamic Science*, Nasr devotes an entire chapter to answering, 'What is Islamic science?'. We shall examine it point by point.[39]

1. 'To understand the nature of this science,' Nasr writes, 'it is important first of all to distinguish it from its application in the form of technology and even from the ethical implications of this science'.[40] To distinguish, of course, does not necessarily mean to divorce. But in his vast output, Nasr has never once discussed the ethical implications of Islamic science or its practical and applied applications. One is forced to conclude: Nasr's Islamic science is divorced from ethics and pragmatic concerns.

2. 'A science worthy of being called Islamic must reflect and lead to unity; it must not hide the interrelation of all things which is a reflection upon the level of multiplicity of unity but rather accent and reveal it.' 'Unity must also be reflected in any Islamic science through its awareness of unity as the divine principle and not only as the principle of integration and interrelation.'[41] A number of questions arise here. How does a science lead to unity? How does one avoid not hiding the interrelations of at least a few things?

Nasr's notion of unity is not what more conventional Muslims understand by *tawheed*, the unity of God. Nasr is talking about some sort of underlying metaphysical unity which does not distinguish between the Creator and the created; both are an extension of the same unity. Elsewhere, we get an explanation of it: 'the metaphysical knowledge of unity comprehends the theological one in both a figurative and literal sense, while the converse is not true'.[42] In other words,

126 Sardar: Explorations in Islamic Science

Nasr's metaphysics of unity is greater than religion itself, and as such it is clearly above our theological understanding of Islam. But if this unity does not distinguish between the Creator and created, then surely only a super-human person, or another deity, can claim not to 'hide interrelationships of all things'. Clearly an absurd assertion.

3. 'The concern of certain mathematical physicists in this century for mathematical symmetry and beauty, almost as scientific argument, represents a philosophy similar to this aspect of Islamic science except that Islamic science connotes invariably this mathematical harmony and beauty to the beauty of God and sees in this harmony an imprint of the wisdom of the Creator'.[43] And in the reference we read: 'This aspect of Islamic science resembles greatly the Pythagorean–Platonic tradition which Islam integrated so easily with its own worldview precisely because this was a wisdom based on unity and harmony, and therefore close to the perspective of Islam but not the cause of it.'[44] Why does Nasr insist on drawing parallels between the Islamic notion of unity and the Pythagorean–Platonic tradition? Because he sees the whole notion of unity in Pythagorean–Platonic terms. If, as the Pythagoreans believed, numbers correspond to heavenly activities, then by decoding these numbers scientists are discovering absolute reality. Thus Nasr believes in mathematics not as an instrument for solving problems, but as a magical system for removing the hidden veil of reality. What this literally means is that the Heisenberg Uncertainty Principle, Schrodinger's Equations, the Maxwell-Boltzmann Distribution, et cetera, reveal the beauty and reality of God!

4. More follows in the same vein: we are told that mathematical models must correspond to reality, largely because Ptolemy said so. 'In Islamic science this nexus between science and reality must exist. Science must correspond to some ontological aspect or aspects of what it studies. It cannot remain satisfied with mathematical models which can predict events and describe phenomena but which do not correspond to physical reality.'[45] Thus, in Islamic science mathematical models are not just tools but have one-to-one correspondence with reality. But this assumes two possibilities: first, that we *know* reality so that we are in a position to tell that the correspondence is exact; for example, we really have to know—as we know a chair or a cat—what are neutrinos, quarks and quantum waves and not just some of their properties. This is clearly an impossibility; and what this assertion does to the Heisenberg Uncertainty Principle I shudder to think. Second, as Parvez Manzoor points out 'the only kind of world that

submits itself to decodification by the ciphers of mathematics is the one that has been encoded so.' So if you believe that God has been writing equations in the heavens you will be on to a good thing. But this possibility also has an ironic side-effect in that it actually writes off God from the whole enterprise. Manzoor again: science 'posits, the existence of a world that is already amenable to mathematical codification and whose "essential" attributes are mathematical. The ultimate reality of science, therefore, is a physical universe that is devoid of any ultimate goal. The universe of mathematical ciphers is a universe without ethical purpose.'[46]

5. Furthermore, 'the goal of any science which can be characterized as being Islamic must be to study the nature of things, or some level of reality in its ontological sense and not only accidents and phenomena independent of substance and the noumena.'[47] So Islamic science is essentially an ontological enterprise, it deals with the nature of being and not with the physical, biological and material aspects of phenomena. It is a metaphysical and not a practical enterprise.

6. 'Conjecture and hypothesis must never be mistaken for science which, in the Islamic context, always implies certitude. There is a place in Islam for a "science" of the physical order which "grows" from the less exact to the more exact but this type of "science" which grows from the knower to the unknown must be subordinated to that highest science which is based on certitude and permanence.'[48] Does that mean that scientific activity should be guided by immutable and certain values? No. Since Nasr equates *ilm* (knowledge) with *al-haqqiqa* (the truth), it is the 'certitude and permanence' of *al-haqqiqa*, or rather the mystical experience of *al-haqqiqa* that becomes the prime mover of science. Such an endeavour has nothing to do with a problem-solving enterprise.

7. 'No science can claim to be Islamic which seeks to study the material universe independent of the higher levels of existence and as if it were an independent order of reality. Nor can a science be Islamic if it does not remain aware of the levels of consciousness and modes of knowing.'[49] How do you integrate 'higher modes of existence' in material phenomena? By ascribing them with symbolic, magical and occult properties, of course.

8. And finally to the crunch: 'Without hierarchy there is no Islamic science no matter how many pious assertions are made about studying nature as God's creation.'[50] One could reasonably assume that by hierarchy Nasr means classification of science to set priorities and

emphasis, to delineate what should be done first and establish an appropriate order for scientific work: solid state physics before high energy physics, diarrhoea research before cancer cures, food research before slimming diets. But one would be wrong. Nasr's obsession with hierarchy and that clear, precise declaration that 'without hierarchy there is no Islamic science' hides a deeper meaning. In Ismaili gnosis and Guenon/Schuon theology, hierarchy has a special significance: it is an integral part of Imamology and angelology. The Angelic world is structured in a strict hierarchy from the level of the Uppermost Heaven, the First Intelligence, the Natiq, who signifies the literal or esoteric statement of positive religion, to the Second Intelligence, the Heaven of the Fixed Stars, where the Asas provides the exegesis of the esoteric meaning, to the Third Intelligence, Heaven of Saturn, the domain of Imam, who has personal mastery over the community, and so on.[51] Accepting this hierarchy, therefore, signifies submitting to the appropriate level of intelligence. A science that submits to this hierarchy becomes subject to the esoteric interpretation of the Imam. Scientists therefore become the devotees of the Master and this is how their science acquires its ontological significance and the ultimate end of science becomes God. Thus, for Nasr, only that science is 'Islamic' which functions on the model of the Pythagorean cult, or a Platonic republic ruled by a master race of purified gnostics, or in a gnostic framework where all owe unqualified allegiance to the Master who gives it a purpose and direction: 'hierarchy also exists in the subject which studies the objective order. There are not only levels of reality to be studied but also levels of consciousness or modes of knowledge of a hierarchic nature capable of studying that objective reality. The Quran itself refers to the level of the soul ranging from the *nafs al-ammarah* to the *lawwamah*, *mutmainnah*, *radiyya* and *mardiyyah*. Likewise, it refers to levels of those who know, distinguishing between those who know and those who do not, and furthermore between those who are "firm in knowledge" (*al-rasikh-un fil-ilm*) and ordinary knower.'[52] Thus those who know the truth (*al-haqqiqa*), like Ismaili Imams, Guenonite Masters, practitioners of alchemy and other esoteric occultism, have a divine right to be accepted as Masters, give esoteric interpretation to science and scientific output, and lead the scientific community to the path of God.

A study of that aspect of Nasr's oeuvre related to his notion of Islamic science leads to the conclusion that he is a nowhere man, occupying a nowhere land: his discourse is neither about Islam, nor about science, but is a purely totalitarian enterprise.

Ground Control to Major Tom

So what do we actually learn from Nasr's discourse on Islamic science? Nasr is telling us that:

1. All religions, including secular worldviews such as Buddhism, are the same at a certain level of reality.
2. Pythagorian cult, neo-Platonism and other ancient esoteric mythologies are the basis of Islamic metaphysics.
3. The Zoroastrian notion of a world perpetually in battle between the forces of light and darkness is a part of the Islamic metaphysical system.
4. The Hindu notion of cyclic time, reincarnation and karma are also an integral part of the Islamic metaphysical system.
5. Gnostics are somehow superior beings who know the truth.
6. Islamic cosmology is essentially a combination of gnosticism and occultism.
7. The history of Islamic science is basically a history of astrology and magic, numerology and alchemy, sacred geography and geometry, gnosis and Greek mystical mythology.
8. Islamic science has nothing to do with the practical realm; it is a purely abstract form of mysticism.
9. Islamic science is divorced from ethics.
10. The goal of Islamic science is unity, but since this unity is so all pervasive that there is no distinction between the Creator and the created it is essentially an elusive goal.
11. Islamic science is the study of ontological reality.
12. Islamic science is hierarchal, which means that it must submit to the authority of the Gnostics and others who know the truth so that the correct esoteric interpretations can be given to Islamic science.

Following Feyerabend, we can say that this system of science is neither superior nor inferior to any other system of science. There are, however, certain social factors associated with this framework that ought to be appreciated. Apart from its Islamic gloss, and the fact that it is a confused, incoherent mixture, the underlying proposition of metaphysics is not entirely new. Throughout history, it has existed in one form or another; indeed, the fact that Nasr can borrow so easily from this ancient cult and that religious cosmology means that the bare bones of the framework have existed since the beginning of history. That it is not an expression of Islamic ideas and ideals should be evident; what may not be apparent is that throughout history, emergence of such gnostic frameworks of thought, and the authoritarianism and extremism which go with it, are associated with certain developments.

For example, the emergence in the late nineteenth century of the *volkisch* ideology in Germany and Austria owes a great deal to this type of metaphysical framework. This ideology emerged as a reactionary response to the problems of nationality and modernity and led to the theories of Aryan German racial excellence and eventually to the emergence of the Third Reich. Occultism was invoked to endorse the enduring validity of an obsolescent and precarious social order. The occultism that formed the basis of *volkisch* ideology, as Nicholas Goodrick-Clarke points out in his powerful and scholarly study, *The Occult Roots of Nazism*,[53] was based on Gnosticism, the Hermetic corpus, Pythagoreanism, neo-Platonism, the Hindu belief in reincarnation, karma and cyclic time, the Cabbala and religious trappings of Christianity. This lethal formula was turned by Helena Petrovna Blavatsky (d. 1891), a Russian occultist, into what came to be known as theosophy and became the foundation stone of Naziism. The founder of the Theosophical Society expressed the basic beliefs of her occult metaphysics in *The Secret Doctrine*. Goodrick-Clarke summarizes her metaphysics in three principles:

> Firstly, the fact of a God, who is omnipotent, eternal, boundless and immutable. . . . Secondly, the rule of periodicity, whereby all creation is subject to an endless cycle of destruction and rebirth . . . .Thirdly, there exists a fundamental unity between all individual souls and the deity, between the microcosm and the macrocosm. But it was hardly this plain theology that guaranteed theosophy its converts. Only the hazy promise of occult initiation shimmering through its countless quotations from ancient beliefs, lost apocryphal writings, and the traditional Gnostic and Hermetic sources of esoteric wisdom can account for the success of her doctrine and the size of her following amongst the educated classes of several countries.[54]

These ideas were adopted by German theosophists such as Guido von List, Jorg Lanz von Liebenfels, Rudolf von Sebottendorf and Karl Maria Wiligut, all practising occult gnostics; and it was these ideas which shaped the mythological mood of the Nazi era. Goodrick-

Clarke demonstrates convincingly that the desire to found a nation of pure Aryans *evolved directly* from the élitism and authoritarianism of gnosis.

In Muslim history itself, there are examples of gnostic totalitarian groups. An obvious example is the Ismaili Order of Assassins which, from the late eleventh to the closing quarter of the thirteenth century, freely and frequently carried out assassinations of their political opponents. The Assassins were organized into a hierarchial secret society and owed blind obedience to their gnostic head, the Grand Master. One of their first victims was the celebrated wazir, Nizam al-Mulk, who founded the famous Nazamiyyah Madrassah and library in 1065 in Baghdad.

The impact on the individual of authoritarianism and blind obedience in following the Master, inherent in Nasr's type of gnostic metaphysics, is quite devastating. It circumscribes thought within a fixed framework, thus introducing intellectual rigidity and killing creativity. The devotee is almost duty bound to limit his thought to the *oeuvre* of the Master and the Master's Master. An illustration of this is provided by Osman Bakr, a recent convert to Guenon/Schuon metaphysics. In 'The Question of Methodology in Islamic Science',[55] Bakr, allegedly presenting a work on Sufi metaphysics, quotes only from Schuon and Nasr despite the fact that he has been introduced to Sufism not by his current Guru, Nasr, but by his original teacher, Naquib al-Attas, whose output on Sufism is truly monumental, and who, no doubt, also introduced Bakr to works of original Sufi masters.[56] Because of the complete surrender of his mind to Guenonite philosophy, Bakr cannot see the contradiction and authoritarianism implicit in the metaphysics presented here. We are thus told that methodology only has meaning if it is related to the 'faculties of powers of discernment within man' (in other words, the hierarchal social structure that Guenonite gnostics wish to perpetuate). Why should methodology be a function of social structure? Clearly, a daft statement unless you believe that certain individuals are superior to others and by virtue of this superiority have access to certain (secret? occult?) methods which are not accessible to ordinary mortals. Bakr also tells us that 'Divine origins of creative ideas should not be denied; neither should the divine origins of that which sustains man be denied.' No Muslim will deny the divine origins of creative ideas; but what is meant by 'divine origins of that which sustains man'? Surely God sustains man; and He is clearly divine. Could it be the soul? No, Bakr is referring to something else (otherwise this statement is tautological): he is attributing divine origins to the hierarchal social structure that Guenonite gnosticism seeks. In other words, accept this hierarchy and become the devotee of my Guru for this is the only methodology that Islam allows. We are then told that the methodology of Islamic science is gnosis. But how can gnosis be a methodology? Bakr explains: 'What is implied here is a spiritual travel, a return of the soul to the divine origins. This is the basis of the purification of the soul, which is an integral part of the methodology of knowledge in Islam. This particular methodology has often been described as a higher form of empiricism. What is now the object of observation and "experimentation" is no longer the external object but the soul of the exprimental itself'.[57] So those engaged in Islamic science should base their work purely on gnosis and after each experiment have their souls checked by the Master of gnosis!

The true nature of Bakr's methodology comes to the fore when he tries to bring the Quran into the whole equation. 'The methodology of *tafsir* of the Holy Book, as it has been developed traditionally, including especially the method of linguistic analysis, must constitute an integral component of the overall methodology of Islamic science that is to be revived in the modern world. This is because the Book of nature is the macrocosmic counterpart of the Holy Quran.'[58] There is nothing wrong with using linguistic methodology to understand science: the suggestion is not as baffling as it sounds, for symbolism inherent in language is similar to that inherent in mathematics. But Bakr has something else in mind which becomes clear when *tafsir* ends and *tawil* begins: 'As applied to the Holy Book itself, where the method of *tafsir* ends that of *tawil* or hermeneutic interpretation refers to the knowledge of the inner meaning of the sacred text.'[59] In other words, Bakr wants to interpret the Quran, not according to the well laid out rules of *tafsir* or even that of Quranic linguistic analysis, but by the magical and alchemical notions of Hermiticism—we are back to the occult. This is taking Greek mythology right to the heart of Islam; if a non-Muslim had suggested this the entire Muslim world would be up in arms!

One of the duties of the devotees is to propagate the ideas and worldview of the Master. Here again, Bakr follows the path of true gnostics. *Critique of Evolutionary Theory*, a collection of essays edited by Bakr, is a tribute to the Guenonite contribution in this area and with one or two exceptions—put there for good measure and to make the whole exercise look more pluralistic—the essays are by noted members of the school. These essays do not present any arguments or evidence against evolution; they simply make statements of metaphysical beliefs. Bakr's own contribution reads like an undergraduate essay, which it is, and clearly demonstrates the circular and confined nature of his thought. Bakr opens his introduction with the assertion that the arguments against the theory of evolution have been suppressed by the scientific community. This allegation may have been true over two or three decades ago; there is now overwhelming evidence that scientists themselves have taken a stand against the theory of evolution; they have criticised it at length and deliberated upon the various perspectives offered by Charles Darwin—although Bakr is simply unaware of this. However, Bakr himself has included in this book an essay by W. R. Thompson, a noted Canadian biologist, which was published as an introduction to the 1958 edition of Darwin's *Origin of Species*. As the very first chapter of this book is a critique of the theory of evolution by a scientist, how can Bakr claim that scientists have tried to silence the critics of evolution? There is, however, truth in Bakr's assertion that the anti-evolutionary view 'is being maintained and upheld only by the non-scientific people, especially those who have their religious views and interest at stake.' How else could he justify his own totally non-scientific view of the theory of evolution, particularly when, from what the scientists are actually saying, he is quite incapable of differentiating between the popularly held myths about evolution? Almost all the essays in the book are obsolete with regard to the prevalent scientific view on the subject. The criticism of this theory within the scientific establishments is based on insights from contemporary knowledge of molecular genetics and not on the preliminary observations on taxonomy of this or that phylum. Had Bakr, instead of reading and re-reading Nasr, Schuon and other members of his gnostic circle, bothered to read Mary Midgley, Gillian Beer, a host of Marxist scholars and even committed Christians such as Alan Hayward, he would have been furnished with arguments and real evidence. But since the entire purpose of this absurd book is to promote the Guenonite worldview, understanding of scientific issues, getting the facts right and up-to-date are irrelevant matters. It is possible that Bakr does not know what he is saying or doing; after all gnosticism has a horribly damaging effect on the mind. I like to believe that.

Apart from the emergence of totalitarianism, suppression of

creativity and blind Guru worship, there is another factor connected with the rise of occult gnosticism: the decline and fall of civilizations. For example, a correlation has been noticed between the proliferation of gnostic and occult sects and the breakdown of the stable agricultural order of the Roman Empire.[60] Given the overall, extreme emphasis on other-worldly activities in occult esotericism, and the insistence on seeing the underlying reality of all physical and material phenomena, it is not surprising that it leads to the degeneration of the material world and the collapse of civilization. After all, since the beginning of time, no civilization has ever been built on occult gnosticism and its sciences of alchemy, astrology and numerology.

Look at All Those Lonely People

The positivist approach to science, however, has been spectacularly successful both in providing civilizations with military muscle and in changing the material world itself. The history of positivist ideas is as old as the history of Gnosticism: both have their origins in Greek philosophy and are part and parcel of the package labelled Western thought. Plato imagined a knowledge untainted by human interests, and Bacon believed he had discovered a method (induction) for attaining it. Similar hope for a true knowledge of reality greeted the discoveries of Galileo; from Galileo to our time is a short step in history. With the full weight of the Western intellectual tradition and its scientific establishment behind it, it is hardly surprising that most Muslim scientists subscribe to the positivist interpretation of science.

The position is exemplified by Jamal Mimouni in his reply to Anees's paper, 'What Islamic Science is Not'. Mimouni's criticisms are the standard since-science-is-neutral-objective-and-universal-what-sense-does-it-make-to-talk-about-Islamic-science   variety.[61] This empiricist's assumption that truth is amoral and facts are autonomous from value also runs throughout Abdus Salam's article on 'Islam and Science'.[62] In the first part of the article, Salam tries to prove that there is no contradiction between science and Islam, there are no real limitations to science, and that some areas in theoretical physics echo metaphysical preoccupations of earlier times: the underlying assumption being that science, particularly physics, from which most of his examples come, is an objective, value-free, neutral and universal enterprise.

This position is also held by scholars who passionately advocate an

Islamic alternative to science. Thus, while acknowledging that ideology is important in every activity, Ali Kettani states quite happily that we should not worry too much about 'values and ideology in science'.[63] The assumption is that the good in Western science is so good and so universal that it transcends ideological and value bias and that if science policy is tailor-made, science can take root in Muslim societies. Some positivists, while acknowledging that science does not reflect reality or truth, still hold firmly to the neutrality of science doctrine. For example, Z. R. El-Nejjar is content with introducing individual elements of piety and metaphysical beliefs while accepting science as it is—a position that introduces a dichotomy between individual beliefs and scientific notions.[64] In a survey I did over a decade ago of positions of Muslim scientists, el-Nejjar said that he was an evolutionist while inside the laboratory and a Muslim when he came out![65] But of all the positivist positions, S. Waqar A. Husaini exemplifies the most ambiguous and the most confused. Husaini's theses, which he has been putting forward for a decade now, centre around the notion of 'innovative–imitation': while Muslims are lagging behind in numerous other things, they are certainly not behind in imitation, for that is what they have done for the past two hundred years and no innovations have taken place. This is because imitation seldom leads to innovation, it yields to enslavement—a position clearly demonstrated by the Muslim world today. It is the belief in the neutrality and universalism of science and technology that led Husaini to the contradictory conclusion, in his *Islamic Environmental Systems Engineering*. In this, his only coherent work (indeed, some of his papers and pamphlets are so confused and full of contradictions that it will require papers two to three times their lengths to point them all out[66]), he states that while historically Islamic science and technology reveal unique characteristics and institutions, the present-day salvation lies in importing from an unIslamic tradition. Despite all the trappings of terminology, such as the consistent use of the *shariah* as an adjective, the underlying assumptions of Husaini are positivist, realist ones. Let me, then, briefly examine the positivist position to settle some of the issues and clarify certain others.

Over the last twenty years, philosophers and historians of science, sociologists and anthropologists of knowledge, and Marxist radicals and environmental activists have shown that the view of science as the pursuit of Platonic Objective Truth, divorced from values and morals, with the results of science being universally valid, to be patently false and misguided. Indeed, there is now so much literature on the subject that it is untenable, nay, naive, for a self-respecting scientist to hold this view. There are a number of ways to prove that science is not neutral, but a value-laden enterprise, and I shall give only the bare bones of the arguments, leaving the interested reader to pursue detailed references.

Observation

Most scientists argue that science starts with observation. From these observations, statements, bearing direct one to one relationship, are made. The singular statements are generalized into universal statements from which the theories and laws of science are derived. These universal laws and theories produce various consequences that serve as explanations and predictions.

There are a number of problems with this model. First, we do not just observe; we observe within a framework. Scientists do not just observe phenomena, they test theories. In other words, observation is theory-dependent; the analytical history of science shows that it is not observation that leads to theory but theory that leads to observation. So scientists look where the theory tells them to look. Moreover, observation is coloured with perception and often scientists see what they expect to see. Ian Mitroff proved this when he examined the perceptions, cherished theories and published results of those scientists who analysed lunar rocks brought back by Apollo 11. In almost all cases, these scientists found what they expected to find, leading Mitrof to conclude that scientific objectivity is nothing but a charade.[67]

Second, how do we get from a single statement about a phenomenon to universal statements? Proponents of this model would argue that, given certain conditions, it is a justified action to generalize from a finite list of observation statements to universal laws, or to take an inductive leap. This generates further problems, not least of which is that induction, as David Hume conclusively demonstrated two hundred years ago, is invalid. In *What is this thing called science?*, A. F. Chalmers illustrates the point by relating the story, attributed to Bertrand Russell, of the inductivist turkey.[68] On the first morning of its arrival at a turkey farm, our turkey was fed at 9 a.m. Being a good inductivist he did not jump to any conclusions from this single observation. But when he had collected a large number of observations of the fact that he was fed at 9 a.m. on different days of the week, under a wide range of circumstances, on rainy days, sunny days and so on, his inductive conscience was satisfied. He concluded: 'I am always fed at 9 a.m..' On Christmas Eve his conclusion was shown to be false when, instead of being fed, he had his throat cut. Inductive inferences with true premises can lead to false conclusions: logic does not justify induction. Moreover, past experience does not help much either. The argument that induction has been observed to work in the past, laws derived from it have been successfully used and tested, therefore it is legitimate to assume that induction is valid is also invalid: it is a circular argument, using induction to justify induction. The shift to the probability theory is also of little help: it is not possible to justify statements making universal claims about an infinite number of possible situations from a finite number of observation statements.

Thus, while on the one hand, it is untenable to see science as starting from statements that can be established as true or probably true in the light of given evidence, on the other, it is not difficult to show that scientific observation in science is selective and biased, coloured with the perception of scientists, and is normally focussed in a particular direction by the narrow confines of a theory.

Problems

An alternative approach for the 'science is objective truth' exponent would be to start from problems. Scientists work with problems associated with the behaviour of phenomena and propose falsifiable hypotheses which can be disproved. These conjectural hypotheses are than tested, critically examined and refuted. The weaker ones will be eliminated while the stronger ones are proved more successful. When an hypothesis which has successfully faced a whole range of stringent tests is falsified, new problems are produced which require new hypotheses and thus the whole scientific exterprise progresses. This is the 'objectivist' argument presented by Karl Popper in his monumental works, *The Logic of Scientific Discovery* and *Conjecture and Refutation*. A more sophisticated approach moves from absolute degrees of falsifiability, from the merits of individual theory, to focus on the relative merits of competing theories. Here again, the fact that observation statements are theory dependent and fallible undermines the whole objective enterprise of science. Chalmers sums up the argument against this position:

> If true observation statements are given, *then* it is possible to logically
> deduce from them the falsity of some universal statements, whereas it is not
> possible to deduce from them the truth of any universal statements. This is
> an unexceptional point, but it is a conditional one based on the assumption
> that perfectly secure observation statements are available. But they are not
> . . . all observation statements are fallible. Consequently, if a universal
> statement of a complex of universal statements constituting a theory or
> part of a theory clashes with some observation statement, it may be the
> observation statement that is at fault. Nothing in the logic of the situation
> requires that it should always be the theory that is rejected on the occasion
> of a clash with observation.[69]

Moreover, the history of science, despite Popper's repeated and
heroic attempts to prove otherwise, does not support the falsificationists. There are numerous instances when observation statements
have been rejected and the theory with which it clashed retained. For
example, naked eye observation that Venus does not change size
appreciably during the course of the year is inconsistent with the
Copernican theory and, therefore, was rejected and the theory
retained. Sometimes major clashes between theory and fact are
recognized, simply ignored and considered to be an unnecessary
interference with the process of research which then leads to important
discovery. This was the fate suffered by Kepler's and Decartes' rule
that an object viewed through a lens is perceived at the point of inter-
section of the rays travelling from the lens towards the eye. The rule
made a connection, and gave an empirical base, between theoretical
optics and vision. It applies that an object situated at the focus will be
seen infinitely far away. Borrow, Newton's teacher and predecessor,
refused to test the theory, announcing that his own ideas were 'manifestly agreeable to reason'.[70] T. S. Kuhn's *The Copernican Revolution*
demonstrates the difficulties that falsificationists face in proving their
claim,[71] and Paul Feyerabend's *Against Method* provides a host of
examples which undermine the falsificationist theses.

Falsification does not actually work in practice either. A typical
scientific theory consists of a whole complex of universal statements;
and when it is tested, further assumptions are added concerning the
actual techniques of the experiments, the laws and rules governing the
use of instruments, the experimental arrangements and so on. Now, if
an experiment set up to record an observation intended to disprove a
theory actually yielded the expected observation, then the only logical
conclusion would be that at least one of the assumptions, from the
whole complex of assumptions, is false. The observation does not

actually help us to identify the faulty assumption.

The falsificationist approach to defending the objectivity of science does not stand up to thorough criticism. Scientists do solve problems, but there is nothing in their enterprise that proves that they do it in an objective, neutral way.

Selection

Values make a major input when it comes to the selection process inherent in science. The problems that scientists select to work on are not chosen for altruistic reasons: they are chosen on the basis of expected benefits—economic returns, military goals, political expediency. The European Council for Nuclear Research, of which Salam speaks with glowing terms, exists not because European nations have some humanistic desire to promote theoretical physics, but because theoretical physics is essential if Europe is to acquire an edge over the rest of the world in nuclear might. The fact that much of the world's research and development budget is geared towards weapons research says a great deal about the ideological dimension of science. Considering the truly gigantic problems of food and famine, health and hygiene, disease and disasters that the people of the planet face, it would seem that most of the world's scientists should be working on these problems; yet four out of five scientists are working on some area of defence and weapons. This means that altruism and the pursuit of truth has little to do with science, but that military control and domination, and the associated rise of the military–industrial complex, everything.[72] Clearly certain values are directing science in a certain direction.

At the individual level also, selection is made on the basis of values. The clearest example of application of values and their subsequent suppression is in the teaching of science. The syllabus is presented to the students as though there were no choice of topics, nor any question of the correctness of the answer either. Yet all teachers know that scientific syllabuses are the results of acts of interpretation and selection. And the principles of selection are determined by considerations of feasibility and values. Similarly when individual scientists choose between problems, values come in; but not just values, also ego, peer pressure, political considerations (where is the funding coming from?) and personal preferences.

Even at the heart of scientific method itself, selection is made on the basis of values, and values are brought to the framing of the problems. To paraphrase Ravetz, in testing the correlation between two variables, one has to take account of the significance of the correlation being made. For a higher significant level, one would design a more rigorous test, with a large sample and lengthy, laborious and careful testing procedures. For a low significant level, one need not be so thorough and painstaking. But what decides the basis of significant levels? What errors can be ignored and what errors can lead to fatal results? If one were testing for something highly dangerous, one would naturally be more rigorous and painstaking; for something quite straightforward, one would not waste too much time and would save money on tests. But ultimately, what is important or dangerous, and what is not so important are decided by value criteria. Thus, even in 'quantitative techniques, we have value loadings put on, which derive from the intended functions of a result and which then shape the hard experimental quantitative work.'[73]

Pressure to save money often leads to expedient value judgements. If one were to ask a dozen nuclear physicists how much radiation an individual can sustain without damaging his or her health, one would get a dozen answers, and all would claim their answers to be experimentally proved scientific facts!

Facts and truths

Scientific realists believe that scientific facts, no matter how they are discovered, are in themselves amoral; there cannot be two views about a given fact. Since facts are a reflection of reality, putting any value connotation on them is quite meaningless.

How does an observation statement become a scientific fact? The transformation involves a social process. Scientific facts are not discovered, they are *constructed*. Every fact has a social history associated with it. For example, two decades ago the scientific community declared safe many substances it now declares poisonous or life-threatening. The pill was declared totally safe, now it is connected with breast cancer. Certain toxins and pesticides were established as safe, now they are declared dangerous. So it seems that these things were not poisonous twenty years ago, but they became so when scientists declared them to be so. Toxicity is thus socially defined. Scientific facts are created within a well-defined theoretical structure and a social process and have significance and meaning only within this structure and process. For example, the 'fact' that light behaves as a wave is conveniently forgotten in photovoltaic effects where it is treated as consisting of photons; but the 'fact' that it behaves as a particle is ignored in explaining the phenomenon of Newton's rings. The nature of calculations determines which 'fact' is regarded as 'fact'.

When we examine the evolution of scientific facts, the social process which goes into constructing them becomes evident. In *Laboratory Life: Social Construction of Scientific Facts*,[74] Bruno Latour and Steve Woolgan examine the detailed history of a single fact: the existence of Thyrotropin Releasing Factor (Harmone), or TRF(H) for short. The existence of TRF(H) is now an established fact; it started with the statement in 1962 that 'the brain controls thyrotropin secretion', to the statement in 1969 that 'TRF(H) is Pyro-Glu-His-Pro-NH2'. To begin with, TRF(H) has meaning and significance according to the context in which it is used: it has a different significance for medical doctors, for endocrinologists, for researchers and graduate students who use it as a tool in setting up bioassays, for a group of specialists who have spent their entire professional career studying it and for whom TRH represents a subfield. But outside this network TRH does not exist. The history of TRH involves many values and choices, including the funding for the project and the crucial moments during the project when it was about to be cut off; choice of strategy involved in the decision to obtain the chemical structure; the imposition of the fourteen criteria which had to be accepted before the existence of a new releasing factor could be accepted; the personalities of the two rival groups in the field and the dispute between them over priority; the dispute over the name of the substance (TRF or TRH); the doubts over the peptidic nature of TRF; and finally, the use of mass spectrometry, which introduced an ontological change in the research and put an end to the dispute. The story of TRH is best told in the words of Latour and Woolgar:

> From their initial inception, members of the laboratory are unable to determine whether statements are true or false, objective or subjective, highly likely or quite probable. While the agonistic process is raging, modalities are constantly added, dropped, inverted or modified. Once the statement begins to stabilize, however, an important change takes place. The *statement becomes a split entity*. On the one hand, it is a set of words which represent a statement about an object. On the other hand, it corresponds to an object in itself which takes on a life of its own. It is as if the original statement had projected a virtual image which exists outside the statement.

Previously scientists were dealing with statements. At the point of stabilization, however, there appear to be both objects and statements about these objects. Before long more and more reality is attributed to the object and less and less to the statement about the object. Consequently, an inversion takes place: the object becomes the reason why the statement was formulated in the first place. At the outset of stabilization, the object was the virtual image of the statement; subsequently, the statement becomes the mirror image of the reality 'out there'. Thus the justification for the statement 'TRF(H) is Pyro-Glu-His-Pro-NH2' is simply that TRF really is Pyro-Glu-His-Pro-NH2. At the same time the past becomes inverted. TRF has been there all along, just waiting to be revealed for all to see. The history of its construction is also transformed from this new vantage point: the process of construction is turned into the pursuit of a single path which led inevitably to the 'actual' structure.[75]

But how do Latour and Woolgar counter the argument that the transformation of statement into fact is itself determined by the 'real TRF' which was there all along, simply waiting to be discovered, since 1969? They point out that this transformation of statement into fact is reversible: that is, reality can also be deconstructed:

TRF may yet turn out to be an artefact. For example, no arguments have yet been advanced which are accepted as proof that TRF is present in the body as Pyro-Glu-His-Pro-NH2 in 'physiological significant' amounts. Although it is accepted that synthetic Pyro-Glu-His-Pro-NH2 is active in assays, it has not yet been possible to measure it in the body. The negative findings of attempts to establish the physiological significance of TRF have thus far been attributed to the insensitivity of the assays being used rather than to the possibility that TRF is an artefact. But some further slight change in context may yet favour the selection of an alternative interpretation and the realization of this latter possibility.[76]

The unavoidable conclusion is that reality cannot be used to explain why a statement becomes a fact, since it is only after a fact has been constructed that the effect of reality is obtained.

The notion that facts are a reflection of some reality out there is increasingly coming under question. The ideas that if phenomena can be described in mathematical terms they must correspond to some reality is now proving to be fallacious. Does the mu-meson actually exist in reality or is it simply a mathematical construct that works in certain models? The weight of evidence is towards the latter interpretation.

Science uses two types of laws: phenomenological and theoretical; the distinction is rooted in epistemology. Phenomenological laws are things which we can, at least in principle, observe directly, whereas theoretical laws can only be known by inference. Theoretical laws are supposed to explain phenomenological laws; and physicists have transformed theoretical laws to fundamental laws, the assumption being that they describe some basic reality in nature. In science, phenomenological laws are meant to describe and they succeed reasonably well; but fundamental equations are meant to explain, and paradoxically enough, the cost of explanatory power is descriptive adequacy. Really powerful explanatory laws of the sort found in theoretical physics do not state the truth. But the explanatory power of fundamental laws does not argue for their truth; in fact, the way they are used in explanation confirms their falsehood. As Nancy Cartwright, the Stanford physicist and philosopher demonstrates in *How the Laws of Physics Lie*, 'we explain by *ceteris paribus* laws, by composition of causes, and by approximations that improve on what the fundamental laws dictate. In all these cases the fundamental laws patently do not get the facts right.'[77] Whenever theory tests reality, a host of approximations and adjustments are required, and as such, 'the application of laws to reality by a series of *ad verum* approximations argues for their falsehood, not their truth'.[78] The so-called fundamental laws of science do not govern objects in reality, they govern only objects in models—and the models are an artificial construction for the sake of convenience.

Both the 'facts' of science and the 'truth' they are supposed to express are socially constructed and manufactured entities. All attempts to argue against this position have come to naught: the shifting of ground by the positivists to argue that science only 'corresponds' to truth, the so-called 'correspondence theory of truth', and its further retreat to the 'approximation to the truth' theory, have not stood the test of logic. Values, it seems, are deeply ingrained in the facts, truths and laws of science and no attempt to ostracize them appears to be fruitful. Indeed, the distinction between facts and values is purely arbitrary, as an entity can shift from side to side in different formulations and sociological conditions. Any 'truth' of science can become an arch value as can be seen in sociobiology[79]; and any value can be transformed into a fact. Consider the complex transformation of a category like essence which in theology is a basic value; it is transformed into a fact in modern axiologies that insist on autonomy of value with respect to all metaphysical-structural elements. As long as every form of existence is seen as serving to express its essence, the essence has a guiding role; it is a value. But the theory of evolution destroys this status of essence; it simply becomes the pattern that happens to be hammered out, so the nature of things ceases to be registered as self-justifying; essence now becomes a fact. Scientific 'facts' and 'truths' are like cows. They are not something we can take for granted as the solid rock upon which knowledge is built. Their nature is impregnated with values and is rather problematic—so much so that any serious confrontation scares them off. Like cows, they have become sufficiently domesticated to deal with mundane, run-of-the-mill events. This means, as radical Marxist scholars have been arguing for decades, that science itself is nothing but social relations.[80]

Method

Science's claim to objectivity is based to a very large extent on its method. Scientific method, the positivists claim, is a detached, clinical and universal mode of inquiry based on reason and devoted to unearthing the truth. As is evident from the previous sections on observation, problems, selection and, facts and truth, scientific method is a myth. If one were to go into a laboratory where this method is allegedly in operation, what would one see? When Karin Knorr-Cetina, an anthropologist, studied scientists—as one would study a tribe—working in the laboratory, she was surprised by what she saw. To discover the scientific method in action, she writes that 'we have had to go into the laboratory and observe the process of knowledge production. In view of the opportunistic logic we found at work in process, ''scientific method'' can be seen as a locally situated, locally proliferating form of practice, rather than a paradigm of non-local universality. It is context-impregnated, rather than context-free. And it can be seen as rooted in a site of local social action, just as other forms of social life are.'[81] Laboratory observations, therefore, do not support a neutral, value-free method; neither does the history of science. We find that every rule of the idealized scientific method is broken at one time or another; indeed, during crucial moments in history, science has advanced not because of its rational but because of its irrational methods. For example, the phenomena that Galileo observed through a telescope could only be explained theoretically with Kepler's theory of vision. But Galileo rejects this theory on the simplest of possible evidence. It is his observation of Mars, which when seen through the telescope does change as Copernican theory

predicts, rather than any deep understanding of cosmology or optics
that Galileo approves of in Copernicus. Galileo wins the day 'because
of his style and his clever techniques of persuasion, because he writes
in Italian rather than Latin, and because he appeals to people who are
temperamentally opposed to the old ideas and the standard of learning
connected with them.'[82] Both the history of science and the contemporary anthropology of knowledge show that the method of science is
'anything goes'.

When Thomas Kuhn surveyed the history of science, he discovered
that two alternative kinds of methodologies were at work. A great
many scientists were engaged in refining scientific ideas within a very
rigid framework of accepted beliefs and patterns. This he described as
normal science, and the framework of fundamental beliefs and
accepted framework he termed paradigm. When normal science is
dominant, the paradigm remains inviolate. However, eventually the
paradigm ceases to yield interesting questions, and problems arise
which, after repeated efforts, cannot be explained by the paradigm. A
crisis begins to develop which forces some scientists to question the
paradigm itself; thus revolutionary science takes over. A number of
different paradigms mushroom, all of which threaten the validity of
much of the work done under normal science. Naturally, this is
resisted by those whose life work faces extinction. Revolutionary
science is short-lived. Alternative paradigms are mercilessly attacked;
eventually a dominant paradigm emerges and a time comes when, for
a scientist to remain a scientist, he or she must subscribe to the new
paradigm. The new paradigm then becomes the foundation of a new
normal science. This continues until the new paradigm is again
threatened by irreconcilable evidence. The process repeats itself. The
selection of the new paradigm during the revolutionary phase is not
free from the political, personal and partisan considerations of scientists, because, in the final analysis, there is no test which enables
individual scientists to select from competing paradigms, for they are,
to use Kuhn's term, 'incommensurable'.

As many positivists have claimed, this analysis hits at the very
foundation of science. If scientists can only choose between competing
paradigms on the basis of personal and partisan criteria, the whole
notion of an objective, value-free science falls to the ground. If there
is a method in science, it is acceptance of the beliefs, practices
and techniques of the dominant paradigm, and solving problems and
puzzles, by any means necessary, within the paradigm.

The Structure of Scientific Revolutions begins with the words 'history, if viewed as a repository for more than anecdote or chronology, could produce decisive transformation in the image of science by which we are not possessed'[83] and ends with the extinction of the following notions:

Realism   that science is an attempt to find out about one real world; that truths about the world are true regardless of what people think; that the truth of science reflects some aspect of reality.

Demarcation   that there is a sharp distinction between scientific theories and other kinds of belief systems.

Cumulation   that science is cumulative and builds on what is already known, Einstein being a generalization of Newton.

Observation–theory distinction   that there is a fairly sharp contrast between reports of observation and statements of theory.

Foundations   that observation and experiment provide the foundations for and justification of hypothesis and theories.

Deductive structure of theories   that tests of theories proceed by deducing observation–reports from theoretical postulates.

Precision   that scientific concepts are rather precise and the terms used in science have fixed meanings.

Justification and discovery   that there is a context of justification and a context of discovery, and we should distinguish the psychological or social circumstances in which a discovery is made from the logical basis for justifying belief in facts that have been discovered.

The unity of science   that there should be one science about the one real world; less profound sciences are reducible to more profound ones, psychology is reducible to biology, biology to chemistry, chemistry to physics.[84]

All this makes those, who still believe and argue for the bygone positivist doctrine of science as a universal, objective pursuit of the truth which is divorced from values, very lonely people. The philosophy of science has proved their position to be a total fallacy; the history of science shows their claims to be spurious; sociologists of knowledge have pulled the rug of scientism from under their feet by revealing that their edifice is based purely on a belief system; anthropologists of knowledge have demonstrated that science far from being an enterprise of discovery is in fact a manufacturing process based on an opportunist logic; and archeologists of knowledge have shown that all knowledge is essentially politics and that truth does not exist outside power. Kuhn slew the notion of value-free, neutral, universal science; Feyerabend buried the corpse. Anyone who holds this view believes in a dead ideal.

I Should Have Known Better

The Aligarh school certainly does not hold this view, as a number of their writings indicate. Their work has been concerned with methodology and criticism of various positions of Islamic science. Zaki Kirmani, for example, argues that Islamic science exists in a specific conceptual framework and states the position of the group in these words:

> When science and technology grow in the perspective developed by *ilm* and *taskheer* a unique blend of 'ethics' and 'knowledge' becomes a reality. Islamic science is therefore simultaneously both science and ethics. If for practical purposes, science is considered as a systematic study of matter and material phenomena and is carried out with the help of sense perception then Islamic science can be characterized as a study conducted with a view to understanding and applying Allah's will. However, if one thinks that an addition of a code of ethics to modern science will be sufficient to make it Islamic it will be gross misunderstanding on (one's) part. In fact, method, techniques and philosophy of Islamic science stem from the Islamic framework and its epistemology. Thus it is the Islamic epistemology which distinguishes Islamic science from other scientific tradition.[85]

Much of the group's work has attempted to relate Islamic ethics to science; not surprisingly, this has meant a focus on methodology.

Rais Ahmad, for example, has produced an interesting critique of reductionism which essentially argues that reduction can only be avoided by a drastic change in worldview and epistemology;[86] in other words, given the assumptions of Western science, reductionism will continue unabated. In another paper, he argues that Islamic methodology comprises three elements: the already acquired knowledge that helps formulate questions; the process of study adopted by a researcher to solve these problems; and the criteria used to verify and validate the conclusions. In the 'already acquired' category he includes revelation as well as knowledge acquired by sense perception. He states that the Quran emphasizes the proper use of sense organs, but unfortunately does not tell us what this 'proper' use is. On research methods he puts no restrictions, but argues that the conclusions should be subjected to verification of the teachings of the Quran. 'To limit the conclusions of a scientific study in this way is obviously to contradict the basic spirit of science and one may object to it. But as science is the study of matter and natural phenomena one of its objectives is to study the purpose of the material world and the occurrences of the natural phenomena.'[87] This conclusion is open to two criticisms: it attributes ontological properties to science (how can science study the purpose of the world?), and even if science does study the purpose of the world, the assertion still does not meet the objection that one is putting limits to science. The dilemma arises from Ahmad's formulation of methodology: only if one works on non-problems or problems that arise outside the epistemological framework of Islam or social needs of the Muslims, would one produce results that will contradict the Quranic framework.

Riaz Kirmani's attempts to tackle the questions of Islamic methodology have been more fruitful. In 'Quranic Method of Enquiry',[88] he outlines the standard approach to knowledge in Islam, its basis being revelation, *taqwa* (which is 'a particular attitude of man towards cosmic phenomena, social phenomena not excluded'), spiritual methods such as intuition and inspiration, history, observation, reason and inference and experimentation. He quickly moves, in 'Structure of Islamic Science', to develop a paradigmic system for Islamic science. There is a problem with the whole concept of 'paradigm': it contains the notion of change in beliefs and value systems. Kirmani overcomes this problem by introducing the notion of absolute macro- and micro-paradigms as well as the idea of absolute hint paradigms. While, Kirmani's formulation of absolute hint-paradigms needs to be investigated much more thoroughly, his formulation of absolute macro- and micro-paradigms are much more specific and clearly point towards a research programme that can be undertaken. For example, Kirmani states that the absolute micro-paradigms for physical science and cosmology are, respectively: perfect cause and effect relationships are known to Allah alone, and there is a role of complementarity in the cosmos. These statements immediately liberate science from the imposed burden of the pursuit of ultimate truth while at the same time suggesting that Muslim physicists could be profitably looking for complementarity and correspondence in micro and macro phenomena.

However, when it comes to applying his framework to practical problems, Kirmani totally fails to cope. In 'Islamic Science on Production and Administration Plane' Kirmani applies the formulation of absolute macro-paradigm to study the production process and the structure of research organizations within the framework of Islamic science. He uses the Quranic concepts of *tawheed, ibadah, khilafah* and *akhirah* as analytical tools.

> The concept of *tawheed* forbids man from developing technologies which may endanger the unitary and ecological functioning of the cosmos. The scientific activity if considered to be an act of *ibadah*, serves to raise its status into a more venerable activity than a mere problem-solving exercise. It also develops a consciousness to participate only in those activities which serve to please the Creator. And God is pleased only with those activities which are good and useful to mankind. Moreover, the concept of *ibadah* is also consistent with the fact of the obedience of the entire cosmos to its Creator. Besides providing stimulation for the study of the cosmic phenomena, the concept of *khilafah* defines man as a trustee of Allah and guardian of nature rather than an irresponsible master of the universe. *Akhirah* serves to inspire man to endeavour to eliminate undesirable ego that usually grows with his predominately earthly attitude to life.[89]

So we are set to delineate the nature of the kind of production technologies that would come within the purview of Islamic science and which could usefully be promoted in Muslim countries. But instead, Kirmani begins to question the relevance of conceptual categories that the Ijmalis have used to pin down a viable notion of Islamic science. First of all he criticizes us for not using the concept of *akhirah*. Correct! But just because we have not used *akhirah* as an analytical category does not mean that others cannot use it; indeed, the Ijmalis have only used a handful of concepts from the Quran and the Shariah; there are numerous others that ought to be used and, no doubt, will be used. Then, Kirmani singles out the concepts of *halal* and *haram, adl* and *zulm*, and *ilm* and *istislah*, and argues that:

> These concepts despite being couched in languages which have not served as a medium for Islamic work done hitherto, are already known to scientists. Language does make things more intelligible and consequently enhances the profoundity of effect, but simple replacement of English or for that matter German words by their Arabic equivalents cannot possibly bring out any radical change. This point apart, there are at least two more important grounds which render these concepts less forceful for production research. Firstly the concepts are reductionist and secondly their prediction value is zero. They are reductionist because the decisions arrived at the bases of these concepts—against or in favour of production research—

have to be taken separately regarding the production of an individual article. By zero prediction value, we mean that these concepts do not foretell anything about the kind of products that have to come under their jurisdiction. Only a long and continuous experience of scientific produce tells us about their benefits and hazards. A large number of products of medicine, pesticide, fertilizer, fabric, cosmetic technologies, and technologies other than these may be quoted. They were, in fact, first strongly recommended but finally rejected by scientists themselves. Islamic science requires more comprehensive, organismic and predictive values on the production plane.[90]

Wrong on all three counts. The concept of *haram*, for example, is not known to Western scientists: if science is considered as the rational pursuit of truth, then everything is permitted; as Feyerabend tells us, the method of science is 'anything goes'. Furthermore, these concepts are not reductive. While they may help in reductive analysis they are *distributive*; that is to say, they operate across a whole spectrum of disciplines and shape synthesis. For example, we can use the concept of *adl* and *zulm* to see if certain agricultural practices promote one or the other. A detailed study in this field (asking such questions as: do these practices increase production? Are these increases at the expense of peasant farmers? What impact do they have on the environment? Do they lead to individual, local or national self-sufficiency or do they induce dependency? And so on.) can lead to the synthesis of a more Islamically appropriate policy. Similarly, they can settle the questions of scientific methodology: do certain experimental techniques lead to *zulm* on animals? Where does reduction become meaningless and pursuit of knowledge cease to be an *ibadah*? Is a particularly expensive methodology being used at the expense of *istislah*? Finally, they do have a strong predictive value. If they can predict the direction of a particular policy, decide between what is desirable and what is not, point out that certain methods, processes, techniques, technologies and policies could be beneficial or harmful they certainly have a high predictive value.

Following Gulzar Haider, Kirmani prefers to use the concept of *taqwa* which he himself admits has 'no predictive value of its own [but] its precautionary value is of immense importance'. Kirmani is wrong here, too, as Haider amply demonstrates in the construction of an Islamic theory of environment.[91] So how does Kirmani intend to solve the problem of generating predictive concepts? To solve the problem of prediction, Kirmani develops three principles of 'naturality' which are said to have a predictive value. But immediately after these principles are stated, it is declared that at least two (or three) 'have no predictive importance of their own'!

Kirmani then moves on to the organization of research in an Islamic framework. He declares that science has ceased to be an individual activity and is now an organizational function; and ultimately, Islamic science will unite research organizations with the state. But this is largely how science is structured; certainly in all of the Third World and also in the industrialized countries where multinational corporations also play a large part in the production of science. The whole exercise seems hardly worth bothering about. It will be the 'wisdom of the personnel' which will guide research, which is what science claims today. No matter how much wisdom, how much *taqwa* individuals claim to have, they are always prone to corruption. This is precisely why distributive concepts like *adl* and *istislah* are needed to place social and societal checks on the development of science. Kirmani further states that 'to bring about efficiency in the administration, it is necessary that one should not impose restrictions from outside (i.e. state level) that may impede the process of inquiry and block the growth of knowledge'.[92] But how will this be possible when all research is in the hands of the state in the first place? Back to the drawing board!

In his 'Preface to Islamic Science', M. Kaleemur Rahman points out that Muslims have not done justice to the art of criticism; and that includes their own history. Muslims have uncritically accepted the whole of their history as Islamic, when despotism and injustice, suppression of knowledge and authoritarian rule has been widespread in the Muslim civilization. This is indeed true; we need to look at our history much more critically and shift what is genuinely Islamic and what is mere *zulm* and error.[93] This is particularly the case with the history of Islamic science and philosophy, which needs to be studied from the perspective of the epistemology of Islam. In the classical period, *falsifa* was essentially Greek philosophy; there was no other philosophy about. This was why al-Ghazzali attacked *falsifa* with such formidable power: he was in fact dethroning Greek philosophy from the position it had been given by Muslim philosophers like al-Farabi. Before we accept uncritically the works of ibn Sina, Mulla Sadra and ibn Rushd as major contributions to Islamic thought, we ought to analyze them from the perspective of the worldview of Islam. Such an exercise will also help us develop a more thorough Islamic critique of modern science. As Manzoor has said, 'All Islamic critique of modern science as a social theory is the problem of *zulm* in history';[94] and we ought to be aware of *zulm* in our own history.

But at the same time, as I pointed out in the previous critique of Nasr's contribution to the history of Islamic science, we should not perpetrate *zulm* against our own history either. We should not present what is minor as a major development, what is a side issue as a norm, and what is only a single trend of thought in a profusion of intellectual activity as the only strand of thought; or wrongfully attribute discoveries in a partisan manner, or wrongfully promote one nationality at the expense of another. Unfortunately, the only concrete example that Rahman gives is unjust and wrong even though it is attributed to ibn Khaldun.

The example in question concerns Seyyidna Umar's letter to Saad-Abi Waqqas, instructing him to destroy large quantities of books and scientific papers he had come across in Persia. Umar is reported to have said: 'Throw them into the water. If what they contain is right guidance, God has given us better guidance. If it is in error, God has protected us against it.'

First, the following questions arise: is it possible for a man who had witnessed the revelation of God, when he is repeatedly asked to seek and respect knowledge, to issue such instructions? Is it possible for a man who was among the first to become a Muslim and who was one of the most trusted companions of the Prophet, who had said that one should go even as far as China to seek knowledge, to present such an attitude to knowledge? The story is utterly groundless and was proved so over fifty years ago (even if it keeps cropping up) by the American library historian Ruth Stellhorn Mackensen, who points a finger towards other quarters:

> Possibly the story arose among a group of scholarly but heretical Moslems who greatly admired the remnants of Greek learning but regretted that so few survived and, at the same time had little use for the early caliphs. One can quite well imagine such among the ranks of Ismaili savants who frequented the courts of the Fatimids, whose heretical caliphate in Egypt was brought to an end by Saladin in 567/1171. As partisans of the house of Ali, whom they believed was foully prevented from succeeding Mohammad as the true head of the Moslem state, they should have felt no scruples against representing Umar and his envoy as ignorant vandals. We know that the academy and library founded and supported by the Fatimid caliphs at Cairo was definitely modeled on the Museum or Serapium and there sciences, of Greek origins, and literature were cultivated along with strictly

religious studies. This institution was closed by Saladin and the books from its library were scattered all over Egypt and Syria. Or is it too far-fetched to imagine that the story may be no older than this event and took form as a protest or a bit of literary revenge on the part of some deposed scholar of the Fatimid House of Science?[95]

After uncritically citing ibn Khaldun, Rahman takes me to task for formulating my norms of Western and Islamic science 'in haste'[96] and says 'he has grouped faith in rationality in the norms of Western science . . . but Islamic science does not reject rationality. . . . 'The interdisciplinary and multidisciplinary work has become a fashion in modern science. Therefore, in this context the categorization of Sardar is unsatisfactory. . . . Sardar has included neutrality as a norm for Western science which in the contemporary sense does not find ground. It is now known that Western science or so-called secular sciences are not value-neutral.'[97] Of Munawar Ahmad Anees, Rahman claims, 'Anees advocates methodological freedom for Islamic science but does not consider the reductive method for Islamic science. To assume that reductive method is always harmful is an error.'[98]

These criticisms do not reveal a proper reading of Ijmali output. Let me make the points clear. Western science, or more appropriately a very large proportion of those who practise it, believes in rationality as the only method of inquiry; we believe in revelation but consider rationality as a viable, indeed, an important tool of studying science. The distinction is between 'belief' and 'tool'. Furthermore, it is not true to say that 'interdisciplinary and multidisciplinary work has become a fashion in modern science'; in fact those who are truly doing interdisciplinary work can be counted on the fingers on one hand. Rahman makes an attempt at counting them but misses a few important figures: 'David Bohm, Ilya Prigogine, Rupert Sheldrake and Karl Pribram have given new dimensions to Western science and have shifted the emphasis of the emerging science of wholeness from epistemology to experiment'. But even if interdisciplinary work has become a fashion this does not negate my categories, for as Rahman points out, this work may introduce 'some changes in the present framework and values but by and large the worldview would remain Western'. (See my criticism of their work further on). I am suggesting interdisciplinary work should be done within the worldview of Islam, quite a different enterprise. When it comes to Rahman's assertion that I am claiming that Western science is neutral, well, I should have known better. I was the first Muslim intellectual to argue that Western science is value-laden,[99] then, as now, I am saying that Western science claims the norm of neutrality for itself; but intellectuals like myself and Rahman are not fooled. And finally to Rahman's criticism of Anees: of course, reduction is a viable methodology and in certain areas one cannot do without it. What Anees is attacking is the fact that reduction has been turned into an overriding, omnipotent methodology, especially in physics and biology, where the Western scientific establishment appreciates no limits to reduction.

We Have Only Just Begun

So what is the Ijmali position among all this? From my criticism of Nasr and the positivist thought, it is obvious that the Ijmalis do not equate Islamic science either with Greek gnosis or with neutrality and truth. The formidable arguments and evidence brought against the positivist, realist view of science not only spell the end of positivism, but also write off much of Platonian and Aristotelian epistemology. This may generate problems for those theological positions which draw sustenance from Greek philosophy and metaphysics, but it is good news for the worldview of Islam.

As I stated earlier, *falsifa* was essentially Greek philosophy; and al-Ghazzali realized that it was intrinsically un-Islamic. He was disturbed by the attribution of divine qualities to Plato, and attacked the followers of Greek epistemology and metaphysics as heretics:

> The heretics of our time have heard the awe-inspiring names of people like Socrates, Hippocrates, Plato, Aristotle, etc. They have been deceived by the exaggerations made by the followers of these philosophers— exaggerations to the effect that the ancient masters possessed extraordinary intellectual powers: that the principles they have discovered are unquestionable: that the mathematical, logical, physical and metaphysical sciences developed by them are the most profound: that their excellent intelligence justifies bold attempts to discover the Hidden Things by deductive methods; and with all the subtlety of their intelligence and the originality of their accomplishments they repudiated the authority of the religious laws: denied the validity of the positive contents of historical religions.[100]

Al-Ghazzali rightly believed that even though some of their beliefs were justified, 'they slipped into error and falsehood'; he was willing, however, to recognize 'the solid achievements which lie beneath the repulsive facade of their thought'.[101]

The Ijmali position is similar to that of al-Ghazzali. The propagandists for science, just like the propagandists for Greek philosophers, have attributed to science things which are beyond its abilities and scope. While we do not, indeed cannot, deny the solid achievements of modern science, we emphasize the 'repulsive facade' of its metaphysical trappings, the arrogance and violence inherent in its methodology, and the ideology of domination and control which has become its hallmark.

However, it would be wrong to assume from this that the Ijmalis are simply Kuhnian; we neither sanction the extreme relativism of Kuhn, nor the anarchistic epistemology of Feyerabend; neither do we support the class-based science of radical Marxists, or a science based on 'evolutionary epistemologies' of the new schools—we do, however, appreciate the positive contribution of each and learn from their expositions, just as we have learned from the positivist interpretation of science. But we do, even though we have only just begun, have a unique position of our own which is derived solely from the ethical, value and conceptual parameters of Islam. The essence of Ijmali thought is *reconstruction, complexicity* and *interconnection*, or what Riaz Kirmani has called complementarity.

Just as we have argued that the Muslim civilization itself has to be reconstructed,[102] and have made efforts to reconstruct a contemporary Islamic theory of environment[103] and areas of knowledge such as Islamic anthropology,[104] so a contemporary Islamic science must be reconstructed. The basic tools for this reconstruction are the eternal concepts of the Quran and Shariah at our disposal, what is genuinely Islamic in our tradition and history, and what we can synthesize and creatively assimilate[105] from the fruitful products of Western science and technology. In this sense, the Ijmalis are neither willing to write off Islamic history and tradition nor to reinvent the wheel.

But the hallmark of the world that we inherit is complexity and interconnection. Nothing amenable to simple, linear, one-dimensional solutions, or black and white metaphysics. There is nothing in the complex web of problems that we face that can instantly and once and for all be solved by further injections of positivist science or by sprinkling the magic from the Hermetic corpus. The mechanical properties of linear cause and effect—like a piano, if you depress a certain key, a certain note is struck every time—may work for a rather simple system but are of little use in complex environments.

In complex systems, the components do not have fixed properties. Moreover, each component changes with time, partly as a result of the learning processes through these interactions. Complexity and multi-dimensional interactions change and obscure cause–effect relationships. In complex environments solutions have to operate on several levels, especially when everything appears to be connected to everything else. Moreover, the past no longer becomes a sure guide to the future. If expectations are repeatedly frustrated, we lose confidence in the validity of our judgement, in our ability to solve problems and in the very processes of structuring reality. Let me explain this further by delineating the Ijmali position vis-á-vis positivism, relativism, the Marxist position on science, the gnostic notion of science, and the thought of the new paradigm and epistemological schools.

Positivism

The Ijmali objection to positivism is that perceptions are not neutral, unequivocal reflections of reality, but depend on non-empirical conceptual categories that are indeed subjective. Thus to talk about neutral, value-free, universal science makes little sense, particularly when we cannot find this category of science in history or in the laboratory, nor see them in the facts and laws of science. As Chalmers puts it, 'there is in general no category 'science' and no concept of truth which is up to the task of characterizing science as a search for truth'.[106] Thus to raise science above values and morals, to try to overlook the ideology inherent in it, is absurd.

Quite apart from epistemological considerations, there is a clear paradox in the notions of a non-conventional, non-political truth. For if science claimed to be independent of established institutions, then it would necessarily constitute a challenge to those institutions, and hence would hardly be above politics. But because the positivists insist on a purist science leading to absolute knowledge, science itself has become an arch morality, an intolerant, authoritarian endeavour based on the perpetuation of metaphysical and physical violence. The relentless pursuit of reason, over and above morality and values, in a supposed search for an elusive truth, has turned science into a nightmare. As Foucault says, 'Look hard enough at the Western notion of reason and you will find madness.'[107] Those who criticize science, object to its mad and meaningless descent into reductionism, and oppose its selfish and shortsighted applications, are the true guardians of its essential humanitarian ideals.

As the positivist view of science is inadequate, should we throw reason and rationality completely overboard and descend into magic and myth—as is the want of so many Western critics of science? This would clearly be an un-Islamic stand, considering the emphasis that the Quran places on reason. However, if one thought that only one kind of reason exists, a single type of rationality, one would be wrong. As Paul Hirst notes, Western philosophy itself presents us with a bewildering array of definitions of rationality from opposed philosophical doctrines, each of which gives its own epistemological guarantees and legislation.[108] Underlying these notions of rationalism are numerous easily challenged assumptions about human beings, knowledge, order, the world, and so on, because the notion of rationality is itself intrinsically linked to worldview.

It goes without saying that observation and sense–perception, empirical work and experimentation are essential features of Islamic science. But on what notion of rationality is it based? The Ijmalis argue for a circumspect rationality which connects pure reason to the conceptual matrix of Islam. Circumspect rationality reflects the complexity of our physical environment where decisions based on reason and canons of logic can sometimes be morally irrational. Only when rationality is synthesized with values and morals does it produce a humanitarian science. In the framework of cautious, circumspect rationality, pure knowledge is never separated from moral knowledge. However, while this rationality is circumscribed by such Islamic conceptual categories as *khilafah, adl, halal, haram, istislah* and *taqwa*, it is limitless in its use—a contradiction that is more apparent than real.

Thus the Ijmalis have the complex position that they are not positivists in the sense that they endorse the fallacy of value/fact distinction, or support the inadequate use/abuse model of science which posits science in the Platonic ideal of the relentless pursuit of objective truth; but they are positivists in the sense that they do believe in an objectivity and rationality which is circumscribed by the value and conceptual framework of Islam. If codes of knowledge determine what is seen then let us bring our own absolute codes of morality to the forefront; let us shape knowledge according to the codes in which we believe and hold dear, for what is contained in the Quran and the Sunnah is the only absolute truth we can be sure of.

Relativism

The Ijmalis agree with the proposition—indeed the weight of evidence in its favour is overwhelming—that theories are not the ideal in bearing a one-to-one relationship with reality. They may be more or less coherent, aesthetically pleasing or morally desirable, but they cannot ultimately be equated with reality as they rest on acts of metaphysical faith. But our opposition to relativism is that the subjectivity inherent in knowledge is itself an objective, socially necessary expression of social forces. In other words, instead of presenting subjectivity as something mysterious and arbitrary which exists in itself, we hold that societical consensus, or *ijma* if you like, selects and shapes reality and nature in a particular way. This consensus is an objective phenomenon because it arises from the basic values of the worldview and from the physical needs and requirements of a society.

Social consensus or *ijma* therefore is an essential part of Ijmali thought. The notion of truth is univocal, for it applies equally to the judgement of lawyers, anthropologists, physicists, philologists, and literary criticism, as well as scientists and technologists. And as relativism demonstrates, there is no way to allot degrees of objectivity or hardness to all of them. But the presence or emergence of unforced agreement, a social consensus, an *ijma*, gives us everything in the way of objective truth which a society may need. Since a society may have consensus on a body of absolute truths, this also undermines the moral objections one has against relativism. Thus the notions of truth, beauty and goodness, on which there is a complete social consensus, an *ijma*, are not changeable artefacts.

Morally, relativism, with its distasteful extensions into a politics of lesser-evils and a practice structured around risk-versus-benefits calculations, can be just as totalitarian as positivism. Indeed, as Feyerabend's dictum 'anything goes' means 'everything stays', the seeming pluralism of a moral democracy has been known to encompass a fascistic ethic as easily as an anarchic one (which raises the interesting problem of how to keep a democracy from voting itself out of existence!). This is why the Ijmalis insist on operating such notions as *adl* and *istislah* to keep extreme relativism in check and introduce a level of objectivity and morality in the enterprise of science. By connecting relativism as well as science to the conceptual matrix of Islam and societal consensus, *ijma*, we transcend both moral relativism as well as the dualism inherent in Western scientific and philosophical tradition which pits humanity against animality, society against nature, freedom against necessity, mind against body, and in its most insidious hierarchical form, men against women. This transcendance also gives an objective base to Islamic science as all elements in society agree with the conceptual categories of the Quran. At the same time it makes Islamic science accountable not just to God, but also to society, its needs, requirements and wishes.

The Ijmali stance on relativism, therefore is a complex one: on the one hand it accepts the relativistic nature of man-made knowledge; on the other it transcends moral relativism by making science accountable to moral conceptual categories and objective social consensus. Subjectivity is therefore demystified by an objective *ijma*.

Radical science

The Ijmalis appreciate the Marxist analysis of science which highlights the ideological characteristics of science and argues that science is an enterprise of competitive struggle, in which the specific issue at stake is the monopoly of scientific authority, defined inseparably as technical capacity and social power. However, our objection to radical science is that in their efforts to describe science in political terms, the Marxists rely on assumed knowledge of bourgeois society and class positions. This knowledge is of a sociological nature and its assumptions can be readily challenged, but the Marxists take it uncritically in order to criticize the contents of medicine, biology or physics that mirror or distort this unjust society. The complexity with which a scientific discipline is constructed does not make it amenable to one-dimensional class analysis; while class may play a part in the social relations of science, it is certainly not the sole factor which influences the social construction of science. The Marxist position is thus too limited and weak. Moreover, it is also self-contradictory because Marxists do not want to apply the criticism they apply to natural sciences to their own position, their own science of society and notions of historical materialism and 'scientific' socialism.

In the final analysis, Marxists are positivists. While they attack science for its ideological bias, they need a real, positivist science to ground their own radical science somewhere and perpetuate their own kind of ideology: while capitalism is exploitation of man by man, Marxism is simply the other way round.

The Ijmalis, therefore, reject Marxism not simply on epistemological and religious grounds, but also on the basis of complexity: it is too simple, too one-dimensional an analysis of a complex reality. And despite its rhetoric, Marxism, as with radical science, has not introduced any real discontinuity: it sits comfortably within an epistemological arrangement that welcomes and considers it its own legitimate child; in return Marxism had no real intention of disturbing, or indeed any real power of changing, the structure of Western civilization. In nineteenth-century European thought and the twentieth-century epistemology of Western science, Marxism exists like a fish in water. All this, however, does not mean that the real contribution of Marxist thought—of revealing the links between science and ideology, politics and racism—should be underestimated.

Mystical science

To the mystics the Ijmalis say: we accept higher levels of consciousness as well as gnosis as a method of understanding metaphysical reality, but it is only a method, and not necessarily the most elevated method either. Gnosis cannot be equated with revelation: as a method of understanding the truth revelation has come to an end with the Prophet of Islam. We have all the absolute truths that a society needs in the Quran. We do not deny the absolute values that exist in other religious traditions; however, the values of a tradition recommending absolute values may be absolute, but the tradition itself is not. And if Islam is a summation of the message of Allah, which is the basic belief of Muslims, then what need is there to look at other traditions for absolute values?

Intuition does play a part in creativity, this much must be recognized. But it should also be recognized that the mystics have appropriated intuition; they have reserved it for an élitist group and denied it to the vast majority of the people. By limiting intuition to organized and structured mysticism, they have mystified it and undermined its social acceptance. Intuition is open to all. Our understanding of knowledge should be derived from both intellect and intuition; not from an intuition that is simply confined to secret orders, occult rituals and magic—but from that intuition which is the natural right of all humanity, which connects personal conscience with consciousness that is the root of the material universe, is cognizant of the whole, and infinitely mobile and capable of great acts of creation and transformation. We need to recognize that intuition plays an important part in the social construction of knowledge, and appreciate its true role in organized and systematic methods of inquiry that seek to solve physical and material problems and gain a limited understanding of the relationships between physical phenomena. But all this has nothing to do with structured and institutionalized gnosticism, authoritarian master–devotee relationships and élitist social politics.

In a way, the mystics want to have the best of all possible worlds: they want to limit their methodology within certain groups while seeking a social consensus on it; they propagate methodological relativism on the one hand, and want their methodology to be an arch, omnipotent methodology on the other; they want nothing to do with the physical world, yet insist that their methodology can help us shape physical reality. One thus finds double standards and moral dualism in the writings of mystics seeking to dominate science and, by implication, society. Reality, whatever it is, is much too complicated to be left solely in the hands of the mystics.

New paradigm and epistemological schools

These schools are exemplified by the work of Fritjof Capra,[109] Francis Verala[110], David Bohm[111] and Ilya Prigogine[112], who reject the mechanistic framework formulated by Descartes, Newton and Bacon and the associated methodology of reduction that goes with it, as well as the belief that in complex systems the dynamic of the whole can be understood from the properties of the parts. In their work these scientists emphasize that the properties of the part can be understood only from the dynamics of the whole; indeed, ultimately there are no parts at all; what we call a part is merely a pattern in an inseparable web of relationships. Moreover, there are no fundamental structures, but every structure is a manifestation of an underlying process. The entire web of relationships is intrinsically dynamic. There is also a shift away from seeing scientific descriptions as objective, independent of the human observer and the process of knowledge, towards epistemology—the understanding of the process of knowledge—which has to be included explicitly in the description of natural phenomena. Thus reality is perceived as a network of relationships, and descriptions of reality form an interconnected network representing the observed phenomena. In such networks there are no hierarchies or foundations. These scholars believe that all scientific concepts and theories are limited and approximate. Science can never provide any

complete and definite understanding. Scientists do not deal with
truth; they deal with limited and approximate descriptions of reality.

The Ijmalis would agree with much of this, but it is worth noting
that while all this looks radically new, it is nothing more than an
acceptance of an imposed situation. It is what positivist science itself is
telling us; and the new paradigm and epistemological schools are
positivist scientists who do not believe in any values because they
believe in all values. Despite their own analysis which shows Western
science to be destructive and inherently violent, they continue to
believe in it and work within its parameters. Because they have
realized that Western science is epistemologically bankrupt, they are
now engaged in a rescue job, casting for epistemologies here and
there. And where have they looked for new epistemologies? Towards
science itself or, in some cases, towards Zen Buddhism. Why?
Because in both cases there are no axiological parameters to worry
about. Modern science offers a secular, highly structured, totalitarian
system of thought that permits no diversity. If it is to survive, it must
look towards secular values: those seeking to enrich the banality and
lack of meaning of Western scientific thought are attracted either
towards such areas as biology and ecology, or secular, highly structured, totalitarian systems of metaphysics such as Zen Buddhism that
permit no diversity. Since it is secularism in a number of different
manifestations, including its manifestation as modern science, which
is the root cause of the contemporary predicament of mankind, a
synthesis of Zen Buddhism and Western thought, or new
epistemologies from the trenches of biology, are hardly likely to move
us forward to the goal of constructing a new, humane science.
However, the exercise here is not so much to construct a new science,
but to produce a final picture. This is science in a new phase of
colonization.[113]

The Ijmali position can be stated in the words of Feyerabend.

> The more recent developments in physical sciences are holistic, emphasize
> historical processes instead of universal laws and let 'reality' arise from an
> (often indivisible) interaction between observer and the thing observed.
> For the authors who encourage the trend (Bohm, Jantsch, Maturana,
> Prigogine, Verala, the proponents of 'evolutionary epistemology' and
> others) defuse cultural variety by showing that and how it fits in their
> scheme. Instead, of providing guidance for personal and social choices they
> withdraw into their theoretical edifices and explain from there how things
> were as they were, are as they are and will be as they will be. This is the old
> objectivism all over again, only wrapped in revolutionary pseudo-

humanitarian language. This is the philosophy that our ways are right and we are not going to change them.[114]

Our criticism of various positions within and without science should throw ample light on our own position, on science in general and on Islamic science in particular. The final point in regard to criticisms of science is that all critics want to maintain the *status quo*. Both Popper and Kuhn are all too protective of the establishment: both believe that science is always true and good, although not true as theories advance, but that the accumulative effect of science is good. Those who have articulated positions in their support are also conservatives: Imre Lakatos,[115] M. Polanyi,[116] even Feyerabend, for ultimately anarchism ends by strengthening the establishment. Marxists would simply like to replace one set of ideologues with another while preserving the same values. The epistemological schools and new paradigm thought aim at saving science by discovering new values in such areas as biology or ecology, or simply by co-opting secular atheistic traditions such as Zen Buddhism. What all these positions make clear is that one can no longer be naive about the relationship between the will to attain knowledge and truth and the will to attain power, between science and politics.

Islamic science, the Ijmalis maintain, is the only scientific enterprise—and this can be proved from history—where the values are played out upfront. Moreover, since these values have their bearings in the epistemological framework of Islam and since many are clearly opposed to the cherished values of positivist science, Islamic science is the only science, at least in its theoretical construction, that presents a challenge to Western science. Such values of Islamic science as *tawheed, khilafah, adl, istislah, ijma* and so many others, make it implicitly anti-status quo; it is the only revolutionary notion of science (in the Kuhnian sense) that is around.

Let me then formulate a working definition of Islamic science that incorporates the Ijmali synthesis:

Islamic science is a subjectively objective enterprise: it is based on a circumspect rationality which connects human rationality to the conceptual matrix of Islam and hence synthesizes pure knowledge with moral knowledge. The subjectivity of Islamic science is itself objective, since it is based on such Islamic conceptual categories as *khilafah, adl, halal, haram, istislah, taqwa* and numerous other concepts of the Quran and the Shariah—in which it has its epistemological being—and on a social consensus, the *ijma,* of the Muslim community and civilization, the *ummah*. It uses methods in conformity with the questions it raises, the problems it seeks to solve, the needs it wishes to fulfil. It is universal not just because Islam itself is universal, but because it is grounded in a rationality and a methodology, empirical and experimental work that is objective and can be duplicated and repeated by people of all cultures. Its nature and contents reflect its metaphysical and epistemological foundations, as well as the needs, requirements and concerns of Muslim people. It seeks not to discover absolute truths but to delineate their exposition and highlight the complex and interconnected nature of reality—thus, it is ultimately a form of worship, *ibadah*, a way towards the glorification of God and elevation of man, as well as a systematic and organized way of solving the physical problems and fulfilling the needs of individuals and society.

Two things can be said about this formulation of Islamic science. The first is obvious: nowhere in the world can we see such a science in operation. The second, that it is a combination of ideational, social, cultural as well as behavioural processes: it is the use of ideas to transform the material world, it is the participation of society to evolve an unforced consensus and give social meaning to scientific work, it is to highlight and shape scientific activity with declared and understood cultural value, and it is the use of skills to create and use appropriate tools and processes. Needless to say, such an endeavour cannot be undertaken in isolation; Islamic science is intrinsically linked to other areas of Muslim society and civilization, as well as to the evolution of a dynamic, thriving Muslim civilization of the future.

The question that we now face is, how are we going to reconstruct this Islamic science?

We Can Work It Out[117]

The reconstruction of Islamic science in our time is based on the firm realization that science is the energy of civilization, and that the science of the future will play an even bigger role than before. From the way I have argued, it is evident that this reconstruction has theoretical as well as empirical dimensions. It is based on a history, an epistemology that is described by the conceptual field of the Quran, and an optimistic but realistic belief in the future.

Indeed, any curative response to the almost total lack of science in the Muslim world, as well as the destructive nature of Western science, requires a confidence in the future. Such confidence involves both a vision of something desirable and a willingness to risk a great deal to attain it. Without sacrifice, commitment and persistence it is impossible to confront successfully a well-entrenched system of beliefs, practices and institutions. It is important to appreciate that the continuing 'success' and resilience of Western science has become the focus for political and ideological loyalty (after all positivism, in its idealized form, goes as far back as Plato), with incredibly large funding behind it, including the power of the military–industrial complex that fuels its expansion. We cannot expect to transform the essential nature of science without challenging these pillars of modern science—a great deal of resistance to Islamic science would come from Muslim scientists themselves and those privileged groups in Muslim societies who benefit from it. The struggle for Islamic science, therefore, is at once theoretical, practical, educational and political. The reconstruction of Islamic science involves not just theory building, but also empirical and experimental work, setting up laboratories, constructing science policies, raising the level of science consciousness among the people, mobilizing resources and popular opinion behind just scientific causes, as well as preparing a generation of committed scientists who understand the ethical and conceptual dimensions of Islam and can thus produce work in quality and quantity to make Islamic science a viable enterprise. The reconstruction of Islamic science is thus a multi-dimensional and multi-generational task.

The reconstruction of Islamic science involves systematic and simultaneous work on at least eight levels. Let me briefly describe each level, the whole description being a preliminary, long-range research programme for the reconstruction of Islamic science.

1. Epistemology

We need detailed articulation of a contemporary epistemology of Islam. Up to now attempts at formulating Islamic epistemology have not gone beyond al-Ghazzali; we need to go beyond al-Ghazzali both in depth and scope. We need to examine every discipline, every branch of knowledge and from the purview of this epistemology to identify common ground as well as areas of conflict. However, we need not just a total articulation of Islamic epistemology, but also a detailed exposition of the segments of this epistemology. For example, what is the Islamic view of man and where does this view come in direct conflict with modern biology? Moreover, we need to develop mechanisms to translate this epistemology into practical steps. How can we, as Hamid Khan suggests, 'evolve a model of "an integrated and closed system of studies" ' in which 'all disciplines of studies, including disciplines of empirical studies, should be integrated inter-relatedly and interdependently with the whole',[118] from this epistemology? How can we take this epistemology right down to the level of the laboratory? How would it help in ethical choices involved in research? How would it help in theory building? What kind of predictions could we make with these theories? Furthermore, we need to evolve a system of priorities for research based on this epistemology, including an Islamic classification of contemporary sciences.[119] We need to use the conceptual categories of Islam to evolve ethical positions in such areas as nuclear power, particle physics, recombinent DNA research, emerging reproductive technologies, sociobiology, high-technology surgery and medicine and so forth. And finally, we need a system to institutionalize this epistemology. What would be the nature of this institutionalization? How can it come about? How would it shape the content of research and science and technology policies? How would it change the nature of research institutions and administration of science? What impact would it have on scientific methodologies? How can we evolve ethical guidelines for scientists and researchers? All these questions need to be answered in considerable detail if the development of a contemporary Islamic epistemology is to have an impact on science.

2. *Methodology*

A vast amount of serious work needs to be done on the question of methodology if Islamic science is to become a viable enterprise. It is the extreme reliance of modern science on reduction and the complete disrespect for other forms of life that have led Foucault to say that 'all knowledge is linked to the essential forms of cruelty.'[120] And it is Bacon's dictum that 'nature yields her secrets under torture' that has become the foundation of the methodology of modern science.[121] How can we combat the intrinsic violence—so vivid in vivisection and experimental theoretical physics—of modern science? We need to examine the methods of modern science in minute detail, shifting every discipline, to see how violence and disrespect for God's creations have become such an important part of it.[122] But we need to do more than simply identify the destructive parts of scientific methodology and denounce them. We need to produce alternative methods. If, for example, we denounce vivisection by Islamic ethical criteria, what do we replace it with? Does a change in methodology also mean a change in the problems that come under the purview of science? Can it be argued that vivisection itself, for example, motivates society to behave in a certain manner and generates the kinds of problems which can only be solved by vivisection? A great deal has been said about synthesis: how can we turn synthesis into a methodology that can be brought down to the level of the laboratory? How can synthesis be introduced in all branches of science including theoretical physics? What problems amenable to synthesis have been overlooked (due to over-emphasis on reductionism)? What ethical criteria can we introduce into scientific work to check the descent of reductionism into destruction and meaninglessness? And to the vexed question of intuition: what needs to be done to ensure that intuition is acknowledged as a viable method for promoting creativity? We also need to explore the question of methods from the perspective of the Shariah: how can the Shariah help shape methodologies for science? What tools does it provide and what do we need to do to put these tools into operation in contemporary society? How do we recapture and operate the Shariah as a problem-solving methodology and a basis for ethical choices?

3. History

The history of Islamic science and technology has been one of the most neglected fields. Considering that many answers to the questions we face today lie in history, this is a dangerous shortcoming. We need to engage in a planned, systematic and organized attempt to reclaim the history of Islamic science and technology, an exposition even greater than that undertaken by Joseph Needham for the history of Chinese science.[123] We need to discover what was genuinely Islamic in Islamic science and to identify the ethical criteria and motivation which shaped the work of Muslim scientists. Up to now, almost all of the history of science has been a tourist guide, identifying major personalities and describing their work, focussing on discoveries and inventions. We need histories that are *about* science, *about* ideas that examine the impact of science and ideas on Muslim society. Furthermore, to be able to shift critically, we need to examine the rich scientific past of the Muslim civilization with the eternal conceptual categories of the Quran and the Shariah. Only by doing this can we distinguish between what is Islamic and what is merely Muslim in the history of Islamic science. In other words we need a questioning history: a history that asks questions about Islamic science and sets out to explore these questions in an historical context. Since Islamic science is intrinsically connected with ethics and the Shariah, we also need a history of the evolution of the Shariah: how did the Shariah shape the connections between science and ethics, what dictates of the Shariah led to establishment of specific institutions, how did the Shariah gave sense and direction to the work of Muslim scientists?

4. Policy

Using the conceptual matrix of Islam, we need to formulate detailed science policies. These policies need to be formulated for individual Muslim countries, at regional level and at the level of the ummah. Moreover, we need to formulate policies for individual areas: agriculture, industry, biology, physics, material science, information technology and communication.[124] In today's complex world, few problems can be solved in isolation; co-operation on interconnection and interdependence is the key to developing a viable ummah-level science policy. Furthermore, we need to develop two kinds of mechanisms: one that connects the science policies of individual Muslim countries to regional situations as well as to the ummah as a whole, encouraging sharing of resources and co-operation, and ensuring that all areas of science get appropriate attention in some segment of the ummah; and another to persuade decision makers to adopt these policies. The old development myth that a country need only spend 1 per cent of its GNP on science to get by needs to be demolished; a country that does not spend a sizeable proportion of its GNP on research and development and does not have clear, precise policies in all areas of science, is writing off its future. Decision makers tend to be particularly blind to this fact; moreover, when political authority intervenes in science it tends to impose its own conception of scientific and technological development. We must therefore work towards the creation of appropriate social and political mechanisms to ensure that science gets the support it needs.

5. Empirical work

Empirical work is the backbone of science, without which all other theoretical constructions collapse like castles in the air. Moreover, as experience of three decades of transfer of technology and know-how teaches us, science does not slowly detach itself from its empirical roots, the initial needs from which it rose, to become pure speculation subject only to the demands of reason. Its development is not tied to the constitution and affirmation of a free subject; rather it creates a progressive enslavement and induces dependency on those who carried out the original empirical work. The notion that science or technology can be imported is dangerously obsolete. Every Muslim country needs to undertake empirical research in such areas as food and basic needs, local health problems, agriculture, essential industry and so on; there are other areas of science where Muslim countries need to work in co-operation with each other: biotechnology, renewable energy, and information and space technologies, disaster management, desertification, soil erosion, environmental problems—to mention just a few. The priorities of research need to be set by examining the needs of individual countries; that is, by evolving science policies on the basis of value and conceptual criteria of Islam. A country where water logging is a major problem, for instance, needs to concentrate on solving this problem rather than to go into high-energy physics; a country that faces regular floods needs to invest in researching this area rather than to back a programme for research on organ transplants—the conceptual categories of the Islamic matrix help shape priorities of research and experimental work. In addition to these, we also need to do empirical work on certain problems that highlight the nature of Islamic science and show its methodology in action. What are these problems? Identifying these problems is itself a research task. This is where the predictive power of the theories built on Islamic epistemology has to be used to pin-point problems which could be solved directly by empirical work within the present nascent framework of Islamic science.

6. Institutions

A major component of the reconstruction of Islamic science is institution building. To begin with we need models of ideal institutions for Islamic science. What kind of institutions would best be suited to research based on synthesis rather than reduction? What would be the administrative and governance structure of such institutions? But it is not just laboratories and centres of excellence in certain disciplines with which we are concerned. We also need institutions devoted to the history of Islamic science and technology, we need science policy and planning bodies, we need institutions pursuing theoretical and ethical research in the area of science, such as the Centre for Science Studies in Aligarh. Moreover, these institutions are needed not just for individual countries, but also to serve the ummah as a whole. How can we go about creating such institutions? What are the hurdles that face the creation of these institutions? Where can they be ideally located? How will they be funded? How can we motivate the decision makers to give political support to such institutions? These and numerous other questions require systematic deliberation and action.

7. Education

As we systematically reconstruct Islamic science, we need to ensure that it is integrated with and becomes part of our education system. To begin with we can present a more accurate picture of science in our textbooks; it is worth noting that so far attempts to produce curricula for natural sciences have been crude and naive, failed to highlight the ideological, value-laden and relativistic nature of science and concentrated on such simple formulas as replacing the term 'nature' with 'God'.[125] We need to introduce elements of Islamic epistemology right at the beginning of science courses: only when students are aware of the ethical dimensions of knowledge will they be in a position to look at the ethics of science critically. A systematic attempt is thus needed to produce sophisticated science textbooks that highlight the limitation as well as strengths of science, delineate the domains of ethical and methodological choices, and relate science to local environment and societal and social needs. Curricula for science education should focus on creativity, original thinking and experimental work. Here the need for appropriate experimental manuals cannot be overemphasized. At the university level, we need to ensure that Islamic epistemology, philosophy, history of science and ethics are an integral part of science education. It is by focussing on the ethical dimension of science that we shall create appropriate Muslim scientists who will take the whole enterprise of Islamic science forward. Writing textbooks and producing new courses is not a once-off exercise; it should be an on-going process; as our ideas of Islamic science get more and more refined, as we become surer of our methodologies and empirical work, it should be incorporated in textbooks and become the standard fare for students.

8. Science consciousness

Just as social consensus, *ijma*, is an integral part of Islamic science, it is also an essential part of the process of reconstruction of Islamic science. We need to develop mechanisms for raising the consciousness of the people about science and the issues of science. People's partici-pation in the issues of science can only be ensured when the dogmatic belief in the excellence of expert knowledge is dethroned, when they have an appreciation of science and understand its importance for the modern world, when the ethical dimension of scientific choice has been presented before them. We need to change the mass perception of science by using the press, radio and television as well as modern information technologies, by constantly bringing issues of science and ethics in front of the public. But more than that: we need to get people involved in science by tackling their own problems, by developing their own tools, by looking after their own health and the health of their immediate environment and by discovering new means of demystifing science. The reconstruction of Islamic science thus involves taking science to the people: production of programmes of village science, participatory science, science for rural development, science for inner cities and so on.

Jean Ladrière has summed up the disruptive character of Western science and technology in the metaphor of 'uprooting'.[126] An appro-priate metaphor for the reconstruction of Islamic science could be 'planting'. At each of the eight levels where basic work is required, we need to plant the seeds which will eventually germinate into a full-fledged body by knowledge that can be universally and objectively seen to be Islamic science. The reason why Western science tends to form a self-directed system as to its ends is that it is driven by a project, a sort of inner motivation or design which is that of its own growth. Once these seeds have germinated into plants, they too will be inter-nally motivated by the 'project' of their own growth and fruition. If the proponents of Islamic science systematically work on the issues related to the eight levels that will collectively reconstruct Islamic science, they would be planting change—a change that will lead to a human and humane science that will benefit not just Muslims but the whole of humanity.

The possibility of rational anticipation, which underlies the project of reconstructing Islamic science, shows the future in a new light: the future is no longer a continuation of past events, miseries and calamities, or entirely unseeable and uncontrollable events; instead it is a field in which action is to take place. The world is no longer *a priori* given an assortment of facts and theories that one may endeavour to understand and is obliged to accept as they are. Instead, the world can be transformed by organized endeavour, by working within ethical boundaries and with nature, by inviting people to participate in science, by evolving a social consensus, by appreciating complexity and complementarity and by synthesis and empirical exposition. We can, indeed, work it out, as we are no longer placed before a reality which comes about of itself and to which we can, at best, attempt to adapt ourselves; instead, we are faced with an incomplete reality that we are responsible for transforming. The universe is no longer a cosmos but a world penetrated by human thought and activity and in which, to an increasing extent, this thought and activity merely rediscovers its own echo.

References

1. Kirmani, 'Issues in Islamic science' and 'Imitative–innovative assimilation; Rahman, 'Preface to Islamic science'.
2. Rahman, 'Perspective of New Science'.
3. By working in groups, scholars create and maintain an 'intellectual space', a piece of intellectual territory that they then defend from all outsiders. See Sardar, 'Intellectual Space and Western Domination'.
4. Manzoor's numerous articles have appeared in the 'Ideas' section of *Inquiry*; see also his 'Environment and values: an Islamic perspective' in Sardar, *The Touch of Midas*. Anees presents an Ijmali perspective on biology in his forthcoming book, *Islam and Biological Futures*, Mansell, London, 1989.
5. Gulzar Haider wrote numerous essays which looked at nature from the conceptual matrix of Islam for *Inquiry*; see also his penetrating essay, 'Habitat and values in Islam: a conceptual formulation of an Islamic city', in Sardar, *The Touch of Midas*. See Davies's brilliant new book, *Knowing One Another*. Iqbal Asaria's many articles on Islamic economics have appeared in *Inquiry*. Ibrahim Sulaiman's ideas are found in *The Islamic State and the Challenge of History*, Mansell, London, 1987; see also his *A Revolution in History*, Mansell, London, 1986, and his forthcoming *The Future of Shariah*, Mansell, London, 1990.
6. Foucault, *The Archaeology of Knowledge*, p. 23.
7. Said and Khan, *Al-Biruni*, p. 34.
8. Paris, 1951, and London, 1953, respectively.
9. Faber and Faber, London, 1953, and Harper and Row, New York, 1975; London, 1959 and reprinted by Perennial Books, London, 1982; and London, 1965, respectively.
10. See Titus Burckhardt, *Mirror of the Intellect: Essays on Traditional Science and Sacred Art*, Quinta Essentia, Cambridge, 1987; see also his *Art of Islam*, World of Islam Festival, London, 1976. See A. K. Coomaraswamy, *Selected Papers—*

Traditional Art and Symbolism, Princeton, 1977. See Martin Ling, *A Sufi Saint of the Twentieth Century*, Berkeley, 1973, and *What is Sufism?*, Berkeley, 1977. See Victor Danner, *The Islamic Tradition: An Introduction*, Amity House, New York, 1988. For a flavour of Needleman's ideas, see his edited work, *The Sword of Gnosis*, Penguin, London, 1974. See Gai Eaton, *The King of the Castle* and *Islam and the Destiny of Man*, Albany. Ali Ashraf and Hadi Sharifi are at the Islamic Academy in Cambridge.

11. The 'Christic embodiment' that Massignon represents is well described by Nasr in *Traditional Islam in the Modern World*, KPI, London, 1987, chapter 15. For Corbin's worldview, see his *Cyclic Time and Ismaili Gnosis*, KPI, London, 1983.

12. Nasr, *Knowledge and the Sacred*, Edinburgh University Press, 1981, p. ix. See also Mohammad Salman Raschid's dissection of this book in 'Philosophia perennis universale imperium', *Religion*, **13**, 155–71 (1983). Raschid concludes: 'As a Muslim I am bound to say that Professor Hossein Nasr's book cannot be read as a Muslim statement since it does not represent the expression of Islamic (i.e. Quranic) ideas. It is rather based upon a confused mixture of what could be characterized as "Neoplatonized Semitic Theism with an admixture of distorted Vedanta". If this sounds like an extraordinary, incoherent formulation I submit that it is a direct reflection of the basic incoherence in Nasr's whole case.' (p. 170).

13. Nasr, *Knowledge and the Sacred*, p. 107. Is he describing a man or a god?

14. *Ibid.*, p. 137.

15. *Islamic Science: An Illustrated Study*, p. 28.

16. *Ibid.*, p. 31.

17. *Ibid.*, pp. 31, 36.

18. *Ibid.*, p. 36.

19. See *The Golden Verses of Pythagoras*, Concord Grove Press, London, 1983, p. 20.

20. See *Hermitica*, edited and translated by Walter Scott, Shambhala, Boston, 1985 (3 vols.), (original edition, 1926).

21. Aristotle's *Physics*, Books I & II, translated and edited by W. Charlton, OUP, 1970; Books III & IV translated and edited by A. Hussey, OUP, 1983. A penguin edition of *De Anima* was published in 1986.

22. Nasr, *Islamic Science*, p. 75.

23. *Ibid.*, p. 79.

24. *Ibid.*, p. 84.

25. *Ibid.*, pp. 126, 127.

26. See his catalogues of absurdities found in 'Islamic science' in *Journal for the History of Astronomy*, **ix**, pp. 212–19 (1978).

27. Nasr, *Islamic science*. p. 135–6.

28. *Ibid.*, p. 54–6.

29. *Ibid.*, p. 68.

30. *Ibid.*, p. 36–7.

31. *Ibid.*, p. 193.

32. It is because of its rather un-Islamic stances that the publication of *Islamic Science* led to protests by members of the Federation of Students Islamic Societies in front of the offices of the Festival of Islam. Despite its name, the

festival had little to do with Islam and more to do with the celebration of Guenonite thought—all publications of the festival were produced by the Guenonite savants.

33. *An Annotated Bibliography of Islamic Science*, p. xiii.
34. Robert Hall, *ISIS*, **69**, 3:248 457–61, (1978).
35. Brill, Leiden, 1972–84 (8 volumes published).
36. These citations occur on pp. 116, 114, 111, respectively, of volume 2 of the *Bibliography*.
37. See Michel Foucault, *The Uses of Pleasure* (volume 2 of *The History of Sexuality*), Penguin, 1984.
38. Al-Ghazzali, *Book of Knowledge*, pp. 76–6.
39. The chapter—What is Islamic science?—will also appear in *Issues in Islamic Science*, edited by Munawar Ahmad Anees and scheduled to be published by Mansell in 1990. The references are from the typescript presented to Anees.
40. *Ibid.*, p. 1.
41. *Ibid.*, p. 2.
42. Nasr, *Knowledge and the Sacred*, p. 138.
43. Nasr, 'What is Islamic Science?', p. 4.
44. *Ibid.*, pp. 18–19.
45. *Ibid.*, p. 5.
46. Manzoor, 'The Paralysed Metaphysical Nerve', p. 45.
47. Nasr, 'What is Islamic Science?', p. 5.
48. *Ibid.*, p. 15.
49. *Ibid.*, p. 8.
50. *Ibid.*, p. 8.
51. See Henry Corbin, *Cyclic Time and Ismaili Gnosis*, op. cit. The table on p. 94 sums it up.
52. Nasr, 'What is Islamic Science?', p. 7.
53. The Aquarian Press, Wellinbgorough, 1985.
54. *Ibid.*, p. 22.
55. In Ahmad and Ahmad, *Quest for a New Science*, pp. 91–110. Following his Master, Bakr describes Islamic science as 'all disciplines relating to the world of nature, of the psyche and of mathematics' and these disciplines 'include psychology, alchemy, astrology and cosmology'. See his 'The Influence of Islamic Science on Medieval Christian Concepts of Nature', *MAAS J. Islamic Sc.* **4** (1), 25–43 (1988).
56. As Naquib al-Attas's output is based on genuine Islamic tradition that owes nothing to Pythagoras, Hermeticism, and other forms of the occult; it is deliberately and totally ignored by Nasr. See his *The Mysticism of Hamzah Fansuri*, University of Malaya Press, Kuala Lumpur, 1970; *A Commentary on the Hujjat Al-Siddiq of Nur Al-Din Al-Raniri*, Ministry of Culture, Kuala Lumpur, 1986; his brilliant *Islam, Secularism and the Philosophy of the Future*; and look out for the book he is now writing, *The Metaphysics of Islam*.
57. Bakr, 'The Question of Methodology in Islamic Science', p. 105.
58. *Ibid.*, p. 102.
59. *Ibid.*, p. 103.
60. See Richard Cavendish, *A History of Magic*, London, 1977.

61. *MAAS J. Islamic Sc.* **3** (1) 85–90 (1987).

62. *MAAS J. Islamic Sc.* **2** (1) 21–46 (1986).

63. Kettani, 'Science and Technology in the Muslim World'.

64. El-Nejjar, 'The Limitations of Science . . .'.

65. Sardar, 'A Revival for Islam, A Boost for Science'.

66. Particular examples of Husaini's confused thinking are presented in two pamphlets: 'Islamic Science and Public Policies: Lessons from the History of Science' and 'Teaching Islamic Science and Engineering', both self-published in Kuala Lumpur, 1985.

67. Mitroff, *The Subjective Side of Science*.

68. Chalmers is a standard textbook on the nature of science.

69. Chalmers, p. 60.

70. See Feyerabend, *Farewell to Reason*, p. 172.

71. University of Chicago Press, 1962; second edition, 1972.

72. See Norman, *The God That Limps*.

73. See 'Science and Values', in Sardar, *Touch of Midas*, p. 47.

74. Sage, London, 1979.

75. These quotations are from John Stewart's excellent review of Latour and Woolgar in *Radical Science Journal*.

76. *Ibid.*, p. 132.

77. Cartwright, p. 3.

78. *Ibid.*, p. 15.

79. The father of sociobiology is E. O. Wilson; see his *Sociobiology: The New Synthesis*, Harvard University Press, Cambridge, Mass., 1975; see also the brilliant critique from the radical left: Steven Rose, R. C. Lewontin and Leon J. Kamin, *Not in Our Genes*, Penguin, London, 1984.

80. The classical paper is by Robert Young, 'Science *is* Social Relations', *Radical Science Journal*, Number 5 (1977), pp. 65–131.

81. Knorr-Cetina, *Manufacture of Knowledge*, p. 47.

82. Feyerabend, *Against Method*, p. 142.

83. Kuhn, *Structure of Scientific Revolutions*, p. 1.

84. This list of positions demolished by Kuhn is from Hacking, *Scientific Revolutions*, pp. 1–2.

85. Kirmani, 'On the Parameters of Islamic Science', p. 175.

86. Ahmad, 'A Preliminary Thought on Reductionism'.

87. Ahmad, 'Some Thoughts on Methodology in Islamic Science'.

88. In Ahmad and Ahmad, *Quest for New Science*, pp. 79–90.

89. Kirmani, 'Islamic Science on Production . . .' p. 48.

90. *Ibid.*, p. 49.

91. See Gulzar Haider's numerous articles on the environment and cities in *Inquiry*, such as 'The City of Learning', **2** (7), 45–51 (1985), and 'Man and Nature', **2** (8), 47–52 (1985).

92. Kirmani, 'Islamic Science on Production . . .' p. 53. There is a further contradiction in this paper which ought to be pointed out. One cannot on the one hand argue that 'modern science cannot possibly claim to have any absolute reality in its worldview', while on the other hand stating: 'if an absolute truth comes into knowledge after a long course of investigation, that too is not considered truth and is looked upon doubtfully because of the very

nature of scientists' minds.' How can absolute truths arise in modern science, if it has already eliminated them from its worldview?

93. I argued the same point, although somewhat differently, in *The Future of Muslim Civilization*, Mansell, London, 1987, chapter 8.

94. Manzoor, 'Paralysed Metaphysical Nerve,' p. 44.

95. Mackensen, 'Background of History of Muslim Libraries', pp. 121–2.

96. M. Kaleemur Rahman, *Arguments for Islamic Science*, Centre for Studies on Science, Aligarh, 1985.

97. Rahman, 'A Preface to Islamic Science', p. 54.

98. *Ibid.*, p. 54.

99. Sardar, *Science, Technology and Development in the Muslim World*.

100. Al-Ghazzali's *Incoherence of the Philosophers*, p. 2.

101. *Ibid.*, p. 4.

102. See Ziauddin Sardar, *Islamic Futures: The Shape of Ideas to Come*, Mansell, London, 1985.

103. See Gulzar Haider's work, reference 5 of this chapter.

104. See Davies, *Knowing One Another*.

105. But synthesis and assimilation can only take place between two scientific cultures of equal status; at present the Muslim world is too weak to exercise synthesis. In this regard see Parvez Manzoor's timely warning, 'Science in Islam and West: Synthesis or Con-fusion?', in Sardar, *Touch of Midas*.

106. Chalmers, *What is This Thing Called Science?* p. 166.

107. See Michel Foucault, *Madness and Civilization*, Tavistock Publications, London, 1967.

108. Paul Hirst, 'Is it rational to reject relativism?'

109. See his *The Toa of Physics* and *The Turning Point*.

110. See Maturana and Verala, *El Arbol de Conscimento*, and Verala, 'Living Ways of Sense-Making.

111. See his *Wholeness and the Implicate Order*.

112. See Prigogine and Stengers, *Order Out of Chaos*.

113. For an insightful critique of Capra from the Hindu perspective see Alvares, 'We Have Been Here Before'.

114. Feyerabend, *Farewell to Reason*, p. 6.

115. Lakatos's classic defence of the falsificationist programme is 'Falsification and the Methodology of Scientific Research Programme'; see also Lakatos, *Philosophical Papers—Volume 1*.

116. See his *Knowing and Being* and *Personal Knowledge*.

117. Just in case the reader has not guessed it by now, I have been having fun at the expense of the lyrics from the late 1960s pop songs: 'Ground control to Major Tom' is attributed to David Bowie; 'We have only just begun' to the Carpenters; the others are from the Beatles. No indirect promotion of pop culture is intended!

118. Hamid Ahmad Khan, 'How to Identify Islamic Science?', p. 199.

119. While the classification of sciences was one of the major activities of the classical Muslim scholars, it has been totally ignored by scholars in our time. For a primitive model of a classification scheme, see Ziauddin Sardar, *Islam: Outline of A Classification Scheme*, K. G. Saur, London, 1979.

120. Michel Foucault, *Mental Illness and Psychology*, Harper and Row, New York, 1976, p. 81.
121. Cited by Aicken, *The Nature of Science*, p. 36.
122. For a detailed analysis of the violent nature of Western science, see Shiva, 'The violence of reductionist science'.
123. Needham, *Science and Civilization in China*.
124. I have recently attempted to develop an *ummah* level information policy. See Ziauddin Sardar, *Information and the Muslim World: A Strategy for the 21st Century*, Mansell, London, 1988.
125. See, for example, Sami and Sajjad, *Planning Curricula for Natural Science*.
126. Ladrière, *The Challenge Presented to Cultures by Science and Technology*, p. 83.

Bibliography

Abir-Am, Pnina. 'The discourse of physical power and biological knowledge in the 1930s: a reappraisal of the Rockefeller Foundation's "policy" in molecular biology', *Social Studies of Science*, **12** (3), 341–82, 1982.

Ahmad, Rais. 'A preliminary thought on reductionism'. *MAAS J. Islamic Sc.*, **2** (1), 107–12, 1986.

———. 'Some thoughts on methodology in Islamic science'. *MAAS J. Islamic Sc.*, **3** (2), 71–8, 1987.

———. and S. N. Ahmad (eds.). *Quest for New Science*. Centre for Science Studies, Aligarh, 1985.

Ahmad, Mashhood. 'Islamic ethos and Muslim scientists'. *MAAS J. Islamic Sc.*, **1** (1), 56–68, 1985.

Aicken, Frederick. *The Nature of Science*. Heinemann, London, 1984.

Al-Attas, Syed Muhammad Naquib. *Islam, Secularism and the Philosophy of the Future*. Mansell, London, 1985.

Al-Biruni. *The Determination of the Co-ordinates of Positions for the Correction of Distances between Cities*. Translated by Jamil Ali, Beirut, 1976.

———. *India*. Abridged and annotated by Ahmad Hasan Dani. University of Islamabad Press, Islamabad, 1973.

Al-Faruqi, I. R. 'Science and traditional values in Islamic society'. *Zygon*, **2** (3), 231–46, 1967.

———. *Islamization of Knowledge*. International Institute of Islamic Thought, Washington, D.C., 1982.

———. 'The causal and telic nature of the universe'. *J. Islamic Sc.*, **2** (2), 9–22, 1986.

Al-Faruqi, I. R. and A. O. Naseef (eds.). *Social and Natural Sciences: the Islamic Perspective*. Hodder and Stoughton, London, 1981.

Al-Ghazzali. *The Book of Knowledge*. Translated by Nabih Amin Faris. Ashraf, Lahore, 1962.

———. *Tahafut al-Falsifah (Incoherence of the Philosophers)*. Translated by Sabih Ahmad Kamali. Pakistan Philosophical Congress, 1963.

Al-Hassan, Ahmad Y. and Donald R. Hill. *Islamic Technology: an Illustrated Study*. CUP, Cambridge, 1986.

Alvares, Claude. 'We have been here before'. In Sardar, *Revenge of Athena*, 1988.

Amilcar, O. H., *et al. Catastrophe or a New Society?* International Development Research Centre, Ottawa, 1976.

Anees, M. A. 'Islamic science—an antidote to reductionism'. *Afkar/Inquiry*, 1 (2), 49, July 1984.

———. 'Islamic values and Western science: a case study of reproductive biology'. In Sardar, *Touch of Midas*, 1984.

———. 'Laying the foundations of Islamic science'. *Inquiry*, 2 (11) 36–43, November 1985.

———. 'What Islamic science is not'. *J. Islamic Sc.*, 2 (1), 9–20, 1986.

——— and A. N. Athar. 'Development of higher education and scientific research in the Arab world'. *J. South Asian and Middle Eastern Studies*, 2 (3), 93–100, Spring 1979.

——— and ———. 'Significance of scientific, technical and social information in the Muslim world'. Al-Ittihad, 17 (1), 46–52, 1980.

Ann Arbor Science for the People Editorial Collective. *Biology as a Social Weapon*. Burgess, Minneapolis, 1977.

Arditti, Rita, Paty Brennan and Steve Cavrak (eds.). *Science and Liberation*. South End Press, Boston, 1980.

Averroes. *Tahafut Al-Tahafut (Incoherence of the Incoherence)*. Translated by Simon van den Bergh. Luzac, London 1954, 2 vols.; reprinted as 1 vol., 1978.

Ayub, Hamid. 'Alternative technology—a cross-section'. *Muslim Scientist*, 8 (4), 1–6, 1979.

Azam, M. N. 'International Conference on Science in Islamic Polity—its past, present and future'. *Science and Technology in the Islamic World*, 1 (4), 294–309, 1983.

Azam, R. M. I. 'Need for a Pakistan futuristics institute'. *Science, Technology and Development*, 1 (4) 23–4, 1982.

Bakr, Osman. 'The question of methodology in Islamic science'. In Ahmad and Ahmad, *Quest for New Science*, 1984.

———. 'The influence of Islamic science on medieval Christian concepts of nature'. *MAAS J. Islamic Sc.*, 4 (1), 25–43, 1988.

———. *Critique of Evolution*. Islamic Academy of Science and Nurin Enterprise, Kuala Lumpur, 1987.

Barnes, B. *T. S. Kuhn and Social Sciences*. Macmillan, London, 1982.

Bateson, Gregory. *Steps to an Ecology of Mind*. Paladin, London, 1973.

Beer, Gillian. *Darwin's Plot*. Routledge, London, 1984.

———. *Evolutionary Narrative in Darwin*. Routledge, London, 1984.

Behbehani, K., M. Girgis and M. S. Marzouk (eds.). *Proceedings of the Symposium on Science and Technology for Development in Kuwait*. Longman, London, 1981.

Berger, Peter L., and Thomas Luckman. *The Social Construction of Reality: a Treatise in the Sociology of Knowledge*. Doubleday, New York, 1967.

Berlin, Isaiah. *The Age of Enlightenment*. Mentor Books, New York, 1956.

Bernal, J. D. *Science in History*. MIT Press, Cambridge, 1979, 4 vols..

Blissett, Marlan. *Politics in Science*. Little Brown, Boston, 1972.

Bloor, D. *Knowledge and Social Imagery*. Routledge, London, 1976.

Bohm, David. *Wholeness and the Implicate Order*. Ark, London, 1983.

Bucaille, Maurice. *The Bible, The Quran and Science*. Seghers, Paris, 1976; North American Trust, Indianapolis, 1978.

Busch, Lawrence, and William B. Lacy. *Science, Agriculture and the Politics of Research*. Westview, Boulder, 1983.

Caplan, Arthur L. (ed.). *The Sociobiology Debate*. Harper and Row, New York, 1978.

Capra, Fritjof. *The Toa of Physics*. Flamingo, London, 1976.

———. *The Turning Point*. Flamingo, London, 1983.

Cartwright, Nancy. *How the Laws of Physics Lie*. Clarendon Press, Oxford, 1983.

Chalmers, A. F. *What is this Thing Called Science?* Open University Press, Milton Keynes, 1982.

Chejne, A. G. *Ibn Hazm*, Kazi Publications, Chicago, 1982.

Chotani, A. H. 'Some aspects of transfer of technology in the Islamic world'. *Science, Technology and Development*, 2 (2), 19–22, 1983.

Chughtai, M. I. D. 'Role of scientific societies in the promotion of science in the Islamic world'. *Science, Technology and Development*, 2 (1), 2–3, 1983.

Collins, H. M. 'Knowledge, norms and rules in the sociology of science'. *Social Studies of Science*, 12 (2), 299–308, 1982.

Collins, H. M. 'Stages in the empirical programme of relativism'. *Social Studies of Science*, 11 (1), 3–10 1981.

Collins, H. M. (ed.). 'Knowledge and controversy: studies of modern natural science'. *Social Studies of Science*, 11 (1), 1981, special issue.

Cotsgrove, S. *Catastrophe or Cornucopia? The Environment, Politics and the Future*. Wiley, Chichester, 1982.

Council for Science and Society. *Superstar Technologies*. Barry Rose, London, 1976.

———. *The Acceptability of Risk*. Barry Rose, London, 1976.

———. *Scholarly Freedom and Human Rights*. Barry Rose, 1977.

Dar, B. A. *Quranic Ethics*. Institute of Islamic Culture, Lahore, 1960.

Davies, Merryl Wyn. *Knowing One Another: Shaping an Islamic Anthropology*. Mansell, London, 1988.

Dickson, David. *The New Politics of Science*. Pantheon, New York, 1984.

Hill, Donald R. *Arabic Water-Clocks*. Institute of History of Arabic Science, Aleppo, 1981.

Durrani, S. A. 'Importance of scientific research in Islamic countries: a blueprint for progress'. *J. Islamic Sc.*, 2 (2), 23–47, 1986.

El-Fandy, M. G. 'Islam and science'. *J. World Muslim League*, 1 (8) 39–40, 1974.

El-Nejjar, Zaghlour R. 'The Limitations of Science and the Teaching of Science from the Islamic Perspective'. *American J. Islamic Social Sciences*, 3 (1), 59–76, 1986.

Farrington, Benjamin. *Greek Science*. Penguin, London, 1983.

Feyerabend, Paul. *Against Method*. NLB, London, 1975.

———. *Science in a Free Society*. Verso, London, 1978.

———. *Farewell to Reason*. Verso, London, 1987.

Ford, G. 'A framework for a new view of Islamic science'. *Adiyat Halab*, 4/5, 68–74, 1978/79.

———. 'Liberating science with Islamic values'. *Afkar/Inquiry*, 1 (2), 50–1, July 1984.

———. 'Rebirth of Islamic science?' In Sardar, *Touch of Midas*, 1984.

Foucault, Michel. *The Archaeology of Knowledge*. Tavistock Publications, London, 1972.

Gilbert, G. Nigel and Michael Mulkay. 'Contexts of scientific discourse: social accounting in experimental papers'. In Knorr-Cetina, Krohn and Whitley, *Social Process of Scientific Investigation*, 1980.

——— and ———. 'Warranting scientific belief'. *Social Studies of Science*, 12 (3), 383–408, 1982.

Goonatilake, Susantha. *Crippled Minds: an exploration into Colonial Culture*. Vikas, Delhi, 1982.

———. *Aborted Discovery: Science and Creativity in the Third World*. Zed Press, London, 1984.

Green, Philip. *Pursuit of Inequality*. Pantheon, New York, 1981.

Hacking, Ian (ed.). *Scientific Revolutions*. OUP, Oxford, 1981.

Haq., S. 'The Quran and modern cosmologies'. *Science and Technology in the Islamic World*, 1, 47–52, 1983.

Hashmi, Z. A. 'Science in the Islamic world'. *Science, Technology and Development*, 1 (1), 2–7, 1982.

———. 'Future opportunities and challenges for science and technology in the Muslim world'. *International Conference on Science in Islamic Polity*, Islamabad, 1983, document ICSIP-5.

Hayward, Alan. *Creation and Evolution*, Triangle, London, 1985.

Heshamaul Haque. 'Research co-operation among the Muslim states for raising food output'. *Science, Technology and Development*, 1 (6), 2–6, 1982.

Hirst, Paul. 'Is it rational to reject relativism?' In Joanna Overing (ed.). *Reason and Morality*. Tavistock Publications, London, 1985, pp. 85–103.

Hoffman, K. and H. Rush. 'Microelectronics industry and the Third World'. *Futures*, 12 (4), 289–302, 1980.

Holton, Gerald and William Blanpied. *Science and Its Public: the Changing Relationships*. Reidel, Boston, 1976.

Hourani, George F. *Reason and Tradition in Islamic Ethics*. CUP, Cambridge, 1985.

Husaini, S. Waqar A. 'Islamic ethics and values in medical science and practice'. *J. Islamic Sc.*, 1 (2), 19–30, 1985.

———. 'Towards the rebirth and development of Shariyyah science and technology'. *J. Islamic Sc.*, 1 (2), 81–94, 1985.

———. 'Birth, decline and rebirth of Islamic science and technology: indigenous causes of decline and their remedies'. *J. Islamic Sc.*, 2 (1), 75–90, 1986.

———. 'What are Islamic, Muslim or Shariyyah Science and Technology? A Tentative Note'. *J. Islamic Sc.*, 2 (2), 75–78, 1986.

Husaini, W. A. *Islamic Environmental Systems Engineering*. Macmillan, London, 1980.

Ibn Khaldun. *The Muqaddimah*. Translated by Franz Rosenthal. Routledge, London, 1967.

Impact of Science on Society. 'Science and the Islamic world'. Special Issue, **26** (3), May–September 1976.

International Islamic University. *Abstracts of Papers Presented at the First International Conference on Scientific Miracles of the Quran and Sunnah.* International Islamic University, Islamabad, and Muslim World League, Makkah al-Mukarramah, 1987.

International Organization of Islamic Medicine. *Islamic Code of Medical Ethics*. Kuwait, 1981.

Kazi, M. A. 'Science, Islam and peace'. *Science, Technology and Development*, **1** (2), 2–7, 1982.

Keeney, Elizabeth Barnaby. 'Science in America or American Science?: relative merits of context and comparison'. *History of Science in America: News and Views*, **4** (2), 1–2 1986.

Kettani, M. Ali. 'Islamic Foundation for Science, Technology and Development and its role'. *Science and Technology in the Islamic World*, **1** (2), 70–6, 1983.

——. 'Science and technology and the Muslim world'. *J. Islamic Sc.*, **2** (2), 49–68, 1986.

Khalifa, Rashad. *Quran: Visual Presentation of the Miracle*. Islamic Productions International, Tucson, 1982.

Khan, A. U. 'Islam and science'. *J. Research Society of Pakistan*, **7** (4), 15–20, 1970.

Khan, Ehsanullah. *Science, Islam and the Modern Age*. Academy of Ijtihad, New Delhi, 1986.

Khan, Hamid Ahmad. 'How to identify Islamic science'. In Ahmad and Ahmad, *Quest for New Science*, 1984.

Kirmani, M. Riaz. 'Structure of Islamic science'. *MAAS J. Islamic Sc.*, **1** (2), 31–8, 1985.

——. 'Islamic science on production and administration plane'. *MAAS J. Islamic Sc.*, **2** (1), 47–54, 1986.

Kirmani, M. Zaki. 'On the parameters of Islamic science'. In Ahmad and Ahmad, *Quest for New Science*, 1984.

——. 'New ideologies on science'. *MAAS J. Islamic Sc.*, **1** (1), 69–74, 1985.

——. 'Ghazzali needs revival'. *MAAS J. Islamic Sc.*, **1** (1), 83–6, 1985.

——. 'A critique of criticism on science'. *MAAS J. Islamic Sc.*, **1** (2), 39–52, 1985.

——. 'Imitative-innovative assimilation: a critique of Waqar A. Husaini's scheme of contemporary Islamic S & T rebirth'. *MAAS J. Islamic Sc.*, **2** (2), 69–74, 1986.

——. 'Issues in Islamic science'. *MAAS J. Islamic Sc.*, **3** (2), 41–70, 1987.

Knorr-Cetina, Karin D. *The Manufacture of Knowledge*. Pergamon, Oxford, 1981.

——. 'The constructivist programme in the sociology of science: retreats or advances?' *Social Studies of Science*, **12** (2), 320–4, 1982.

——. Roger Krohn and Richard Whitle. *The Social Process of Scientific Investigation*. Reidel, Boston, 1980.

—— and Michael Mulkay (eds.). *Science Observed: Perspective on the Social Study of Science.* Sage, Beverley Hills, 1983.

——. Hermann Strasser and Hans Georg Zilian (eds.). *Determinants and Controls of Scientific Development.* Reidel, Boston, 1975.

Kocabas, S. 'In search of Islamic epistemology'. *J. Islamic Sc.*, **2** (2), 79–86, 1986.

Koestler, A. and J. Smythies (ed.). *Beyond Reductionism.* Hutchinson, London, 1969.

Kuhn, T. S. *The Structure of Scientific Revolution.* University of Chicago Press, 1962; second edition, 1972.

——. 'The historical structure of scientific discovery'. *Science,* **136**, 760–4, 1962.

Ladrière, Jean. *The Challenge Presented to Cultures by Science and Technology.* Unesco, Paris, 1977.

Lakatos, Imre. *Philosophical Papers—Volume 1: the Methodology of Scientific Research Programmes.* Edited by J. Worrall and G. Currie. CUP, Cambridge, 1978.

—— and Alan Musgrave. *Criticism and the Growth of Knowledge.* CUP, Cambridge, 1970.

Lakoff, Sanford A. (ed.). *Science and Ethical Responsibility.* Addison-Wesley, Reading, 1980.

Leaman, Oliver. *An Introduction to Mediaeval Islamic Philosophy.* CUP, Cambridge, 1985.

Mackensen, Ruth Stellhorn. 'Background of history of Muslim libraries'. *American J. Semitic Languages and Literatures,* **51**, 114–25, 1934–35.

Manzoor, S. Parvez. 'The paralysed metaphysical nerve'. *Inquiry,* **4** (11), 42–9.

Mashhood, Ahmad. 'Islamic ethos and Muslim scientists'. *MAAS J. Islamic Sc.*, **1** (1), 56–68, 1985.

Matin, Abdul. 'Industrial Co-operation among Muslim Countries'. *Science and Technology in the Islamic World,* **1** (1), 1–19, 1983.

Maturana, Humberto and Francisco Verala. *El Arbol de Conscimento.* Editorial Universitaria, Santiago, 1984.

Maula, Erkka J. 'On the impact of the past upon the future of Islamic science: juxtaposition of the two crucial periods 850–1450 and 1980–2000'. *Science and Technology in the Islamic World,* **1** (1), 40–6, 1983.

Maxwell, Nicholas. *From Knowledge to Wisdom.* Basil Blackwell, Oxford, 1984.

Mendelsohn, E. 'Should science survive its success?' *For Dirk Struik.* Edited by R. S. Cohen, *et al.* Reidel, Dordrecht, 1974.

——. 'The social construction of scientific knowledge'. In *Social Production of Scientific Knowledge.* Reidel, Dordrecht, 1977.

Mendelssohn, K. *Science and Western Domination.* Thames and Hudson, London, 1976.

Midgley, Mary. *Beast and Men.* Methuen, London, 1980.

——. *Evolution as a Religion.* Methuen, London, 1985.

Ministry of Science and Technology, International Conference on Science in Islamic Polity. *S and T Potential and its Development in the Muslim World*

(2 vols.), and *Islamic Scientific Thought and Muslim Achievements in Science* (2 vols.). Islamabad, 1983.

Mitroff, Ian. *The Subjective Side of Science*. Elzevier, Amsterdam, 1974.

Mohammad Ayoob (ed.). *The Politics of Islamic Reassertion*. Croom Helm, London, 1981.

Moore, Keith L. 'Highlights of human embryology in the Quran and the Hadith'. *Proceedings of the Seventh Saudi Medical Meeting.* Riyadh, pp. 51–8, 1982.

Moorehouse, W. 'Confronting a four-dimensional problem: science, technology, society and tradition in India and Pakistan'. *Technology and Culture*, **8**, 363, 1967.

Moorehouse, W. (ed.). *Science and the Human Condition in India and Pakistan*. Rockefeller University Press, New York, 1968.

Moraze, C., *et al. Science and the Factors of Inequality*. Unesco, Paris, 1979.

Morley, David. *The Sensitive Scientist*. SCM Press, London, 1978.

Muslim, The. 'Science and values', **15** (5), 99, 1979.

Nandy, Ashis. 'Science severed from source'. *Resurgence*, **11** (5), 4–7, 1980.

Naseef, Abdullah Omar. 'The role of faith and Islamic ethics in the teaching of natural and applied sciences'. *Islamic Quarterly*, **26** (3), 131–7, 1982.

Nasr, S. H. *Science and Civilization in Islam.* Harvard University Press, Cambridge, 1968.

———. *Encounter of Man and Nature*. Allen and Unwin, London, 1978.

———. *Islamic Science: an Illustrated Study*. World of Islam Festival, London, 1976.

———. W. C. Chittick and P. Zirmis. *An Annotated Bibliography of Islamic Science.* Tehran, vol. 1, 1975; vol. 2, 1979.

Nature. 'Development in the Muslim world'. *Nature*, **272**, 195, 16 March 1978.

———. 'Pakistan needs indigenous medicine'. *Nature*, **275**, 1, 7 September 1978.

Needham, Joseph. *Science and Civilization in China.* CUP, Cambridge, 1956–   , 6 vols.

Norman, Colin. *The God That Limps*. Norton, New York, 1981.

Nowotny, H. and H. Rose (eds.). *Counter-movements in Science*. Reidel, Dordrecht, 1979.

Osiris, second series 1, 1985.

Pacy, Arnold. *The Culture of Technology*. Basil Blackwell, Oxford, 1983.

Philips, Abu Ameenah Bilal. 'The theory of 19: hoax and heresy'. To be published.

Pinch, Trevor J. 'The sun-set: the presentation of certainty in scientific life'. *Social Studies of Science*, **11** (1), 131–58, 1981.

Polanyi, M. *Knowing and Being*. Routledge, London, 1969.

———. *Personal Knowledge*. Routledge, London, 1973.

Popper, K. *The Logic of Scientific Discovery*. Hutchinson, London, 1959.

———. *Conjecture and Refutation*. Routledge, London, 1963.

———. *Objective Knowledge*. OUP, Oxford, 1972.

Prigogine, Ilya and Isabelle Stengers. *Order Out of Chaos*. Bantam Books, New York, 1984.

Qurashi, M. M. 'Research unit for science in Islamic polity'. *Science, Technology and Development*, **1** (5), 15–20, 1982.

——. 'Creative spans of Muslim scientists in Pakistan—a review'. *Science and Technology in the Islamic World*, **4** (4), 187–203, 1986.

Rahman, M. Kaleemur. 'The Islamic renaissance and the contemporary problems of Islamic science'. In Ahmad and Ahmad, *Quest for New Science*, 1984.

——. 'Perspective of new science'. *MAAS J. Islamic Sc.*, **1** (2), 75–80, 1985.

——. 'Environmental awareness in Islam'. *MAAS J. Islamic Sc.*, **2** (1), 99–106, 1986.

——. 'Preface to Islamic science', *MAAS J. Islamic Sc.*, **3** (1), 45–56, 1987.

Rao, P. R. K. 'Metaphors and myths in science'. *MAAS J. Islamic Sc.*, **1** (2), 53–68, July 1985.

Rashid, Salim. 'Science and values: some comments'. *MAAS . Islamic Sc.*, **2** (1), 113–14, 1986.

Ravetz, J. R. *Scientific Knowledge and its Social Problems*. OUP, Oxford, 1971.

——. 'Marxism and the history of science: Bernal's Marxist vision of history'. *ISIS*, **72** (263), 393–402, 1981.

——. 'Science and values'. In Sardar, *Touch of Midas*, 1984.

Rose, H. and S. Rose (eds.). *Ideology of/in the Natural Sciences*. Macmillan, London, 1976, 2 vols.

Rosenthal, F. *Knowledge Triumphant*. Brill, Leiden, 1970.

Said, Hakim Mohammad (ed.). *Ibn Al-Haitham: Proceedings of the Celebration of 1000th Anniversary*. Hamdard National Foundation, Karachi, 1970.

——. *Al-Biruni Commemorative Volume*. Hamdard National Foundation, Karachi, 1979.

——— and Ansar Zahid Khan. *Al-Biruni: His Times, Life and Works*. Hamdard Foundation, Karachi, 1981.

Salam, Mohammad Abdus. 'Science: the shared heritage of mankind'. *Science, Technology and Development*, **1** (1), 8–14, 1982.

——. 'Islam and science'. *MAAS J. Islamic Sc.*, **2** (1), 21–46, 1986.

Sami, Mohammad Abdus and Muslim Sajjad. *Planning Curricula for Natural Sciences: the Islamic Perspective*. Institute of Policy Studies, Islamabad, 1983.

Sardar, Ziauddin. *Science, Technology and Development in the Muslim World*. Croom Helm, London, 1977.

——. 'Incalculating an appropriate sense of confidence'. *Nature*,**280**, 530–1, 1979.

——. 'A revival for Islam, a boost for science?' *Nature*, **282**, 354–7, 1979.

——. 'Scientific thinking behind Khomeini'. *Nature*, **282**, 439–1, 1979.

——. 'The day the Saudis discovered technology'. *New Scientist*, **90**, 481–4, 1981.

——. 'Integrated technology transfer'. *Technology and Culture*, **22** (3), 683–6, 1981.

——. 'Islamic science'. *British J. History Sc.*, **14** (48), 285–6, 1981.

——. *Science and Technology in the Middle East*. Longman, London, 1982.

——. 'Intellectual space and Western domination: abstracts, bibliographies and current awareness'. *Muslim World Book Review*, **4** (2), 3–8, 1984.

——. 'Science and technology in the Muslim world: a select bibliography'. *Muslim World Book Review*, **4** (3), 58–65, 1984.

——. 'The need for Islamic science'. *Afkar/Inquiry*, **1** (2), 47–8, July 1984.

—— (ed.). *The Touch of Midas: Science, Values and the Environment in Islam and the West*. University of Manchester Press, Manchester, 1984.

—— (ed.). *The Revenge of Athena: Science, Exploitation and the Third World*. Mansell, London, 1988.

—— and D. G. Rosserowen. 'Science policy and developing countries'. In *Science, Technology and Society; a Cross-Disciplinary Perspective*. Edited by I. Spiegal-Rosing and D. de Solla Price. Sage, London, 1977.

Sarton, George. *Introduction to the History of Science*. Baltimore, 1927.

——. 'Islamic science'. In T. C. Young (ed.), *Near Eastern Culture and Society*. Princeton University Press, pp. 187–99, 1951.

Shah, Amanullah. 'Pan-Islamism in the field of science and technology. *Science and Technology in the Islamic World*, **1** (1), 33–6, 1983.

Sharif, M. M. (ed.). *A History of Muslim Philosophy*. Otto Harrassowitz, Wiesbaden, 1963, 2 vols.

Sharma, K. D. and M. A. Qureshi (eds.). *Science, Technology and Society*. Sterling, Delhi, 1978.

Sheikh, M. Saeed. *Studies in Muslim Philosophy*. Ashraf, Lahore, 1962.

Sherif, M. A. 'Re-examining scientific knowledge'. *The Muslim*, **16** (94), 82–3, 1980.

Shiva, Vandana. 'The violence of reductionist science'. *Alternatives*, **12** (2), 243–61, 1987.

Siddiqui, Hafizur Rahman. 'The development of scientific methodology by the Muslim scientists'. *J. Islamic Sc.*, **1** (1), 45–55, 1985.

Siddiqui, Muhammad Raziuddin. 'Planning for scientific and technological education, research and development in the Muslim countries'. *Science, Technology and Development*, **1** (1), 19–25, 1982.

Stewart, John. 'Facts as commodities'. *Radical Science Journal*, No. 12, 129–37, 1982.

Technical University of Istanbul. *Proceedings of the First International Conference on the History of Turkish–Islamic Science and Technology*. Istanbul, 1981 (4 vols.).

Umarudding, Muhammad. *The Ethical Philosophy of Al-Ghazzali*. Ashraf, Lahore, 1962.

University of Aleppo. *The Second International Symposium for the History of Arabic Science*. Aleppo, 1979.

University of Riyadh. *Islamic Solidarity Conference in Science and Technology*. Riyadh, 1976.

Verala, Francis. 'Living ways of sense-making: the middle path of neuroscience'. In P. Livingstone (ed.), *Disorder and Order*. Stanford University Press, Stanford, 1985.

Walgate, R. 'Science in Islam and the West: synthesis by dialogue'. In Sardar, *Touch of Midas*.

White, Jr. Lynn. 'The historical roots of our ecological crisis'. *Science*, **155**, 1203–7, 1967.

Whitley, Richard (ed.). *Social Processes of Scientific Development*. Routledge, London, 1974.

Willard, Beatrice. 'Ethics of biospheral survival'. In *Growth or Ecodisaster?*, edited by N. Polunin. Macmillan, 1980.

Young, M. J. L. 'Polymathy in Islam'. *The Australian Bulletin of Comparative Religion*, **1**, 35–44, 1961.

Young, Robert. 'Science is social relations'. *Radical Science Journal*, No. 5, 65–131, 1977.

Zukav, Gary. *The Dancing Wu Li Masters: an Overview of the New Physics*. Fontana, London, 1980.

Index

Entries are in word-by-word alphabetical order except subheadings beginning 'on . . .', where the preposition is ignored in determining the position of the entries.